The
Positive
Deviant

'To be truly radical is to make hope possible
rather than despair convincing.'

Raymond Williams

For Colin and Douglas and their generation's future

The Positive Deviant

Sustainability Leadership in a Perverse World

SARA PARKIN

publishing for a sustainable future

London • Washington, DC

Earthscan Ltd
Dunstan House,
14a St Cross Street,
London EC1N 8XA, UK

Earthscan LLC
1616 P Street,
NW, Washington,
DC 20036, USA

Earthscan publishes in association with the International Institute for Environment and Development

For more information on Earthscan publications, see www.earthscan.co.uk or write to earthinfo@earthscan.co.uk

ISBN: 978-1-84971-118-0 hardback

Typeset by Kerrypress Ltd, Luton, Bedfordshire
Cover design by Rob Watts

A catalogue record for this book is available from the British Library

Library of Congress Cataloging-in-Publication Data

Parkin, Sara.
    The positive deviant: sustainability leadership in a perverse world/Sara Parkin – 1st ed.
        p. cm.
    Includes bibliographical references and index.
    ISBN 978-1-84971-118-0 (hardback)
1. Leadership.   2. Sustainable development.   I. Title.
    HD57.7.P3653 2010
    658.4'092–dc22   2010005170

Contents

List of Figures, Tables and Boxes

Figures

Tables

Boxes

About the Author

Sara Parkin is Founder Director of Forum for the Future, the UK's foremost sustainable development charity, where she designed the well-regarded Leadership for Sustainable Development Masters course. She is Chair of the Richard Sandbrook Trust, sits on the board of the European Training Foundation and the Science in Society advisory group of the multi-agency Living With Environmental Change research programme, and has just completed terms of office on the boards of the Natural Environment Research Council and Leadership Foundation for Higher Education. After starting her working life in nursing, Sara played leadership roles in the UK and European Green parties. She received an OBE for services to education and sustainability in 2001.

Forum for the Future was launched in 1996 as the first of the new generation of charities to take a solutions-oriented and systemic approach to accelerating change to a sustainable way of life. Forum works internationally with over 100 partners in government, business and the public sector, and favours leadership, innovation and futures thinking amongst the means of helping them integrate sustainability into their policies, strategies and practices. Learning is widely shared through publications and the magazine *Green Futures*.
www.forumforthefuture.org

Acknowledgements

To list all those who have contributed to my thinking down the years or even those who have commented on various drafts of this book would almost certainly take me over my word limit. Nevertheless, my gratitude to them is without limit. My lifelong journey owes you so much. More than a trace of your inspiration and insights has shaped this book, though I of course absolve you from any responsibility for my representation of your wisdom and advice. Thanks to colleagues at Forum for the Future, with Jackie van Bueren, Jane Wilkinson and Iain Watt deserving a special mention in dispatches, as do the scholars on the Leadership for Sustainable Development Masters programme, who, down the years have helped shape a distinctive view of what kind of leadership sustainability needs. I'm grateful to Deborah Seddon, Tim O'Riordan, Ian Christie and Kate Rawles for commenting on the nearly whole manuscript, to the TNS students at Blekinge Institute of Technology for an early brainstorm around some concepts, to Agustina O'Farrell for research help and to the many who allowed me to quiz them for their scientific and other expertise, or their personal experiences of leadership. At Earthscan, I am grateful to Jonathan Sinclair-Wilson, Claire Lamont and Camille Bramall and their colleagues who chivvied me amiably to a publishable conclusion. My husband dared me to say that without my family this book would have been finished in half the time. So I will, because it is true! However, as I would have forgone so much fun along the way, I thank them for that instead.

List of Acronyms and Abbreviations

A4S	Accounting for Sustainability
AACSB	Association to Advance Collegiate Schools of Business (US)
ACCA	Association of Chartered Certified Accountants
ALOE+US	all life on Earth including us
ANC	African National Congress
BAU	business as usual
BCSD	Business Council for Sustainable Development
C	carbon
CCC	Committee on Climate Change
CCS	carbon capture and storage
CEML	Council for Excellence in Management and Leadership
CEO	chief executive officer
CIPFA	Chartered Institute of Public Finance and Accountancy
CO_2	carbon dioxide
CO_2e	carbon dioxide equivalents
CR	corporate responsibility
CSR	corporate social responsibility
EMS	environmental management system
EPOCA	European Project on Ocean Acidification
ETS	Emissions Trading Scheme
FAO	Food and Agriculture Organization
FT	*Financial Times*
GDR	German Democratic Republic
GDP	gross domestic product
GHG	greenhouse gas
GWP	global warming potential
ICT	information and communications technology
IEA	International Energy Authority

IFPRI	International Food Policy Research Institute
IMF	International Monetary Fund
IPCC	Intergovernmental Panel on Climate Change
ISEW	Index of Sustainable Economic Welfare
IUCN	International Union for Conservation of Nature
LCA	life cycle analysis
LSDM	Leadership for Sustainable Development Masters
LTG	*Limits to Growth*
MBA	Masters in Business Administration
MDG	Millennium Development Goal
MEA	Millennium Ecosystem Assessment
MIT	Massachusetts Institute of Technology
MPA	Masters in Public Administration
MSLS	Masters programme, for Strategic Leadership towards Sustainability
mt/yr	million tonnes per year
MW	megawatt
NATO	North Atlantic Treaty Organization
NEF	new economics foundation
NERC	Natural Environment Research Council
NESTA	National Endowment for Science, Technology and the Arts
NFP	not-for-profit
NGO	non-governmental organization
NHS	National Health Service
NIC	National Intelligence Council
OECD	Organisation for Economic Co-operation and Development
PCB	polychlorinated biphenyl
PDI	Positive Deviance Initiative
PESTLE	Political, Economic, Social, Technology, Legislative, Environmental
pp/yr	per person per year
ppm	parts per million
PPP	purchasing power parity
PTA	Parent–Teacher Association
PTFE	polytetrafluoroethylene

SC   Seikatsu Club
SD   sustainable development
TNS   The Natural Step
UN   United Nations
UNEP   United Nations Environment Programme
UNESCO   United Nations Educational, Scientific and Cultural Organization
UNFCCC   United Nations Framework Convention on Climate Change
WBCSD   World Business Council for Sustainable Development
WHO   World Health Organization
WWF   World Wide Fund for Nature

Introduction

Positive deviance: A 21st century revolution

Don't go round saying the world owes you a living. The world owes you nothing. It was here first.

Mark Twain

Positive deviant: a person who does the right thing for sustainability, *despite* being surrounded by the wrong institutional structures, the wrong processes and stubbornly uncooperative people.

Perverse: obstinately in the wrong; wrongheaded; against the evidence; turned aside from right or truth.

The odd title of this book was born of much frustration and not a little anger. For over 40 years I have campaigned for a great awakening from the fantasy that the natural world's capacity to support unconstrained demand from us humans is infinite. 'Think of your grandchildren', we used to argue, 'think of your children'. Now the cost of those decades of inaction means worrying about future generations has been overtaken by worries about this one. University leavers, where most of tomorrow's leaders are being prepared, can expect over 60 years of healthy active life. Yet long before the end of that time, scientists predict possibly catastrophic rises in global temperature – unless, that is, we change our carbon-addicted ways. We've got about ten years to kick the habit and avert the worst case scenarios. United Nations (UN) Secretary General Ban Ki-Moon has made a parallel between the economic crisis and the ecological one: 'continuing to pour trillions of dollars into fossil-fuel subsidies is like investing in sub-prime real estate. Our carbon-based infrastructure is like a toxic asset that threatens the portfolio of global goods, from public health to food security.'[1]

Most people admit something must be done – and quickly. But what and how remains unclear. Coming out of a senior management masterclass on sustainability, one participant complained: 'But I still don't know what to do differently on Monday!' She is not alone. If survey after survey is to be believed, many people are ready to get cracking on finding more sustainable ways of living and working, but don't feel confident they know the right way to go about it. What they learnt at school or college has simply not equipped them with the right knowledge or skills. Missing too are unambiguous leadership signals from government or workplace. UK cabinet members, like the boards of most firms large and small, are split on whether climate change is (a) happening; (b) urgent; and (c) their responsibility anyway. Bewitched by the pond-skaters of public opinion – the pollsters, focus groups and the twittering media – leadership everywhere seems to have lost its macro-political compass. The poor preparation and chaotic process at the 2009 Copenhagen UN Climate Change Summit epitomized what is wrong with global leadership. As does the weak ambition of the Millennium Development Goals (MDGs) where *halving* global poverty by 2015 is deemed to be a legitimate target, and all goals are imperilled by the perversity of a global economic system that is dependent on overdosing on resources and underperforming on basic human rights.

Hence the title of this book. We have left it so late to put our human house in order, that the only strategy left is that of positive deviance. We can't wait for the international treaties, institutional reform or wise government leadership that will be too long coming. The only option is for as many people as possible to get on and do the right thing – wherever we are. It is a very positive revolution: *against* everything that leads back to behaviours that caused the ecological (and economic) breakdown in the first place, and *for* a stampede towards a future that puts improving the quality of life for people and the environment as the primary purpose of everything we do. In a Robin Hood sort of way, I'm inviting you to join the growing and merry band of positive deviants committed to doing the right thing, despite everything and everyone, and recruiting like mad as we go. A sense of urgency and passion about sustainability are the only joining qualifications.

But what about that Monday question? How do we work out what are the right things to do? There are next to no courses and no single book to help you get going quickly. You are likely to have some ideas and knowledge already, but perhaps do not yet feel sufficiently confident in your decision making. This book aims to fill the gaps – in your confidence as well as in the marketplace for such books. An early warning though – it will not tell you *what* to do. My purpose is to stimulate you and help you build or refresh your own leadership 'persona' so you are confidently sustainability-literate and effective as a positive deviant. In my experience one size rarely fits all, particularly when it comes to leadership. To be authentic, and therefore trusted and worthy of being followed, you have to be true to yourself. Your personal sustainability leadership model is therefore as unique as a snowflake, and in the case of an organization, as singular as its logo. With this book as your companion you should find all you need to work out *how* to identify the right thing to do, in whatever circumstances you find yourself. Plus some tools so you can get started straight away.

As sustainability leadership may be exercised from everywhere in an organization, this book will be relevant to people in very different sorts of jobs. And I hope it will provoke a revolution too in those places where management and leadership development takes place. In fact, I hope it has a broader influence on education in general. If I had my way no one would leave any publically funded educational institution who isn't sustainability-literate. Ideally, it will become one of the things good parents, teachers and friends inculcate in children from the earliest age so they become responsible and happy adults capable of bringing up the following generation in much the same way.

Box 0.1 What is sustainability-literate leadership?

Keith Grint says leadership 'is not a science, but an art; it is a performance not a recipe; it is an invention not a discovery'. And I agree. As I agree that it is primarily a product of the imagination. A leader imagines a better future and persuades people to follow (Grint, 2000). There is, however, a difference between leadership for anything else, and leadership for sustainability. Leadership for sustainable development (SD) is definitely about imagining a better future, but not one that is constrained by an organizational or geographical boundary, as most leadership is. It is for something far greater than an individual, his or her organization, or even family and country. It is for a greater good that embraces all life on Earth, including all humanity and future generations. As we recently celebrated the 200th anniversary of Darwin's birth, it seems appropriate to say that sustainability leadership is about the continuing participation of our species in evolution. Get it wrong and we are fossils.

You will note from the Contents pages that the book is in four sections. The first deals with the symptoms of *un*sustainability, how it has come about and the choice we have about where we go from here, the second with what is unsatisfactory about the way leadership (mostly as management) education is done (including a critique of corporate responsibility). Section Three is devoted to the ways of thinking, knowledge bases, some principles of practice and key tools for any sustainability-literate leader, particularly those in positive deviant mode. A final section provides a overview of what needs to happen at global level, in a way that makes it easier to see how many local actions can all add up to globally significant contributions. Keeping faith that local efforts can make a difference is critical to being a successful positive deviant.

It may seem perverse of me to end with a Prologue, but that is simply because the future really does start now. It's what we do in the next decade that will determine whether we can speak with pride about our efforts or not.

First, though, I need to introduce you to a couple of overarching themes and some threading concepts that influence how I look upon sustainability leadership and therefore shape this book. They will explain my spin, if you like, on where we went wrong, where we want to end up, and how.

Introducing Adam Smith, James Hutton and the compound error theory of history

When I first became involved in thinking about how unsustainable patterns for human development came about, I was living in Edinburgh, where I learnt about two of the city's former denizens: Adam Smith and James Hutton. Lifelong friends (Hutton was executor of Smith's will) and born within a few years of each other in the 1720s, both produced blockbuster books: Smith on economics, and Hutton on the geophysics of the Earth.

Today, Adam Smith's head adorns the £20 note and some of the ideas he set out in *The Wealth of Nations* (1776) dominate the way we run the global economy (e.g. the invisible hand of the market). Less well known is James Hutton, who was a farmer, doctor, geologist and philosopher. Yet he attracted headlines too for his *Theory of the Earth* (1795), which punched an early hole in the Bible-based belief that the Earth was only 6000 years old. Hutton observed that 'this world has neither beginning nor an end' and described the continual renewal cycles of the natural world as having one purpose – that of life itself. 'We are thus led to see a circulation in the matter of this globe, and a system of beautiful economy in the works of nature.' His conclusion was called 'sublime' by contemporaries, because it represented 'nature as having provided for a constant succession of land on the surface of the earth, according to a plan having no termination …'.[2]

For me, these two Enlightenment heroes symbolize choices made 23 decades ago about what rules would govern the way we humans ran our lives. Even though Adam Smith saw his marketplace contingent on people and natural resources ('… the demand for men, like the demand for any other commodity, necessarily regulates the production of men') it is clear neither he, nor his disciples, nor even Hutton himself, viewed Hutton's natural marketplace as a better model upon which to base the human economy. The historical and still compounding error is the ongoing separation between the two models. Throughout the book, I use the terms **biogeochemical economy** and **human economy** to differentiate between, respectively, the workings of the physical world, of which we are a part, and the workings of the human economy, of which nature is not a part, and which has been constructed out of over-simplistic theories about how we humans think and behave.

What is the purpose of life?

Though I know this puts me into a minority, I am chronically unable to think in anything but outcomes. Even fewer people contemplate what they would like to say about their life when it reaches an end. It might well be that because so few of us have an idea of what 'good' would look like for our own life journey, that we struggle to do it collectively – as a community, country or as a species. It really should be no wonder that politicians flounder within their five-year horizons, if we – their citizens – are unable to articulate what we want for the longer term.

Obviously, the immediate purpose of life is to avoid death. Few would disagree with that. But as our current ways of life – even in the richest of countries – does not seem to provide the meaning and satisfaction – the happiness – we say we crave, it seems worth having what Amital Etzioni calls a 'moral megalogue' – a big public dialogue about whether there is a shared idea about the purpose of life, and how we might go about defining a good one well spent (Etzioni and Carney, 1997). Thankfully, over the last decade there has been a series of books, collectively known as the 'happiness literature', to set the ball rolling. (e.g. Lane, 2000; Grayling, 2003; Layard, 2005; McMahon, 2006; Gilbert, 2006). This has also made it easier for me to propose that the purpose for what Adam Smith called the 'toil and bustle' of our economy should be happiness. Even though the idea is far from new, for ages people thought I was daft to suggest it. Now, as we are all (re)discovering, happiness is there in all religions and non-organized spiritual traditions, whether achieved after life, through meditation or in obedience to a particular God's rules for right behaviour. It is even in the American Declaration of Independence: 'We hold these truths to be self-evident – that all men are created equal: that they are endowed by their Creator with certain unalienable rights; that among these are life, liberty and the pursuit of happiness.'

The really big question, though, is what does the good life where happiness – or at the very least, contentment – may be found look like? Socrates said it was the 'perfection of the soul' and Plato, his disciple, explained that wisdom and goodness give value to wealth and success, not the reverse, and when Socrates said 'virtue is knowledge' he meant that once a person understands what good is, he cannot do otherwise (Grayling, 2003, p21). Thanks to new neurological research we can add some physiological evidence to philosophical and instinctive definitions of what makes us happy. The physical responses of our brain in various trials even suggest we have an innate sense of right and wrong.[3] Moral judgement, long considered to be culturally relative, just might be hard-wired to the way our brains work. And it looks like we've evolved that way. We are happier being cooperative and honest and struggle in a world that rewards the opposite.[4] As Robert Lane points out, the way we 'toil and struggle' right now is bad for personal relationships. There is a 'kind of famine of warm interpersonal relations, of easy-to-reach neighbours, of encircling, inclusive memberships and of solidary family life'. And evidence that for people lacking this kind of social capital, 'unemployment has more serious effects, illnesses are more deadly, disappointment with one's children is harder to bear, bouts of depression last longer, and frustration and failed expectations of all kinds are more traumatic' (Lane, 2000, p9). Our personal happiness and resilience in face of difficulty is heavily tied up in how successful we are in our relationships with others.

Boil down all the surveys and studies and it does seem that, most of all, people want to feel good about themselves, their relationships and the places where they live. How perverse is it that none of these are criteria for success, of an individual or an economy? Figure 0.1 is a graph from just one of the many exercises in many countries that finds happiness – or more accurately life satisfaction – does not parallel growth of *per capita* GDP, but flatlines above about $15,000 per annum.

A sustainability critique of the research on what makes up human happiness would say that, like so much social enquiry, it is disconnected from the physical environment in which people act out their lives. Even without bringing forward evidence from poets, writers, painters and musicians of all cultures, there is plenty of evidence a healthy, attractive environment raises our spirits, and makes us happier and healthier.

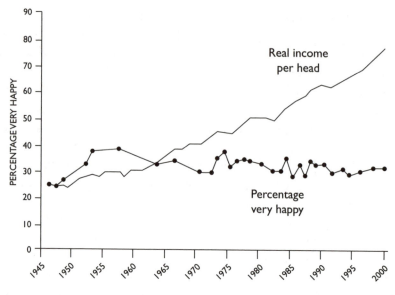

Source: Layard, 2005

Figure 0.1 Happiness and GDP in the USA

When we are sick or stressed, the sight of trees and the sound of water and birds sooths us and speeds our recovery. Recently a student argued that happiness was an anthropocentric concept, but I wonder if that is true. Surely the ultimate human-centred conceit is to imagine other species to be incapable of happiness, albeit in ways that may be largely beyond our comprehension. The Greek word for happiness translates most literally as 'flourishing', something that I like to think applies to all living things.

For me, the joy of happiness as a goal for our lives is that, because it is *not only about feeling good but being good*, it is – or could be – the 'big idea' around which to build the sustainability project as a positive and engaging view of the future.

Threading concepts

There are some other concepts and shorthand expressions that crop up throughout the book and need some introduction. Some, like the 'four habits of thought', are developed in later chapters. The others simply require an early warning of their meaning.

Four habits of thought

In the daily bustle of deciding and doing I use the ideas of resilience, relationships, reflection and reverence as a mental checklist to keep me thinking from a sustainability perspective. Will this or that decision, policy or action increase resilience or not? Are relationships increased or improved this way? Has enough reflection taken place, and are the right people involved? Does that respect what we know (and maybe don't know) about the way the biogeochemical economy works?

Resilience

Resilience is the capacity of a system (or a person) to bounce back after shocks. The more resilient a system, the larger the disturbance it can absorb without shifting to an alternative regime. Increasing resilience is the main strategy of evolution. The strength of an ecological system (like a river valley or forest) is based on the number and density of the connections (relationships) between different components. Resilience of social and economic systems may be obtained in the same way, but only if embedded in ecological resilience.

Relationships

Good and many relationships is how resilience is achieved and sustained in any system or by any person. Increasing the number of right (i.e. sustainability-oriented) relationships between people, their institutions and processes and the environment, is what sustainability-literate leadership does.

Reflection

Extracting the learning from any experience helps avoid or further compounding past mistakes. It also raises the chance of good judgement now, however complex and uncertain the future may appear. Applying what is known to work, and being imaginative about making good practice better, is what has made evolution a success. If we learn to pause and reflect before we decide and act, we can do the same.

Reverence

Respectful awe, or reverence, for the power and beauty of the natural world, and for the intimacy of our biogeochemical relationship with it, is the default spiritual and practical position. It protects us from hubris or ideas of scientific omni-competence, and helps us proceed with confidence and caution. We are less likely to hurt what we love and revere.

All life on Earth including us (ALOE+US)

If we are to correct the error that finds us believing our human story can evolve separate from the rest of life on Earth, at the very least we can use a language that acknowledges the shared storyline. Too many environmentalists talk of the environment and neglect the people bit, just as too many social scientists, politicians, economists, financiers and so on (almost everybody else in fact!), talk only about people (and often a rather small aspect of our humanity at that), neglecting the rest of life on Earth, even though it is the inescapable home-base for everything and everybody.

To emphasize the indivisibility of everything, in parts of the text I've substituted the rather inelegant acronym ALOE+US for the words 'all life on Earth including us'.

The notions of sufficient and good enough

Many people are put off getting to grips with sustainable development because they believe it is too complicated and more the domain of specialists sporting PhDs. And it can be daunting to realize that sustainability is about everything. How on Earth can one person, or one organization, know about everything?

No one can, of course. Which is why sustainability literacy is about having *sufficient* knowledge and understanding to make a *good enough* choice or decision. By definition, we've not done sustainable development before (certainly not on the scale we have to now), so we are all learning as we go. Hence the importance of reflection as an important habit of thought. You may not get it right every time, but with a *good enough* insight into a broad enough range of old and new ideas, you should be able to work out when it is wise to ask for help, or to just go ahead with *sufficient* confidence you've got the direction of travel more right than not. The words are used frequently throughout the book and appear in italics to remind you that *enough* is often *sufficient*.

Direct action: Deviating around the political and economic filters

Quite a lot of the writing about sustainable development is couched in terms of policy, often recommending sums of money to be spent on this or that. Like the Stern Report on *The Economics of Climate Change* (2006), in which the author thought 1 per cent of GDP per annum should be enough to decarbonize the UK economy. Within months, Sir Nicholas had to revise his estimate upwards, with any stable meaning for money subsequently lost in the economic collapse. Moreover, the mobilization of trillions of pounds to bail out banks proves that any sum can be found if the policy maker considers it important enough. Moreover again, the last decades have shown that decision makers in government and all sectors appear to be immune to pre-cooked policy prescriptions. And a final moreover, policy, like a budget, has a short shelf life.

So, as far as I have been able to restrain myself, I've steered clear of giving policy recommendations or price tags for this or that action. That is not because I don't think policy and budgets are important. They are. It is just that we are up to the eyebrows in policies, treaties and funding recommendations for sustainable development. They are not in short supply. So why add more? The crisis, as Kofi Annan has been pointing out for years, is in implementation; we know what to do, but are not doing it. Why? This is the home territory of the positive deviant. It is *your* task to work out the right thing to do where you are and deviate round or remove the policy, funding and other impediments to making it happen.

Starring positive deviants ✱

For the same reason, mostly I have avoided offering case studies of companies or countries. Too many examples of what is irritatingly called 'best practice' (do they really mean it cannot get any better?) have been degraded by time and transparency.

Instead, I include a number of examples of positive deviants (see the appendix) – people who, if mentioned in the text, have a ✻ beside their name. Most are individuals, some are organizations, and each offers an inspiring example of different ways to be a positive deviant in the 21st century.

Section One

The Anatomy and Physiology of *Un*sustainable Development

This natural inequality of the two powers, of population, and of production of the earth, and that great law of our nature which must constantly keep their effects equal, form the great difficulty that appears to me insurmountable in the way to the perfectibility of society.
Thomas Malthus, First essay on population, 1789

Section One

Introduction

Getting the diagnosis right matters

As a one-time nurse, I know only too well that a successful treatment depends on a good diagnosis. Treating someone for a stomach ulcer when they are suffering from a heart attack, for example, may even make things worse. The best diagnosticians know enough about the body's anatomy and physiology (how everything works) to quickly appraise the symptoms, make a good diagnosis and get on with the treatment.

Exactly the same principles apply when it comes to diagnosing and treating *un*sustainable development. Indeed, James Lovelock describes himself as a 'general practitioner of planetary medicine'. This is not a bad metaphor for positive deviants to adopt, though it is well to remember St Luke's injunction that first the physician has to heal himself.

In Chapter 1, therefore, I try to give you a *good enough* overview of the various symptoms of *un*sustainable development, enough for anyone unfamiliar with them to be able to explain them to others. I draw parallels with the human body, so, for example, biological resource depletion represents a wasting of the flesh and scarring of the skin of the Earth.

Like the human body, the anatomy of the Earth operates according to certain principles, which I have called 'laws'. Chapter 2 starts by looking at how we have broken, and are still breaking, these laws. For a long time I would have said we did this out of ignorance or for want of reflection, but now there is a strong element of wilfulness as the consequences become more obvious. Which is why one symptom – a heart attack in the human economic system – is presented as a whole system or physiological failure. A diagnosis is made.

The treatment proposed in Chapter 3 is not so much a detailed prescription, but a consideration of the sort of treatment that will be needed to get the patient (i.e. ALOE+US) back on its feet. The idea is to help you differentiate between good and bad planetary medicine, and perhaps concoct a few remedies of your own.

Subsequent chapters are about leadership, and how to grow your capacity to offer sustainability-literate leadership in such critical times, becoming an effective planetary physician yourself. But this section is about why it matters, and why positive deviants have such an important role to play in what happens next.

Chapter 1

The symptoms

Examine the whole patient

A good diagnostician starts by standing back a bit and surveying the patient as a whole. One such planetary physician is Herman Daly. He describes the world as being 'full up': 'as the world becomes full of us and our stuff, it becomes empty of what was here before [natural resources]'.[1]

Figure 1.1 is my attempt to illustrate Daly's observation. The large square in the middle represents the human economy with estimates that it sucks in over 40 per cent of the biological production of the Earth (including forests and green cover) each year, sometimes so degrading the land that it is no longer productive (1).[2] At the same time, some non-renewable minerals like zinc, uranium, tantalum and copper are anticipated to run out within 50 years (2). Moreover, the resources we do use (biological and mineral) are processed in a humongously wasteful way, generating waste and pollution (including greenhouse gases (GHGs)) that is as damaging as it is unnecessary (3). Included in that profligacy with resources is the way we use fossil fuels as a source of heat, power and light (4). Finally, despite massive 'growth' of the human economy, poverty and inequality remain as intractable as ever (5).

Each symptom is described in more detail in this chapter. Inevitably this is a bit of an Emergency Room examination, but should be *sufficient* to get most positive deviants up to a reasonable speed. For the already knowledgeable or more forensically interested, references and the annotated bibliography should take you further.

Symptom 1: Biological resource depletion (affecting the flesh and skin)

The *angst* around depletion of so-called non-renewable resources like minerals and oil can mask complacency about biological resources such

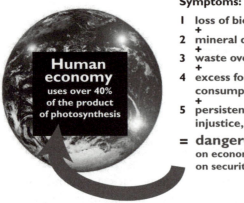

Symptoms:

1 loss of biomass and diversity
   +
2 mineral depletion
   +
3 waste overdose
   +
4 excess fossil fuel
   consumption
   +
5 persistent poverty,
   injustice, inequality

= **dangerous feedback**
   on economy; on well-being;
   on security; on life itself

Figure 1.1 *Un*sustainable development

as water, soil fertility, forests, and grass and wetlands that should be renewable on an annual basis. World Wide Fund for Nature (WWF) calculates we are exceeding the planet's regenerative capacity by around 30 per cent. It is as if we've forgotten that the motor for life on Earth (the biogeochemical economy) is the 'green stuff' covering the Earth and its fuel the sun. Our dependence is not partial, it is absolute.[3]

The consequence of our forgetfulness has been evaluated by the Millennium Ecosystem Assessment (MEA) – considered the biological equivalent of the Intergovernmental Panel on Climate Change (IPCC). The MEA 2005 benchmarking assessment of the state of the global environment found that 'approximately 60% (15 out of 24) of the ecosystem services examined are being degraded or used unsustainably, including fresh water'. The report is highly recommended for its careful plotting of the links between the state of the biological world and our own well-being. The main findings are summarized here:

- Over the past 50 years, humans have changed ecosystems more rapidly and extensively than in any comparable period of time in human history, largely to meet rapidly growing demands for food, fresh water, timber, fibre and fuel. This has resulted in a substantial and largely irreversible loss in the diversity of life on Earth.
- The changes that have been made to ecosystems have contributed to substantial net gains in human well-being and economic development, but these gains have been achieved at growing costs in the

form of the degradation of many ecosystem services, increasing risks of non-linear changes, and the exacerbation of poverty for some groups of people. These problems, unless addressed, will substantially diminish the benefits that future generations obtain from ecosystems.

- The degradation of ecosystem services could grow significantly worse during the first half of this century and is a barrier to achieving the Millennium Development Goals.
- The challenge of reversing the degradation of ecosystems while meeting increasing demands for their services can be partially met under some scenarios that the MEA has considered, but these involve significant changes in policies, institutions and practices that are not currently underway. Many options exist to conserve or enhance specific ecosystem services in ways that reduce negative tradeoffs or that provide positive synergies with other ecosystem services (MEA, 2005).

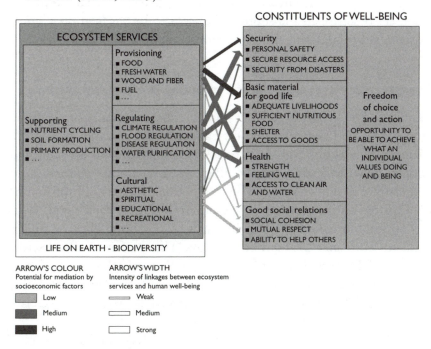

Source: MEA (2005) Figure A Page vi, www.millenniumassessment.org/documents

Figure 1.2 Linkages between ecosystem services and human well-being

Since the MEA reported, no significant trend has slowed, never mind reversed, as competition for the 'biological product' of the Earth intensifies. Rising numbers of people put pressure on land and sea for food and water and places to live, even when they live in extreme poverty. Already, nearly two billion people are severely affected by lack of sufficient water, and the UN predicts that by 2030 nearly half the world's people will live in areas with acute water shortages. Saudi Arabia sources three quarters of its water with fossil fuel intensive desalination plants. Fish stocks are depleting rapidly, and the shift of diets to more animal products means we are less efficient in how we consume plants and grains. A kilogram of beef, for example, takes 6 kilograms of grain and 16,000 litres of water to produce. Around one fifth of all carbon dioxide (CO_2) emissions comes from deforestation yet the rate of trees cleared for cattle ranges and other agricultural use is accelerating.

Collapses in human civilizations, like the Roman Empire, are thought to have happened because human demand for environmental resources outstripped the supply. We seem to be engaged on a similar experiment, though this time on a global scale.

Symptom 2: Mineral depletion (affecting the skeletal system)

Conflicts over mineral resources are on the increase. Over precious stones in Sierra Leone, Angola and Cambodia, for example, while in the Democratic Republic of the Congo diamonds and oil are joined by copper, gold, lead, zinc and tantalum (used in mobile phones) as the sources of ongoing civil war. The UN Human Rights Commission has commented on the violence on the eastern border of the Congo, saying it is wrong to treat what is happening as score settling between militias loyal to Tutsi and Hutu tribal groups: 'This has been about seizing territory.'[4] These violent conflicts are part of an overall picture of shortages of non-biological (and therefore non-renewable) resources worldwide. The United Nations Environmental Programme (UNEP) reckons there have been at least 18 since 1990.[5]

In 2007 the *New Scientist* magazine published a global audit of 19 minerals, calculating how many years' stocks were left if consumption continued at today's rate, and what would happen if consumption were to grow to 50 per cent of the US rate (see Table 1.1).

Table 1.1 Mineral consumption rates

Mineral	Use	Years left at different rates of consumption		Percent-age recycled	Consumed per person in US
		At current rate	Every-one at 50% of US rate		average lifetime (77.8 yrs)
Platinum	Jewellery, catalysts, fuel cells for cars	360	42	0	45g
Phosphorus	Fertilizer, Animal feed	345	142	0	8322kg
Nickel	Batteries, Turbine blades	90	57	35	58.4kg
Lead	Lead pipes, batteries	42	8	72	410kg
Indium	LCDs	13	4	0	10g
Hafnium	Computer chips, power stations	?	?	?	?
Gold	Jewellery, dental	45	36	43	48g
Germanium	Infrared optics, semiconductors	?	?	35	10g
Gallium	LEDs, solar cells, lasers	?	?	0	5g
Copper	Wire, coins, plumbing	61	38	31	630kg
Chromium	Chrome plating, paint	143	40	25	131kg
Antimony	Drugs	30	13	?	7.13kg
Aluminium	Transport, electrical, consumer durables	1027	510	49	
Zinc	Galvanizing	46	34	26	349kg
Uranium	Weapons, power stations	59	19	0	5.95kg
Tin	Coins, solder	40	17	26	15kg
Tantalum	Cellphones, camera lenses	116	70	20	180g
Silver	Jewellery, catalytic converters	9	29	16	1.58kg
Rhodium	X-rays, catalytic converters	?	?	?	4g

Source: Adapted from David Cohen, 'Earth's natural wealth: An audit', *New Scientist*, 23 May 2007

This is a pretty scary table. Many minerals at the heart of modern life, especially digital and telecommunications and renewable energy technologies, are already in very short supply or hard to extract, including indium and gallium, essential to the semi-conducting material at the heart of the new generation of hyper-efficient fuel cells.

When it comes to fossil fuels like oil and coal there are similar panics about diminishing stocks. Coal supplies, according to the World Coal Institute are sufficient for 122 years at today's consumption rates.[6] More immediately alarming is what is happening with oil supplies. Conventional oil (easy to access by drilling into reservoirs) is at or very near its peak.[7] A trend visible for some time now. According to the International Energy Agency, plugging the gap between stalling supply and rising demand (estimated to grow from 85 million barrels a day in 2010 to 105 million by 2030) will be exploration of tar sands, oil shale, and synthetic fuel from coal and gas. All of these come with either poor or unknown ratios for the number of barrels that need to be invested in extraction to the number produced. Moreover, around 50kg CO_2 is emitted per barrel conventionally extracted, with tar sand extraction causing emissions of between 70 and 200kg.[8]

As responding to climate change means we'll have to stop using fossil fuels faster than supplies run out, it seems perverse that competition for access to it is intensifying as it is with other mineral deposits. 'Resource nationalism', as the US Council of Foreign Relations calls it, is on the rise. Europe still has some coal and oil of its own, but not much, and next to none of the minerals in Table 1.1.[9]

Symptom 3: Waste generation (affecting the digestive system)

Belongs to the Climate Change family of understanding (see page 26 for explanation)

No waste recycling system is as efficient as the natural environment. Not a molecule is wasted. Unless, that is, the Earth's systems are overwhelmed by substances that are alien, like plastic and man-made chemicals, or with which they are very familiar, like carbon dioxide but in unfamiliar, excessive volumes. Then they gag and suffer indigestion.

Classically, waste is thought of as visible – like plastic bags, mobile phones, rubble, packaging, old bedsteads, when in reality much of it is invisible, like CO_2, radiation, and air-, soil- and water-borne chemicals. What are called signal indicators of the damage caused by less visible waste and pollution include the increase in number of birds species falling into BirdLife International's 'threatened' category (1212 in

2005, 12 per cent of all bird species). Lifeless watercourses are the result of run-off of agricultural fertilizers, and chemicals from Europe and Asia are to be found in the snows and ice of north and south poles.

As a child I used to earn a comfortable living collecting some of the visible waste, like reusable bottles, and returning them to the right distribution point – the pub, the corner shop, the milkman. Our household didn't generate much rubbish either, almost everything was put to use: paper to the fire (rolled up tightly into logs); vegetable waste to the compost heap (via the soup pot); string into a jar; and there was a healthy rotation of clothes and furniture around family, friends, neighbours and jumble sales. Though not wealthy, life was not as sepia as the photos of that time imply; we were healthy and happy enough. Everyone was thrifty – it was normal behaviour.

I am not being nostalgic, only comparing the volume of waste that my household generated then with what it does today – and I am trying hard to keep it down! It is really difficult. The volume of food, or hardware, or toiletries I buy is dictated more by the packager/vendor than it is by me, the customer. Instead of reusing things like bottles, I put them to be recycled, which causes an additional application of energy to the journey of materials through our economy. Sending plastic bottles to China or grinding glass ones up for road-making may make sense to the cash economy, but does it to the biogeochemical one? The waste stream from households and businesses is growing. Despite an increase in recycling and composting, packaging waste has doubled, with an overall increase in use of materials like paper and aluminum. Perversely, the generation of waste, rather than its reduction, has become incentivized. For example, recycling rates are often judged by weight, which keeps bottles from rising up the waste hierarchy (see Figure 1.3) and can neglect aluminium cans, which are worth recycling rather than making anew. And, lacking alternatives, some local authorities in the UK are locking themselves into 25-year deals that guarantee a stream of waste to incinerating companies. Figure 1.3 is, in fact, ultra-perverse, in that it shows disposal as the biggest portion of the waste management hierarchy, with prevention the tiniest. This is exactly the opposite of what needs to happen – masses of prevention, and very little arriving at the point of end-disposal.

Concern about the human health impacts of chemical exposure (including damage to the immune and neurological systems) is also on the rise. A

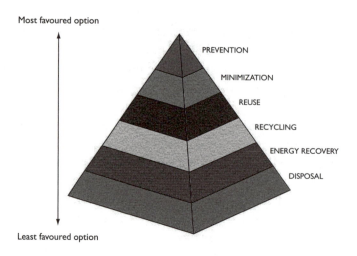

Source: www.rpak.ie/best_practice. This figure is perverse. The bulk of material should be prevented from becoming waste, and only a tiny amount sent to disposal – yet the proportions shown in this government sponsored figure are the opposite

Figure 1.3 The UK government waste hierarchy

test done by WWF on volunteers from 17 EU countries in 2003 found that everyone tested positive for each of the five groups of chemicals involved: pesticides, flame retardants, plasticizers (phalates), stain and water repellants (perfluoroalkyl chemicals) and even polychlorinated biphenyls (PCBs), which were banned in the 1970s.[10] The World Health Organization (WHO) and UNEP Health and Environment Linkages Initiative estimates that 25 per cent of ill health is caused by environmental hazards (rising to 35 per cent in sub-Saharan Africa) a significant proportion of which is due to waste and pollution.[11] Tony McMichael has proposed that the health profile of humans becomes a signal indicator for prevailing environmental and social conditions.[12]

Figure 1.4 shows a different perspective on waste, or rather resource management, to that of government.[13] It illustrates how, for each tonne of 'stuff' bought by a UK adult, ten times that weight of material (rock, energy, water etc.) needs to be moved or used to make the purchase possible. In some cases the ratio is worse. For example, it takes 21 times its weight to produce a unit of steel, 85 times for aluminum (3.5 times if

Start a new industrial revolution?

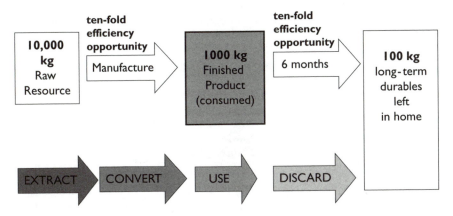

Source: Based on Biffa Waste Services Limited (2000) report, *A Question of Balance*, www.biffa.co.uk/files/aqbreport.pdf

Figure 1.4 Opportunities to squeeze waste out of the system

from recyclates) and, famously, 540,000 times for gold. Imagine carrying a 5.4 tonne rucksack on your back as the real environmental cost of a 10 gram wedding ring![14]

Certainly, that one tonne of shopping per adult per year is a statistic that feels true! But just how wasteful we are is illustrated not only by the waste of the item on its way to the shop shelves, but by the amount we waste once we've bought it. Roughly half of what we buy is food, with about 40 per cent of that thrown away. Of the other half, only one tenth is thought to be still in the home six months later. There are clearly many, many opportunities to squeeze waste out of that continuum of resource use – both pre- and post-shopping. How to use less resources and energy in the first place, and how to squeeze out every drop of waste from that which you do use, is a top priority for sustainability-literate leadership. Cutting out all waste, making thrift normal again, and using fewer resources in the first place not only saves on materials, it drastically reduces the amount of carbon we mobilize, and therefore the amount of CO_2 we emit. It is what a low carbon economy means!

Symptom 4: Fossil fuel burning (affecting the respiratory system)

Different aspects of climate change and carbon management and measurement appear in several parts of this book. The sections and page numbers are given in the schema below. If you are a carbon-novice, you may find it helpful to read first the Accounting for Carbon box in Chapter Eight.

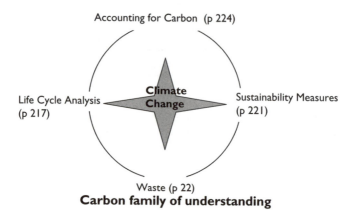

Carbon family of understanding

Although you wouldn't know from the press it gets, carbon dioxide in the right amounts is good stuff. It makes up only a small part of the atmosphere (0.04 per cent), but alongside nitrogen (78 per cent), oxygen (21 per cent), argon (1 per cent) and water (between 0 and 4 per cent) enjoys a complicated but entirely useful lifestyle, continually on the move as part of the carbon cycle. It is a product of animal metabolism (we breathe it out), a food for green plants and soil fertility too. It is the most important of the human produced 'greenhouse gases', so called because they help retain in the atmosphere enough infrared radiation from the Earth to keep the temperature cosy enough for life.

Normally, CO_2 moves in continual chemical interaction between the air, sea and earth (soil, plants and animals including us), in a natural process established over evolutionary timescales. But in the last couple of hundred years, through human activity – particularly the burning of highly carboniferous fossil fuels like coal and oil and changes to land use (deforestation, agriculture) – the concentrations of CO_2 and other greenhouse gases in the atmosphere have increased (see Chapter 8, page 224 for more detail). So much so, the earth and sea parts of the global carbon recycling system are overwhelmed, leaving a growing proportion of the gases in the atmosphere (see Figure 1.5). The now unnaturally high levels of greenhouse gases in the atmosphere cause the excessive heating of the Earth's atmosphere that is changing the way the climate operates. Climate change is a *symptom* of *un*sustainable development. In excess, CO_2 becomes a pollutant. As well as changing the climate, one example is given in a 2009 European Project on Ocean Acidification (EPOCA) report that finds excess CO_2 is making the sea more acidic. This disrupts whale and dolphin navigation systems, damages coral reefs (important fish breeding grounds) and kills off plankton and other organisms at the bottom of an intricate food chain.[15]

   The hypothesis that the most recent warming of the Earth's atmosphere is due to greenhouse gases added by human activity has not been disproved despite a lot of effort over the last 40 years. This hypothesis developed from the fact that we've known since the 19th century that certain gases warm the atmosphere, and that humans now generate a lot of these gases. Less certain are the predictions of what will happen when. This leaves the mind-stretching dilemma of deciding what is *sufficient* evidence to trigger the sort of intervention that has a chance to prevent the worst happening. The demand by policy makers for more precise 'climate forecasts' – as if that was easy and would make their job simpler – is

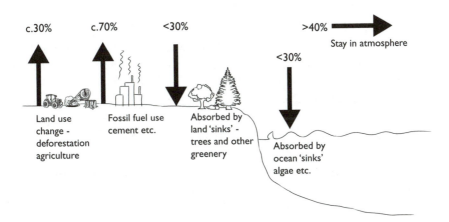

Source: various, including www.globalcarbonproject.org and Le Quéré et al 'Trends in the sources and sinks of carbon dioxide' in *Nature Geoscience* 2, 831836 (November 2009), which suggests the proportion retained in the atmosphere is rising, and that absorbed by land and sea is shrinking

Figure 1.5 Approximate proportions of global CO_2 emitted, absorbed and left in the atmosphere each year

dangerous prevarication; the more precision there is, the nearer we will be to the point when it becomes too late to intervene in a meaningful way.

This makes it off-puttingly hard for aspiring sustainability-literate leaders to make sense of the science itself, never mind the implications of climate change to their organizations or families. The complexity of it all and continually revealed new knowledge about the scale and breadth of the interactions in the global ecological systems are one thing, but layered on top of the science are the political and economic arguments about what is and isn't possible, plus the dust kicked into our eyes by the inevitable 'naysayers' – people who deny or obfuscate the science for ideological or financial reasons.

To try to stay on top of everything, I anchor my understanding of the science in the reports of the IPCC and recommend you do too. Its Fourth Annual Report, published in 2007, is the output of 2500 expert reviewers, 800 authors and 140 political leaders from 130+ countries. Six years' work, four volumes, and a single report representing an unprecedented scientific consensus process, plus the agreement of all governments of the world, seems suitably solid ground on which to stand. The Synthesis Report: 'Summary for Policy Makers' is very comprehensible and will fit the needs of most people. Its top-level conclusions about the science are paraphrased here:

1   Warming of the climate system is unequivocal, all continents and most oceans show many natural systems affected, with some evidence of other effects at regional level, though these are difficult to differentiate from adaption and non-climatic drivers.

2   Global greenhouse gas emissions due to human activities have grown since pre-industrial times (1750), with 70 per cent of that increase happening between 1970 and 2004. This rate of change far exceeds pre-industrial values determined from ice cores spanning many thousands of years. Most of the observed increase in global average temperatures since the mid-20th century is *very likely* (i.e. 90 per cent certain) due to observed increase in anthropogenic (human caused) greenhouse gas concentrations. (The observed temperature rise matches climate models when human emissions are added to natural occurrence.) (IPCC, 2007)

To help ordinary mortals judge the level of confidence around their experiments, observations and different predictions, the IPCC scientists have produced a helpful scale of confidence, which is given in Table 1.2. Nothing in the 'scandals' around leaked e-mails from climate scientists in the UK University of East Anglia, or some sloppiness in the IPCC's 1000 page Working Group II report, weakens the basic hypothesis that global warming is happening and that it is *very* likely (i.e. 90 per cent certain) that human activities are contributing. These levels of likelihood of a big impact event would flash very red on corporate risk registers.

Table 1.2 *IPCC Assessment of the likelihood of certain events*

Virtually certain	> 99%	NB for readers: this way of classifying
Extremely likely	> 95%	confidence in climate change science is also
Very likely	> 90%	useful for classifying risks and opportunities
Likely	> 66%	of any sort, including the potential impact
More likely than not	> 50%	of any mitigation or adaption activity
Unlikely	> 33%	
Very unlikely	> 10%	
Extremely unlikely	> 5%	

Note: > means more than.
Source: Taken from IPCC (2007) 'Summary for Policy Makers', p53

The 2007 IPCC report used 2005 scientific evidence. Since then, of course, research has continued, and has only strengthened the evidence of 'dangerous, long-term and potentially irreversible climate change'. For example:

- Global carbon dioxide concentrations continue to rise, and methane concentrations have started to increase again after a decade of near stability.
- The decade 2000–2009 has been warmer, on average, than any other decade in the previous 150 years.
- Observed changes in precipitation (decreases in the subtropics and increases in high latitudes) have been at the upper limit of model projections.
- Arctic summer ice cover suddenly declined in 2007 and 2008, prompting the realization that the environment may be far more vulnerable to change than previously thought.
- There is increasing evidence of continued and accelerating sea-level rises around the world.[16]

UK government Chief Scientist John Beddington describes a 'perfect storm' where increased demand for water, food and energy not only contribute to emissions of greenhouse gases, but are also further jeopardized by the worsening climate.[17]

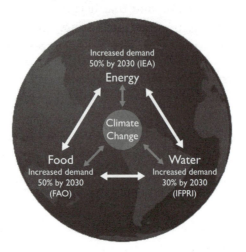

Source: John Beddington, speech to UK Sustainable Development Conference, 19th March 2009

Figure 1.6 The 'perfect storm' of physical constraints on the Earth's capacity to provide

See Box 8.1 Accounting for Carbon on page 224 for more on the language, the science and the numbers of carbon management, but in a nutshell this is the climate change challenge:

> In 2007 and adjusted for ozone and various cooling aerosols, the concentration of greenhouse gases in the atmosphere was 396 parts per million (ppm) of CO_2 equivalents. In order to have at least a 50 per cent chance of keeping the temperature increase to less than 2° Celsius over that of 1750 (not safe but probably the least bad situation possible) the greenhouse gas concentrations need to stabilize at 450ppm. Currently the concentrations are rising at around 2.2ppm per year. (Note: all greenhouse gases from all sources considered here.) (IPCC, 2007)

> Put another way, since 1750 we have burnt half a trillion tonnes of carbon, and are on track to burn the second half trillion in less than 40 years. The cumulative consequences of that first 500 billion tonnes suggest the next 500 billion (and the rest) ought to stay underground. (Note: only pollution from burning fossil fuels considered here.) (Mackay, 2009)

Despite the fuss, the easiest way to keep up with the science and the implications is via the IPCC and the independent UK Committee on Climate Change (CCC), www.theccc.org.uk. Expect more, not less, rigour in future, but be a discerning consumer of newspaper headlines that don't trade in uncertainty as accurately as they should.

The politics (and economics) of climate change

Which brings me unavoidably to the politics (and therefore the economics) of climate change.

Not very long ago a taxi driver told me I needn't worry too much about climate change because 'if it was that serious, they [meaning politicians] would be doing something serious about it'. I found it hard to counter that comment. Although the UK made a world first at the end of 2008 by passing a Climate Change Bill to set legally binding ceilings for UK emissions, the signals government sends to citizens, business and investors remain – to be polite – confused. Just as the bill was published, for example, the government announced a third runway at Heathrow, and when it came to stimulating the economy after the financial crash, incentives to replace old cars trumped loft insulation and double glazing.[18]

The UK government is signed up to the Kyoto Protocol of the UN Framework Convention on Climate Change, with the Climate Change Bill enshrining the UK share of global emissions in domestic legislation. The CCC now sets a series of (legally binding) carbon budgets up to 2022, to be adjusted according to progress and the unfolding science. However, its 2009 report on the period 2003–2007 points out a step change will be needed to meet targets and suggests the policy regime (main features summarized in Table 1.3) is inadequate. The Committee fears recession-induced drops in emissions may produce an over-rosy impression of progress, and that long-term progress is undermined by the low price of carbon. It is right.

Even though the recession has done more for reducing CO_2 emissions than the carbon trading schemes, there has, without a doubt, been an acceleration of awareness and political discussion (if not action) about climate change over the last five years. When HM Treasury published *The Economics of Climate Change* in 2006, the author, Sir

Nicholas Stern, was feted the world over. Campaigners fell on his neck with gratitude. Here at last the financial implications of climate change were set out in a language even the most blinkered finance minister could understand. Along with Al Gore's lucid PowerPoint exposition about the climate science, the Stern Report ended forever the excuse of any politician that 'they did not know' (Gore, 2006; Stern, 2006). The sight of polar bears stranded on melting ice combined with the experience of uptorn trees and floods in their own backyards clinched the reality of climate change in the minds of politicians' constituents, with nearly 80 per cent of their voters saying they are fairly or very concerned about climate change. Most people wanted to see more government action. A couple of years later and over half of people say they don't have confidence government will do anything anyway.[19] So my taxi driver is not alone in interpreting lack of action – and increase of air travel – as evidence that climate change is just another political fad and not as serious as the scientists claim it to be. Like most ordinary people, he will probably not be aware that the Climate Change Committee agrees with him, and is tightening the (legally binding) screw on policy makers as they fail to hit the (legally binding) targets.

The principle reasons for government prevarication fall into three categories:

- entrapment by an economy that depends on profligacy for success;
- an impoverished imagination about policy;
- fear that the cost of rectifying current, never mind historic, inequitable behaviour will be very great.

In the first category sits the reason the UK Treasury was significantly less enthusiastic about the Stern Report than climate change scientists and campaigners. The cost of doing nothing might be 20 per cent of GDP (or worse in the shape of environmental and human disaster), and the bill for tackling climate change a trifling 1 per cent of GDP (quickly updated by Sir Nicholas to 2 per cent), but the implication of the

Table 1.3 Summary of UK policy regime designed to tackle climate change (More details may be found on the websites provided)

United Nations Framework Convention on Climate Change (UNFCCC)

Signed in 1992, it sets non-legally binding targets to stabilize GHG emissions. Adopted in 1997, with 183 signatures by 2008, industrialized countries (Annex 1) agree to reduce collective emissions by 5.2 per cent by 2012 compared to 1990 (Kyoto Protocol). A clean development mechanism and joint implementation schemes allow Annex 1 countries to 'purchase' permits to emit greenhouse gases from poorer countries (non-Annex 1) by paying for reductions in their emissions. UK 'share' is to cut 12.5 per cent emissions by 2012. In December 2009, the Copenhagen meeting to decide what would happen after 2013 failed to agree any concrete outcomes.
www.unfccc.int

UK Climate Change Levy

Came into effect in 2001, and charges a 'levy' on each unit of energy used in the industrial and commercial and public sector. The levy part funds the Carbon Trust established to help reduction strategies and use and development of new technologies, and the Enhanced Capital Allowance for investment in such technologies. Energy intensive sectors have an 80 per cent discount on the levy to protect their competititiveness. Fuels used for domestic energy and transport, and for generating other forms of energy – e.g. electricity – are exempt.
www.cclevy.com

Discount rates

When considering sums of money to be spent now on mitigating climate change in the future, discount rates are used to determine the 'net present value' of future benefits, in order to judge whether the expenditure is worthwhile. They are used in cost–benefit analyses and to profile risk, as in, for example, the future benefit of a third runway at Heathrow. The value of money over a period of time is built into the calculation. The higher the discount rate, the lower the future benefits are deemed to be, so setting the discount rate is the source of much argument. For example, when it comes to climate change a 2% rate would indicate mitigation expenditure now is warranted.

Nicholas Stern used a 1.4% discount rate in his report (Stern, 2006). The waters have been much muddied by the financial crash, as predicting the value of money now, never mind in the future, is difficult. The concept of a 'social' discount rate is no less controversial – setting a 'net present value' of people in the future. Stern used a 0% rate, arguing it was unethical to do otherwise. There is broad agreement that Stern made reasonable choices when determining the costs of doing something or nothing about climate change.
www.hm-treasury.gov.uk

Low-carbon transition policies

In the summer of 2009 the UK government published a suite of policy papers laying out how they see the transition to a low-carbon society happening. The responsibility for reducing part of the total UK annual carbon emissions has been allocated to every department. Scotland have published a carbon assessment of their 2010/11 budget, differentiating between direct, indirect and induced (caused by increased consuming power) emissions.
How effective these initiatives are depend on what actions follow.
www.decc.gov.uk; www.scotland.gov.uk

EU Emissions Trading Scheme (ETS)

The largest emissions trading scheme in the world, the EU ETS affects around 12,000 large energy suppliers and heavy industry, with the target of a 20 per cent reduction of carbon dioxide equivalent (CO_2e) emissions (from 1990 levels) and a 20 per cent increase in use of renewables designed to help countries meet UNFCCC commitments. A national allocation of 'permits to pollute' is made under a total overall cap, with trading of permits facilitated. Dependent on the market price of carbon to be effective.
www.europa.eu/environment/climat/emissions/index

UK Climate Change Bill

Made mandatory a reduction of greenhouse gas emissions by at least 34 per cent by 2020

through domestic action alone, with 2050 reductions of 80 per cent from 1990 baseline the objective. An independent Climate Change Committee will set 'carbon' budgets for three five-year periods from 2008 to 2022 to meet these targets. A Carbon Reduction Commitment energy efficiency scheme was introduced by the bill for organizations not covered by the EU ETS but with energy consumption exceeding 6000 megawatt hours (MWh) per year. Those required to register in 2010/11 will include supermarkets, Network Rail, universities, hospitals, water companies, local authorities including schools, and all central government departments. They will have to buy allowances at £12/tonne for all CO_2 emissions on top of their power bills, retrospectively for the past year, and prospectively for 2011/12. Under-purchasing will mean buying allowances on the open market. League tables will reveal who does well (and gets their money back). Again a lot depends on the right pricing of 'carbon'.
www.decc.gov.uk
www.hm-treasury.gov.uk

Carbon pricing

CO_2 trading schemes have a bad name. Globally Kyoto emissions targets will only be met because of the drop in emissions in east Europe in the 1990s. Under EU ETS emissions have risen. Blamed is weak carbon prices and/or too many of them. In the EU ETS a 2009 permit is half its supposed 2009 price of £21 a tonne, and many argue it should be much higher than that. As Paul Ekins puts it: 'the price [of carbon in or out] should be high enough, when allied to other appropriate policies, to drive the behavioural change in consumption and stimulate the development and deployment of low-carbon technologies that are sufficient to prevent climate change getting really out of hand'.[20] There is also a debate about a 'shadow' price to be used outside the trading schemes – in policy appraisal for example. The limitations of market instruments for handling such a complex and uncertain field as climate change are showing. See ENDS REPORT 415, August 2009 for a discussion about this. www.ends.co.uk

necessary actions jangled Treasury nerves horribly. It would mean changing the basis of economic growth away from increasing consumption of *stuff*, a fundamental restructuring that, until the financial crash at any rate, even the Treasury tea-boy knew was uncontemplatable.

Moreover, government is under a heavy lobby from 'big energy' – the companies that have everything to lose from a shift to energy efficiency with more renewable and distributed generation. Their influencing strategies are legendarily sophisticated, relentless and luxuriously funded, whether it is policing the words in a piece of European legislation, influencing the rewriting of the 2003 UK Energy Paper, or a publicity campaign to block a bill on Capitol Hill. Thinking about a future low in carbon use, and thus low in CO_2 emissions, clashes directly with the energy sector's predictions for growth in future energy needs in the UK and globally and therefore the whole purpose of their companies.

The perverse logic that makes economic growth and therefore success predicated on using more, not less, energy and other resources is one reason why most environmental legislation has concentrated on end-of-pipe pollution and waste going into the air, water or onto dumps (see Symptom 3: Waste generation, page 22) This has led to a huge growth in monitoring equipment and other technologies for separating and treating pollution or waste *once it has been created*, scrubbing gases out of chimneys and so on. Not to mention a growth in the sector devoted to enforcing compliance and catching and prosecuting sinners.

And so it is with climate change. The end-of-pipe mentality has got governments obsessing about CO_2 once it has been emitted and 'permits to pollute' that may be traded. To go upstream to prevent carbon from being mobilized in the first place, and to squeeze all waste out of what we do use, strikes a dagger blow to the perverse logic on which we have built our economy. Less may be more for the environment and even the quality of our life, but it is death to the way the current economy works. Whether in the form of kit to plug onto the end of your pipe or CO_2 emission permits to buy and sell, where there is muck there is a great deal of brass to be made. Consequently, governments are in a fret about more than the loss of some corporation tax from a few large energy generators, they are gripped by an icy dread of an imploding economy. Reflect for a moment on the 3 per cent drop in greenhouse gas emissions credited to economic recession in 2008. That was from fossil fuel energy and other resources not used, widgets not made, thermostats turned down and journeys not taken.

As well as being trapped by the perversity of what constitutes economic growth, policy makers struggle to imagine the wider benefits of shifting to low-carbon lifestyles, so don't allocate money most effectively. This is partly because of poor knowledge about the physics of resource use and partly because of the segregated way policy is made and implemented. Legislators and their civil service find it hard to see that there are many more health and other crossover social benefits, like jobs and innovation, as well as climate change gains to be had in *less* resource use, than there are in trying to keep things going as they are now. Running nuclear power stations, cleaning up pollution or policing CO_2 trading schemes offer few, unattractive jobs devoid of entrepreneurial opportunity.

The very public appointment by President Obama of some serious scientists to advise him, and the chief scientific advisors in UK government departments promise to improve things from the physical science side, though missing from the mix are the social scientists to advise on how to turn citizens like my taxi driver into willing and knowledgeable collaborators instead of unskilled and sceptical antagonists. Which brings me to the last point about why governments – including the UK – are, and have been for a shameful number of decades, dragging their feet over the sort of international agreement that will drive radical, just and swift action. The clue lies in the word 'just'. David Mackay is a scientist who deals in refreshingly round figures. He looks for ways of talking about climate change and energy that are *sufficiently* accurate, but widely comprehensible. For instance, if we were to divide the total global greenhouse gas emissions for 2007 – say, around 40 billion tonnes of CO_2-equivalents – by a world population rounded to seven billion, we'd arrive at around 5.5 tonnes as the average annual emission of a global citizen (Mackay, 2009).

But we are not equal. Figure 1.7 shows some of the variations between countries. In the UK, for example, our emissions are middling compared to other EU countries, but twice the world average at around 11 tonnes per person per year (pp/yr), and nearly six times the average in Africa. China may have roughly the same total greenhouse gas pollution rates as the US, but per person it averages around 5 tonnes compared to the US citizen's 24 tonnes pp/yr. These huge differences are what make richer, high CO_2 emitting countries fearful of what justice, for current as well as historical inequalities, might look like. Discussions at climate change negotiations are steeped in this fear, with the complicating factor that, nowadays, poorer countries are producing many of the things that we consume in the richer world. If we repatriated (took responsibility for) the greenhouse gases embodied in our imports, our personal emissions in the UK would be a great deal larger.

The three big spooks of economic implosion, policy incoherence and fear of the price of justice rode on the shoulders of governments into the 2009 UNFCCC meeting in Copenhagen, and combined with a disgracefully inappropriate process to scupper the sort of agreement the world needed. The days when a fortnight of chaotic negotiation between a self-selected bunch of people before the political leaders jet in to dot the odd 'i' and cross the final credit-grabbing 't' are clearly over. Even with a decent process (run with top quality leadership) the task is enormous; in essence 192 countries are trying to create a common world energy policy. The difference between when the Kyoto Protocol was

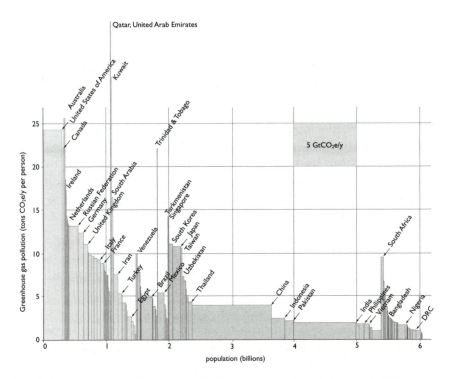

Note: Each square on the graph is equal to $5GtCO_2e$ per year, and the global average is 5.5 tonnes per person per year.
Source: Taken from David Mackay (2009), www.inference.phy.cam.ac.uk/withouthotair/c1/page_13.shtml

Figure 1.7 Greenhouse gas pollution per person/per country

negotiated and now is that no country is in any doubt about what the stakes are – either in the science of climate change or the global power-shifting potential of any agreement.

According to some critics, over-dependence on international treaties means the discussion on alternative policy approaches that recognize the complexity and urgency of climate change are stifled.[21] For instance, the Green Fiscal Commission argues that by going properly upstream and shifting taxation off things valued by society, like jobs, incomes and profits, and onto carbon use and environmental damage, the low-carbon economy will be incentivized, jobs created, a stable income for government created and, properly implemented, the less well off protected.[22]

A US group has suggested a new twist by proposing a cap and trade scheme for carbon entering the economy, where the revenues from auctioning permits (could be between \$400 and \$1600 billion per year) go via an Earth Atmosphere Trust in two different directions. First, a fraction divided up in a *per capita* payment to all people on Earth (could be \$71–\$285 per year depending on the price of carbon), and second into protecting the asset (the atmosphere) through renewable technologies, research and so on.[23] David Fleming proposes a more local rationing system – Tradable Energy Quotas.[24] Impatient at the slow and opaque world of carbon trading, seasoned climate campaigner Bryony Worthington has set up an organization, Sandbag*, which will purchase a permit to pollute for you, but rather than pollute with it or sell it on, Sandbag retires it for you.[25]

Believing that there is a big-tech silver bullet that will solve everything, the technological optimists are agitating for what are called geoengineering solutions, of which there are two types. The first wants to remove excess CO_2 through, for example, carbon capture and storage (CCS), which takes CO_2 from the atmosphere and stores it underground, or seeding seas with iron to increase growth of CO_2-absorbing algae. The other type wants to deflect sunlight reaching the Earth and includes things like adding sulphate to the atmosphere. According to the normally technologically gung-ho *Economist* magazine, all of these are highly risky and extraordinarily complex and expensive.[26] The UK Royal Society has published a scientific evaluation of each, but points out the risks and calls for the application of the technologies we know about already.[27]

How can sustainability-literate leadership get a grip on what needs to be done in the swirl of international negotiations, markets with yo-yoing prices for carbon or 'permits to pollute', flaccid and incoherent policy making, and a certainty that justice is *very likely* to be done, if not agreeably, then brutally through interrupted supply chains for energy or food? My guess about what happens next is that there will be ongoing international negotiations and, in the best of all possible worlds, wonder if agreements to tackle climate change together and in a just way might even create a positive dynamic for international relations. A healthy life-supporting environment for everyone could – repeat could – become the new 'neutral' territory for diplomacy, peacemaking and trade.

Even in that dream scenario, the most ambitious international agreement will be meaningless without the leadership and imagination to turn it into reality back home. So here are some scientific and policy considerations to help positive deviants cope in what are certain to be muddled times.

In preparation for the 2009 Copenhagen meeting, climate scientists summarized the current situation as follows:

- Observations confirm IPCC *worst-case* trajectories are being realized.
- Many societies are highly vulnerable to even modest levels of climate change.
- Rapid, sustained and effective mitigation is required to avoid 'dangerous climate change'.
- Climate change will have strongly differential effects on people (intra and intergenerational) and biodiversity.
- Many of the tools and approaches to deal effectively with the climate change challenge already exist.
- Need to overcome significant constraints (e.g. inertia in economic and social systems) and seize critical opportunities (development of the green economy).[28]

This is a *good enough* summary from the scientists to inform decisions by sustainability-literate leaders. You will need some numbers, but precision is superfluous. As David MacKay reminds us, equity on a global scale means the UK will have to cut its emissions by over 85 per cent, bringing UK individual annual carbon budgets down from 11 tonnes to around 1 tonne. To all intents and purposes that means no fossil fuels – and the sooner the better (Mackay, 2009, p15).

Here is a very distilled climate policy To Do list to help you make your own decisions about what to do, what to support and what to lobby for. If the 2° warming limit is to be met, it looks like a 5 per cent reduction in greenhouse gas emissions from now to 2050 rather than the current 1 per cent increase. So for the next 40 years, *everything* will have to be on the fastest of tracks and as front-loaded as possible to secure reductions later on. Doing what we know works is therefore a priority. For example, planting trees and installing double glazing is less risky than stimulating ocean algae blooms and surely cheaper than machines to suck CO_2 out of the air. The question you must ask is not what is politically or economically possible, but what is scientifically most effective, given our timescales?

Table 1.4 Climate policy to do list

What needs to be done?	What should politicians do?
• Rapidly reduce carbon coming into the economy/organization/home (taxes, carbon budgets, levies etc.)	• Set a high price for carbon
• Quickly become ultra-efficient about the carbon we do use	• Regulate and tax in a way that makes a real difference
• Drive both less C in and more efficient use of it with seriously tough 'cap and trade schemes' on CO_2e emissions	• Target public investment
• Protect existing and plant lots of trees fast, put nature back in control of ecosystems	• Protect the vulnerable
(NB not one or two of the above, but all, simultaneously)	• Send consistent policy signals – to citizens, markets, internationally
	(NB not one or two of the above, but all, simultaneously)

Naysayers (bad) and contrarians (good): Know the difference

Naysayers – people who deny, refuse, oppose or are cynical about something – are everywhere, so it is not surprising they turn up in discussions about climate change. They are often wrongly called contrarians or sceptics. Contrarians are a good and essential part of any debate because, although they may take a contrary position or attitude, they are thinking forward, differently and not always negatively, as naysayers do. Bob May, past President of the Royal Society, says the process by which science moves forward is organized scepticism, and is one of many who are cross that the word has been hijacked. Some naysayers are in denial or opposition because of a psychological fear of – in the case of climate change – death, suffering or extreme change. Troublesome though they may be they are a different category to the malicious naysayer.

Malicious naysayers are usually very active and well funded and get more airtime than they deserve, not least because the media love a for and against argument, regardless of the balance of views. According to Barak Obama's climate science advisor John Holdren, it is the malicious naysayers who 'infest talk shows, internet blogs, letters to the editor, op-ed pieces, and cocktail-party conversations' and they need to be challenged head on.[29] They were particularly active in the build up to the Copenhagen Conference at the end of 2009.

How to do it? Here are some questions to ask:

- Who is employing or paying? For example, some of the most active climate science deniers receive financial support (or consultancy fees) from the commercial interests behind the ideas they champion (e.g. tobacco, oil). In 2006 the UK Royal Society even wrote to Exxon Mobile to ask them to stop funding misrepresentations of the science of climate change.
- Whom do they associate with? The director of the controversial Channel 4 TV programme *The Great Climate Change Swindle* (4 March 2007), Martin Durkin, is connected to a group of people with views that would be recognizable to the further reaches of both right or left political ideologies, but are consistently anti-environmental (see note 32).
- Are they arguing from 'straw man' or a falsely constructed premise? A classic tactic exemplified by Bjørn Lomborg in *The Skeptical Environmentalist*. A statistician, Lomborg attacked what he called 'the litany' of environmentalist claims that he culled, not from a review of their speeches, articles, books and so on, but from a couple of articles in *New Scientist* and *Wired* magazine and a book co-authored by science-fiction writer Isaac Asimov. His loose approach to statistical methodology prompted a rebuke from the Danish Committee on Scientific Dishonesty.[30]
- Is the source a reliable one? In the UK, the International Policy Network is not to be confused with the Policy Network (Blairite left) or Policy Exchange (Conservative centre right). Its executive director regularly provides the 'opposite' point of view in media stories about climate change and the environment, helped Nigel Lawson with his naysaying book (Lawson, 2009) and in July 2008 launched the *Electronic Journal of Sustainable Development*, from the private University of Buckingham. The journal is well populated by naysayers, but test it out yourself, particularly the first issues. Sometimes the naysayers dissemble cleverly. For example a group called The Scientific Alliance lodge in the prestigious Cambridge Network. Some of its members focus on getting naysaying articles into professional and other publications.[31]

How to get answers to those four questions?

- Time spent in reconnaissance is never wasted. But don't get obsessive about exploring the mires of naysayer networks, calumnies and distortions, though do know where they are and where they come from *sufficiently well* to avoid being trapped. There are reliable websites to help.[32] And many naysayers got together at a conference in March 2009, sponsored by the Heartland Institute in the US, if you want to check that out.[33]
- Look out for a robust and good rebuttal. Laying the lie is vital, so public networks, including Google and Wikipedia, need a rebuttal from a respected source. Even David Miliband, when Secretary of State for the Environment weighed in to counter Martin Durkin's arguments, and Channel 4 gave the then Director of the Met Office a Q&A slot on their website. For a dissection of Bjørn Lomborg see Tom Burke, currently advisor to the UK Foreign Office. The Royal Society is good for rebuttals of bad science, and excellent on climate change controversies.[34]

When in doubt, ask someone you trust. When confident, put the record straight yourself.

Symptom 5: Persistent poverty, injustice and inequality of opportunity for many people (affecting mental and psychological health)

In August 2008, the World Bank adjusted the yardstick it uses to measure global poverty. Inflation hit the poverty line, raising it from $1 per day to $1.25, so the number of people now classified as living in extreme poverty went up from the convenient one billion, to 1.4 billion.[35] Around one quarter of people alive today are still struggling for survival, ill from lack of food and easily preventable diseases, while, in the rich part of the world that generates these statistics, around the same number are menaced with another kind of malnutrition: the diseases and mortality that goes with being excessively fat. A gruesomely visible manifestation of the inequality of all sorts of opportunity experienced by people in all parts of the world, as fatness in the rich world is often worst amongst the poor.

The year 2010 marks the start of the last lap for achieving the UN's Millennium Development Goals for 2015.

1   End poverty and hunger (the goal is actually only to halve it).
2   Achieve universal primary education.
3   Promote gender equality and empower women.
4   Reduce child mortality.
5   Improve maternal health.
6   Combat HIV/AIDS, malaria and other diseases.
7   Ensure environmental sustainability.
8   Develop a global partnership for development.[36]

In a report to the UN General Assembly early in 2010, the Secretary General, Ban Ki-Moon notes 'some key successes' in primary school enrolment, drop in disease incidence, the rise of interventions by private sector foundations like that of Bill Gates and Vodafone in providing accessibility to drugs and mobile telephony. But also some persistent negative trends: poverty targets will not be met in some of the poorest areas, like sub-Saharan Africa and parts of Asia and Latin America, with hopes of meeting the goal of halving, never mind ending, poverty by 2015 further jeopardized by rising commodity prices, especially food. About a quarter of all children remain so undernourished their life chances are at risk, and there is only marginal improvements in preventing maternal deaths. Some 2.5 billion people, around half of those living in development countries have poor or no sanitation. The report makes depressing reading.[37] Official development assistance at an all time high of $119.8 billion in 2008 is still only 0.3 per cent of developed country combined income, well short of the long-standing target of 0.7 per cent. With the relentless rise of CO_2 emissions worldwide making matters more difficult, hope is receding that the goals will be achieved by 2015.

The UN High Commissioner for Refugees, António Guterres, warned a 2008 gathering of his 76 member states that 'rather than the universal peace and prosperity that some anticipated in the early 1990s, we are now confronted with an accumulation of adverse trends'. He cited rising numbers of refugees (11.4 million at the end of 2007) who have left their countries but remain in their original regions, many living in urban areas. Internally displaced persons are on the rise too, with around 26 million people on the move. 'Competition for scarce resources has become an increasingly important factor in provoking and perpetuating violence. We are confronted with a series of interlinked conflicts in an arc of crises that stretches from south-west Asia to the Middle East and the Horn of Africa... Climate change, extreme poverty, and conflict are becoming more interrelated.'

Summing up the moral hazard of living in a world with such vast humanitarian challenges, Mr Guterres, bravely (given the audience) quoted Bob Marley who observed in one of his songs that 'a hungry man is an angry man'. Guterres told his audience of ministers and ambassadors they had one year's grace only to debate the 'growing scale and complexity of forced displacement' and to say what they mean when they talk of assuring 'human security' or exercising their 'responsibility to protect'.[38]

The biblical observation that the poor are always with us is not the articulation of a physical law. Like the economists' protestation that boom and bust is inevitable in the financial system, the idea that poverty and massive inequality are social givens is nonsense. There is something systemically wrong when 25 per cent of the world's population is struggling to survive, and when one in five people in a country like the UK are considered to be deprived and two to three million in deep poverty.[39] The image of the former chief executive officer (CEO) of the collapsed investment bank Lehman Brothers explaining that a salary of $45 million was not unreasonable has underscored just how much the gap between rich and poor has widened over the past few decades within and between countries. Economist Paul Krugman points out that this is not just a class phenomenon: high-school teachers and hedge-fund managers have post-graduate degrees, but the top hedge-fund managers earn more than the annual salaries of all 80,000 teachers in New York three times over.[40] Globally, the UN Development Programme estimates that 1 per cent of the world's population earns more than the poorest 57 per cent together.[41]

As a symptom of *un*sustainability, persistent poverty and growing inequality is analogous to mental and psychological health for two reasons. First, for the anguish associated with hopelessness and lack of power over your own destiny and that of your family, of watching your children die of hunger or easy to prevent diseases, of living in fear of conflict and chronic injustice and chaos. And second, for the capacity of so many of the rest of us to blot all that out of our minds even as we contribute to its perpetuation.

Summary of symptoms

So, what does our examination of the patient reveal?

As Figure 1.1 tried to illustrate, there are multiple systems affected by the disease of *un*sustainable development, each manifesting different symptoms. Burning fossil fuels has so affected the Earth's 'respiratory system' that it has caused the climate to become more unpredictable and prone to extreme events. As well as aggravating climate change by being less able to mop up CO_2, loss of biological mass (wasting of the flesh) and diversity (thinning of the skin) through agriculture or thoughtless urbanization, means less resilient ecological systems; resources, like soil fertility and fresh water, or services, like clean air and the pleasure of the company of other species, are in ever shorter supply.

Contributing to this loss of biological mass and diversity is the waste from human activities. Under normal circumstances, the Earth operates a hyper-efficient waste recycling system. In fact it doesn't recognize waste. Everything has a purpose, and can be thought of as a nutrient for another species or a suite of molecules for future construction into a plant or animal. Yet, the waste from the human economy now gives the gastrointestinal system of the Earth indigestion! Whether by chemicals and products it has never seen before and can't digest (like plastic bottles), or an overdose of materials it does recognize (like CO_2, nitrates, phosphorus) its digestive processes are overwhelmed. This contributes to climate change and further harm to biological resources. And, of course, to making us sick.

There are symptoms of bone disease too, the implications of which are only just becoming apparent. The massive damage of quarries and mines has long concerned campaigners and led some of the biggest companies to collaborate around improvements of practice. But the symptom is not restricted to the bigger bones of oil, coal and aggregate. The malaise is very pervasive, found throughout the body Earth, and getting worse as the human economy depends more and more on increasingly rare minerals. Over these we compete intensely now, and fight and go to war.

The final symptom of *un*sustainable development seems to be the failure of human endeavour to achieve even the simplest of its ambitions as set out in so many of our own religious and spiritual teachings, institutional missions and policies. According to academic enquiry, we want to feel good about ourselves, to enjoy satisfactory relationships and live in a fair and caring community, all things that don't require a massive mobilization of biogeochemical resources. We are suffering from what psychologists call cognitive dissonance – a disjunction between what is on offer in the world around us, and what we really, really want. Roger Liddle finds what he calls a 'social pessimism' right across Europe, about family relationships, closing the gap between rich and poor, about life getting better. The glass is definitely half empty.[42] Psychiatrists would say we are depressed and demoralized, low in hope.

As the big arrow in Figure 1.1 implies (page 18) there are not only multiple feedback loops between the various symptoms, but also between them and the human economy. For example, shopping therapy (prescribed as an antidote to winter blues, say) would lead to more mineral extraction (for the latest mobile perhaps) and more energy used to grow, make, package and ship our purchases. Waste and pollution would be increased. All that would register as a plus on the national accounts, but would we be any healthier or happier as a result?

How could we so neglect the evidence that every single part of the body Earth is displaying symptoms of disease? The simultaneous blisters of biological degradation, the clogged lungs of the atmosphere, the chronic indigestion of the ecological cycles, and our restless dissatisfaction with our lives suggest a common cause.

The next chapter explores that question.

Chapter 2
Anatomy and physiology

The rather ugly word obesogenic has been coined to describe the modern lifestyles and behaviours that result in a person becoming too fat. The calorie equation is straightforward – more taken in than expended = weight gain. Obesogenic describes the environment – physical, social and psychological that influences the overconsumption of calories: the hours in front of a TV or computer screen; the loss of cooking skills and the social benefits of a shared meal table; 'comfort' eating as compensation for disappointments.

In some cultures carrying a lot of fat is considered a sign of prosperity and an insurance against times of food scarcity. But the inverse is happening in rich countries today, where prosperity and social status are signalled by expensively maintained and clothed bodies. For the rest of us, however, it is much easier and cheaper to eat badly and to excess.

Our loss of knowledge and understanding about nutrition and the practical and social skills around preparing and enjoying food is paralleled by our forgetfulness about our place in the evolutionary adventure that is life on Earth. Like the facts of good nutrition, the non-negotiable rules about how to get along with the natural world are rarely taught nowadays, and certainly do not inform those who design and run the human economic system. We live in what some call an anthropocentric – human-centred – world, thinking of nothing but ourselves. It is so much worse than that I think narcissogenic would be a better word. In Greek mythology, Narcissus was so caught up with his own beauty he was disdainful and cruel to others, and so condemned to perish for his self-love.

Staying with the theme of diagnosing our dilemma before moving to considering the treatment, this chapter first considers the anatomy of our relationship with the Earth. What has our self-obsession caused us to neglect in our relationship with the rest of life on Earth – to the extent that our survival is threatened? And what is it about our narcissogenic lifestyles – the physiology of our chosen way of getting things done – that consistently make matters worse?

The anatomy: Laws of nature have been broken

Although I have called these five elements of our relationship with life on Earth 'laws' they are really 'wisdoms' that have, by and large, governed our shared evolutionary journey with the rest of life on Earth. When our ancestors crawled out of the primeval swamp, or even when they took up agriculture, it is unlikely they could have codified these laws. Nevertheless, with an instinct akin to that used by birds and whales when following migratory paths, and a great deal of empirical learning, most of our human story has unfolded by living in harmony with them.

All life on Earth operates according to scientific laws that also apply to us

The provision of the most essential elements for human life – air, water, nutrition – depend totally on the proper functioning of the planetary ecological systems. These are the carbon, nitrogen and sulphur cycles, the hydrological (water) and climate systems and so on. They do not work separately, but interdependently. Different species require different conditions for life, and humans are amongst the most vulnerable, because we have quite narrow criteria for survival. We need food regularly (unlike some snakes that may eat only once a year), water even more regularly (unlike some desert plants that can survive for years without water), and unlike organisms such as some Archaea (not a bacteria but close) we do not thrive in extremes of temperature or pollution.

Without benefit of a microscope St Paul noted that 'all flesh is grass', but how many of us remember that the only net producers of energy and raw material (matter) in a concentrated or structured (and therefore useful) form are green cells of plants? Would we cut down so many trees and tarmac over so much green space if we did? It is the sun that provides the energy to assemble a range of chemical and molecular ingredients into a tree, potato or flower. We can obtain shade, furniture, food, medicine and fuel from a tree, eat the potato and enjoy the flower's beauty, but not so the elemental ingredients of each if they are dispersed. Indeed, all our nutrition comes from green plants either directly or via other animals.

Our bodies share the same principle biochemical elements as ALOE – carbon, nitrogen, oxygen, hydrogen, sulphur and phosphorus – and participate in the same continuous molecule recycling process that involves the air and the sea on a planetary scale. How many of us, however, understand the global chemical intimacy in which we live, and take account of it when we make decisions near to where we live? It is odd that the more science has confirmed this interdependency the less we seem to honour it. Most spiritual traditions have recognized this physical reality for centuries, in the Christian 'from dust to dust', for example, or the Hindu belief in reincarnation.

Certainly not taught in business schools is the physical fact that in the Earth's biogeochemical economy energy and raw material (matter) are neither created nor destroyed. Would we be so profligate in our use of energy and other natural resources if it was? In the biogeochemical economy, elements can only appear in different states: either structured by nature (like a tree or coal) or by ourselves (like a brick or a piece of steel), or broken down into individual elements by being eaten, rusting, rotting or eroded by weather. So when we set fire to a piece of wood (or coal, or oil, or plastic, or a corpse) for example, the elements do not disappear, but are returned to the environment in the form of ash, heat and gases. Bin it or burn it, the ingredients persist. The science that explains that nothing 'goes away' is in an aptly named Conservation Law.

In close partnership with the Conservation Laws is what is unhelpfully called the Second Law of Thermodynamics. This states that the overall tendency is for everything to return to its elemental state. However complex the structure, everything, including trees, plants and our own bodies, eventually reverts to its original atoms. For human-made structure like buildings, cars, bridges or roads huge efforts have to be made to stop them from eroding or rusting. The power of nature is often illustrated by an image of green shoots pushing through concrete or tarmac, and I have watched a disused wartime airfield in Lincolnshire become a wild wood in less than two decades. This suggests to me we cannot win any war with nature, though we behave as if we believe we can, mainly because we don't understand the physical laws that govern the competition.

There is no chain of being: Successful evolution is a collaborative venture; it is the result of great networking

Nature, believe it or not, is highly organized. Although evolution appears to be a continual trial and error experiment, it goes about it systematically. Its purpose is order and resilience, but its process is mightily devolved and distributed. Where there is liquid water, organic molecules and an energy source there is organized life.

The idea of a hierarchical Chain of Being with the human species at the top derived from otherwise helpful methods of classifying living organisms. Darwin was not alone in using the simile of a tree to think of species past and present and how they might be organized, and it is not too hard to see how we got it into our heads that we were dominant rather than team players (see Figure 2.1).

But now we can study DNA we find there to be less difference between the branches than we thought; we are more like 'variations on a theme'. Differentiating between a frog and a fungus may be interesting, points out Colin Tudge, but it is not crucial to understanding how life works. In fact, we might be wise to stop thinking of ourselves as outside or even on top of the fantastically rich and organized meta-system that is life on Earth and operate a more humble understanding of just how much we are a part of and dependent on it, and how little it might be dependent on us. Colin Tudge also points out that the actual number of living organisms – known and unknown – may be vastly over the current 30 million estimate (Tudge, 2000, p8). And, as J. B. S. Haldane remarked, for someone who saw humankind as His ultimate creation, 'God is inordinately fond of beetles' (Tudge, 2000, p7). 'We *Homo sapiens sapiens* and our primate relatives are not special but recent', is how Lynn Margulis puts it. 'We are newcomers on the evolutionary stage' (Margulis, 1998, p4).

Margulis also pointed out that the human species, like all others, is the result of a collaborative experimental work programme consisting of 'thousands of millions of years of interaction amongst highly responsive

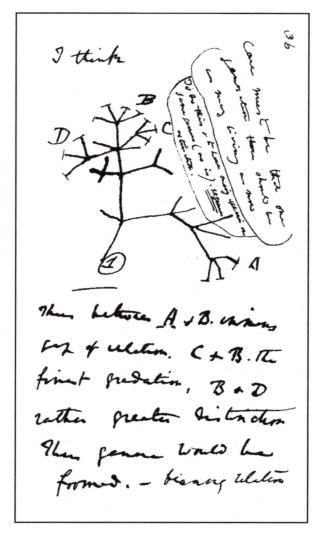

Source: reproduced from Charles Darwin's first notebook on Transmutation of Species (1837) p36. Original in Metropolitan Museum, New York

Figure 2.1 Darwin's tree of life

microbes' (Margulis, 1998, p5). Certainly, the idea that evolution was about competition and 'the survival of the fittest' was not how Charles Darwin saw it. The term was coined by Herbert Spencer in *The Principles of Biology* (1864) as he tried to find parallels between the *theories* of human economics and evolution. Darwin and modern biologists prefer the term natural selection, and there are many examples of how the best outcome for the gene pool is achieved through sometimes sophisticated and mutually beneficial cooperative behaviours. For example: pollinators, some of which are plant specific; vetch and clover and nitrogen fixing bacteria; the human extended kinship systems. Successful life is the result of a massive networking exercise.

The notion that we humans are, by default, competitive and selfish (i.e. natural sinners), has been undermined by research that suggests the opposite. Richard Layard, for example, describes experiments where the brains of volunteers registered pleasure when cooperative moves were made in the Prisoners' Dilemma game. This happened even before participants knew the outcome of the game or whether others had cooperated too. Virtue, it seems, can have its own reward (Layard, 2005). Daniel Goleman suggests we have a 'neural WiFi' that causes us to respond differently to a happy smile or a sad or menacing expression. He cites Giacomo Rizzolatti who says what he calls 'mirror neurones' in the brain 'allow us to grasp the minds of others not through conceptual reasoning, but through direct stimulation: by feeling, not by thinking' (Goleman, 2007, p43). So why have we ended up in a social arrangement that makes virtue uncool, fosters competition over mutuality, and admires ruthlessness, especially amongst politicians, businessmen and gangsters?

Without a doubt, the capacity for rapid reaction has played a large role in our ability to differentiate between friends and foes as we go through life, but it looks as if a more reflective and patient approach to building cooperative relationships with people and the environment, founded on mutuality of interest, might be more fruitful for creating a more sustainable way of life.

Big, fierce, predatory animals are rare

Despite our status as new kids on the evolutionary block, the human species is undeniably a super-efficient predator. Colin Tudge describes us as less strong than a lion and less patient than a crocodile, but far more cunning, and able, as they are not, to kill at a distance, without personal risk. Also, through agriculture, we are able not simply to predate but 'to shape the entire landscape to our needs and whims' (Tudge, 2000, p610).

The ecological law we have broken here is the one that says big, fierce, predatory animals are rare. Very few large animals, let alone predators, can be counted in millions, or even hundreds of thousands, except perhaps the crabeater seal of Antarctica.

Ten thousand years after the end of the Ice Age when archaeological records showed us starting to farm on a significant scale, there were probably around ten million human beings on Earth. Now we are nearly seven billion, and adding to our number by around 80 million a year. As other big mammals like tigers and gorillas struggle for evolutionary survival through loss of habitat, so too does our own species. The difference is that we are doing it knowingly.

When I was born, the population of the world was 2.2 billion. In another 15 years I will be able to say that within my lifetime it has double twice. A rate of growth that Paul Ehrlich called, with controversial perspicacity, 'the population bomb' (Ehrlich, 1968). As Chapter 1 shows, the bomb effect of the human species on an all too finite planet is responsible for all the symptoms of *un*sustainable development. Why, therefore, has more not been done to limit our own numbers? The shorter answer to this question comes in three parts: more people and therefore more consumption of goods and services are the motor of a modern economy; linked to that an incomprehensible (to me at any rate) argument that it is anti-development; and finally a pathetic reluctance to engage with a topic that involves sex, with a dark strand of sexism involved as well.

First of all, it is worth noting that worrying about the number of people and the capacity of the environment to provide is not new. What is new is that it is now a global rather than a local worry. Overpopulation so great that 'the land was bellowing like a bull' is recorded in the Babylonian *Atrahasis Epic* written sometime before 1600BC, and Plato's argument that governments should maintain a stable population through the regulation of marriage owed much to his observation of changes to the local environment caused by deforestation and impoverished soil (Engelman, 2008).

There is equally ancient evidence of the use of contraception as a way of dealing with unwanted births.[1] Cleopatra is reputed to have used the peel of half an orange as a spermicidal cap for the entrance of her womb.

In more modern times, however, 'population' has been considered a matter mainly for poor countries with high birth rates that interfere with western-style development. In richer countries the concern is about insufficient recruits to the workforce (births) to support the pensions of their longer living parents. Yemen, for example, became interested in better family planning after noting in 2005 that its population was growing at 3.2 per cent annually, the same rate as its economic growth, diminishing water supplies and leading to no net improvement in wealth. Meanwhile, countries like France and UK use pro-natalist policies that are respectively explicit (extra state support for *famille nombreuse*) and implicit (child benefit) to grow the number of taxpayers and consumers who will keep the wheels of the economy spinning. Perversely, richer countries, instead of celebrating hard gained advances in longevity at home (and despite promoting longer living as a goal of international development) are now accusing whole generations of being a costly burden to the economy. More thoughtfully, Adair Turner points out the ludicrousness of a system that would require the UK and EU populations to double by 2050 just to maintain the numbers of working age people. Young people, more likely to be unemployed, needing education, homes and health care are much more expensive than the elderly.[2]

From the perspective of global sustainability, an older population profile with lower birth rates is evidence that a country is entering what might be called the Ecological Demographic Transition, and is therefore to be welcomed. The transition is quite advanced in Italy, for example, where population growth has more or less stopped rising, and is predicted to fall steadily between 2015 and 2050. By contrast, the UK population is predicted to rise by ten million by 2033, the equivalent of adding a city the size of Bristol every year.

The second argument about population and sustainability is that absolute numbers do not matter, it is how people impact on the environment. As Figure 2.2 shows, this is a false argument. Even though there are substantial variations in population density and personal greenhouse gas emissions, both matter – a lot.

England and Wales, for example is one of the most densely populated parts of the world, where people have a very high CO_2 emitting lifestyle, while in even more space-challenged Bangladesh CO_2 emis-

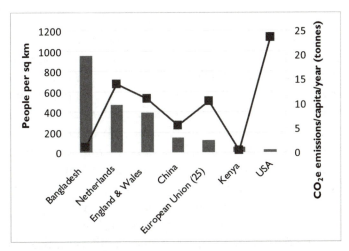

Figure 2.2 Space and impact matter, but so do numbers

sions are low per person and in total. But look at China. For total emissions it now beats the US, although average emissions per citizen are much lower. Which makes it incomprehensible – to me at any rate – that otherwise sensible people working with poor communities around the world should say that it doesn't matter if populations rise in poor countries, because their CO_2 emissions per person are so low compared to that of the rich.[3] This despite the fact that most of the extra 80 or so million new mouths needing to be fed, housed, watered and given a future of hope and happiness, will be born in poor countries. The rather ugly perversity of the logic here is that it is OK for populations to rise in poor countries – *as long as people stay poor and don't emit too much CO_2.*[4] By 2050 Africa is predicted to add one billion to its population, and India half a billion. How do you think that will benefit the environment or the people on either continent?

Which brings me to the final theme of why population struggles to be given serious consideration in many policy areas but especially in environmental and development circles. Sex. Although family planning programmes have helped the significant drop in the global *average* number of children born to a women today (from 5 to 2.6 per woman) there are still 200–300 million women who say they want help in planning their families, but can't get it. In her fertile lifetime, a woman may have intercourse many hundreds of times, so restricting her pregnancies to five, never mind two, is quite a challenge. Sad to say just contemplating that fact stirs up all sorts of prejudices and complexes everywhere, but mostly amongst men of many cultures and in key leadership institutions, like governments and religions.

Improving the literacy of women and their personal circumstances so they have greater confidence the children they do have will live to adulthood is extremely important, but no substitute (as was conveniently assumed for a long time) for access to contraceptives. Statistics suggest that, in the UK, as it is globally, around 30–40 per cent of women become pregnant unintentionally – inside and outside marriage. This means there is a long way to go before every child is plannned, but a tremendous opportunity to intervene to bring about that happy state. Which is where the sexism comes in. Whatever their motive, those who argue against an intentional Ecological Demographic Transition through proper policies to bring down birth rates are not only arguing against protecting the environment, but against the rights of women to be in charge of their own fertility and to have the best chance possible that the children they do have will survive and thrive.

The safety catch of evolution is its slowness

The cumulative impact of the absolute numbers of people on Earth is important, but so too is understanding how the human species has managed to override (so far at any rate) the slow pace of evolution. The development of a crossed bill by some birds, the better to winkle out pine-cone seeds, has evolved over millions of years, yet, as Vaclav Smil points out, our own species has experienced the most profound changes of its 5000 years of recorded history in the last 150 years. A 20th century 'expansive civilization', complex, high-energy, machine dependent, was made possible by a synergy of fossil fuels, science and technical innovation in the latter half of the 19th century. He finds 'much in the record to be proud of, and much that is disappointing and abhorrent', including the 'possibly irreparable harm that technological advances inflict on the biosphere' (Smil, 2006, p311).

We humans are not the only species to develop tools to achieve certain aims. A Galapagos finch, for example, trims bits of stick to poke into holes in trees to get at bugs. Beavers dam rivers and sea otters use stones to crack open molluscs. But unlike other animals, human tools and technologies are not so easily biodegradable. We are one of the few species to span the whole of the Earth, but unlike other global animals (e.g. birds, whales) we are damaging our habitat (and theirs) on a monstrous scale. Evolution has a safety catch – it proceeds slowly and its trials are small enough for any errors that threaten the whole system to be snipped out before too much damage is done. In a twinkling of an evolutionary eye, human technologies have enabled us to go faster than any animal and higher than any bird with no heed to the consequences.

Smil points out that despite the technological advances, and 'armies of scientists and engineers, our observational and analytical capabilities, complex computer models, think tanks and expert meetings' we have no clearer idea of what the end of the 21st century will be like than we did about the end of the 20th century in 1900. The promise, he reflects gloomily, remains the same: 'of yet greater ascent and of unprecedented failure' though thankfully he ends on a note of optimism by saying neither is preordained (Smil, 2006, p311).

As with so many of our technological choices, we tend to do it because we can, not because it is necessarily good for us. We are not particularly good at accounting properly for the potential impact of innovation on people and the environment. Chemicals in food and solitary computer games seem to cause damage as well as good, yet this is not reflected in their price. For years the information and communication technology industry considered itself without environmental impact, for example, but now accepts its necessary infrastructure emits roughly the same amount of CO_2e as the international aviation industry.

There should be no ideological battle between high and low technology, simply a proper reflection on social and environmental impacts, with a proper energy or biogeochemical budget done to check whether the choices we make really are saving resources and preventing pollution. Sheila Jasanoff argues for 'technologies of humility' better suited for coping with the unknown, the uncertain, the ambiguous and the uncontrollable at what she calls the 'ragged fringes of human understanding'.[5] Her prescription for involving citizens in major scientific choices is appropriate to the current discussion about technologies of hubris – the big geo-engineering projects to tackle climate change –

because it does seem odd that the prescription for resolving the negative consequences of large-scale human technological innovation on the geochemistry of the Earth should involve more large-scale technological intervention. Brian Arthur points out the irony of it: 'for all of human existence we have been at home in nature – we <u>trust</u> nature, not technology. And yet we look to technology to take care of our future – we <u>hope</u> in technology' (Arthur, 2009, p215).

But as Smil says, nothing is preordained, so reflection, taking time to consider and test the environmental and social consequences of our choices is the way to render them evolutionarily sensitive. Will they make us more resilient as individuals and as a species? In scale and risk are they appropriate to the unknowns and uncertainties of the future? Will they affirm or diminish our humanness?

Our spirit has evolved with and throughout the rest of life

Fascination with the human mind, soul and spirit and their relationship with the natural world permeate all of human history. The question about why the human brain is so big and commands so much fuel (20 per cent of our metabolism) has been answered. Not it appears for reproduction or hunting hairy mammoth. These are not complicated activities, whereas fostering the sociability of groups to help us survive when hairy mammoths run short, judging when to fight and when to sue for peace, and how to build trusting and loving relationships most certainly is (Tudge, 2000, p498).

By the time we settled as agriculturalists we were already sophisticated social animals with a track record (e.g. cave paintings, artefacts) to prove we enjoyed a rich spiritual element to our physical relationship with each other and the natural world. As Fritjof Capra points out, in different languages the words for 'soul' and for 'spirit' also mean 'breath' (Capra, 1996, p257).

Soul/Breath		Spirit/Breath	
Greek	psyche	Greek	pneuma
Sanskrit	atman	Hebrew	ruah
Latin	anima	Latin	spiritus

Nowadays, thinking about the connection between the breath of our inner life and that of our outer one may not work for everyone. But most people are searching for a deeper meaning for life other than a purely materialist one, and it doesn't take much to reconnect our own physical and mental well-being with that of the environment. To be the 'life and soul' of the party, family or of an organization means your animation (animate: to give life to) of events is as much spiritual as physical.

However diffidently they approach the ineffable, many of the works referenced in this book end up contemplating the metaphysical dimensions of sustainability as well as the practical physical ones. It doesn't take long for any logical train of thought about sustainability to arrive at the steps of our deepest relationship – with ourselves, with our values, with our own souls. Tim Jackson, for example, gives one of the most easy to understand explanations of the physical laws that govern the material world. But in the final section of his book, *Beyond Material Concerns*, he points out that, by accepting material definitions of wealth, society has

> accepted a kind of poisoned chalice. Offering sanctity of choice, fulfilment of our desires, and the greater good of fellow human beings, it has delivered environmental destruction, economic instability and new alarming kinds of poverty: poverty of identity, poverty of community, and poverty of spirit. (Jackson, 1996, p193)

It is this impoverishment – over and above material poverty – that creates the sort of black hole of the soul that too easily sucks in extremist and simplistic representations of any spiritual certainty whether touted by high priests of Anglicanism, Islam, the New Age or nihilism.

To be fair, there have been efforts by the various faiths of the world to connect their history and current proselytizing to concerns about the natural world, and organizations like WWF International, in partnership with the Alliance of Religions and Conservation has produced a fascinating survey of religious sites and their larger meaning, in ancient history and today.[6] Rowan Williams, the UK Archbishop of Canterbury has been quite open that economics 'cannot be separated from ecology'. Ecological fallout, he says, is a 'depletion of real wealth, of human and natural capital'.[7] Less useful is the debate about the role of atheism and humanism in causing and/or reversing *un*sustainable development patterns (see for example Dawkins, 2006). The conclusion for the moment has to be that neither a-theists nor theists present a barrier or carry an advantage that should distract either from contributing to sustainability at full throttle.

These 'laws' or forgotten wisdoms have been described in a way that I hope will give you a bit of depth, as well as enough modern information and insights to inform you in your learning journey. The common theme is that all five 'laws' concern ways of living in and with our environment, not apart from it. Some are very practical – like knowing about the physics that governs all life. Using fewer resources and being ultra-efficient with energy will depend on applying it correctly. Others are evolutionary warnings to go more slowly – we are too numerous as a species, and too prone to Wizard of Oz like behaviour, brandishing shiny expensive kit at problems instead of collaborating with nature and each other using more humble technologies. Perhaps most important of all, we've become so wrapped up in ourselves – so narcissistic – we've forgotten that not so very long ago we lived intimately with nature, very cognizant of our dependence on her for spiritual and physical nourishment.

The physiology: Home economics (the cardiovascular system)

Which brings me to the final symptom, a seizure of the human economic system triggered by a collapse of its financial sector. In Figure 1.1, which summarized how human development has become *un*sustainable, our economy is shown as a large square, commandeering large proportions of the biological economy to its own purposes (page 18). Because of its significance to all the other symptoms and to the eventual treatment, it is presented here as a failure of the physiology of the whole body. Our chosen way of meeting our needs and generally getting things done has not only been flouting the laws of nature, but also it has failed in its own terms.

For us humans the circulatory system sustains the whole body with the pumping of the heart keeping everything on the move. For the Earth it is the global ecological cycles – especially the hydrological pump –

that maintain life. Quite simply, if there is no water there is no life. But the human economy operates a circulatory system not with something real like water, carbon or even blood, but with money. Moreover, not only does money have no intrinsic value, it is also mostly manifests as a negative – as debt. Consequently, instead of being oxygenated by a healthy volume of nice-sounding and well-connected (to something real) credit, the arteries of the human economy have been furring up with lots of nasty cholesterol-laden debt. Defaulting sub-prime mortgages sent off the first fatty plaques towards the heart. Now the whole human economy is flat on its back.

'Why did nobody notice?' asked HM The Queen on a visit to the London School of Economics. Such a good question. Why indeed did no one notice that the patient, on top of everything else, had serious heart disease? Replied economist Professor Luis Garicano: 'Someone was relying on someone else … and everyone thought they were doing the right thing.'[8] Such a poor answer. And a wrong one at that. People did notice, and knew that what was happening in the financial sector was wrong. To take just one example from off the beaten track of ecological economists, former UK Chancellor, Denis Healey, noted 20 years ago:

> The desire to hedge against unpredictable changes in exchange rates and interest rates led to a feverish rash of new financial instruments, starting with swaps, futures, option, and options on futures … Most of the new activities spawned by the financial revolution … assume all trees grow up to the sky – that there will never be another recession. If the United States does have a recession, even one as modest as the Carter years [US President from 1977 to 1981], its whole financial system could collapse like a pack of cards.[9]

Which is precisely what happened – what is happening. Adam Smith himself described money as a lubricant for the 'great wheel of circulation' of human commerce – the trade or traffic in goods and services and all the dealings between people in a market place. A little credit helps the flow when the blood becomes a bit thin, but as the father of accountancy, Luca Pacioli (1445–1541) advised, don't go to sleep until the debits equal the credits.[10] A balancing act that the inter-bank lending mechanism was supposed to do – until there was so little liquid money and such vast volumes of sticky, gooey debt in the system, they lost confidence. The government (i.e. the taxpayer) had to be called in with a life-support machine (i.e. so many billions of pounds that they are now counted in trillions).

The fallout from the unveiled venality of the financial sector will go on for some time. There are many signs of worse to come, as so vast are the transactions (and the debt) racked up by the financial sector compared to what is called (without apparent irony) the *real* economy, Niall Ferguson found that 'Planet Finance is beginning to dwarf Planet Earth' (Ferguson, 2008, p4).

Does this mean that *inevitably* economic growth and prosperity as we currently define and practise it are in conflict with environmental protection and social justice? And that if we resuscitate the patient's heart, the other symptoms will become worse again?

The final part of this chapter, The diagnosis, tries to answer these questions.

The diagnosis: A compound error theory of history

The short answer to both those questions is yes. But not necessarily so, if we choose to reflect deeply about what we want our economy to do for us, and then organize it accordingly. Some of the reasons we don't I've rehearsed in the section on the politics of climate change (pages 31–35). But our economy is not bound by physically inviolable laws, as the use of energy is; it is entirely constructed by us, so therefore it can be changed by us. We do not have to lead narcissogenic lifestyles. We can choose to develop healthy ways of living that include just relationships with the environment and each other. We can go on a low-cholesterol diet (cut out that fatty debt), and start an exercise regime that brings our economy back in line with that of the natural world (more on this in Chapter 9).

But none of that will happen with a few tweaks here and there. More fundamental changes will have to be made. Which is why my formal diagnosis for all the symptoms of *un*sustainable development is that we are living the consequences of what might most kindly be called a compound error in the way we have conceptualized and run the human economy. This conclusion has nothing to do with political or economic ideology; in their theorizing, Marx was as blind to the environment as were John Maynard Keynes and Milton Friedman. Rather it is every-thing to do with the 'great disconnection' of the human economy from that of the physical world. Historically, it was all more complex and long-winded than I suggest, of course, but our friends from Edinburgh, whom we met in the introduction – James Hutton and Adam Smith – serve as a *good enough* metaphor for understanding that disconnection.

As Figure 2.3 illustrates, the basic error is that though they were close friends, Hutton, as a father of the physical sciences, and Smith, as a father of human economics, saw neither the significance of the connection between their ideas, nor the dangers of developing them separately. The compounding factor has been caused by generations of Smith and Hutton disciples who deepened the disconnect – not only between the economics of the natural world and that of us humans, but also of each from the fullness of what it means to be human. Natural scientists are only interested in people for their atoms and not much concerned with the quality of their lives or feelings. Economic scientists, in order to make their mathematical models of human behaviour work, shave off all the incalculable nuances and unpredictabilities of what it means to be human. Now the outcome, *homo oeconomicus*, like a denatured tailor's dummy, represents real people in all the models used by political and economic decision making.

At the time Hutton and Smith were active, there must have been opportunities for synergy. Hutton wrote of the 'beautiful economy of

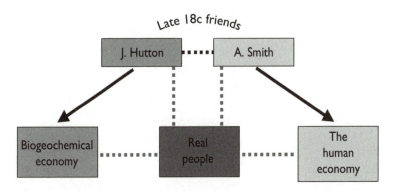

Key: Dotted lines show weak connections; arrows show strong ones.

Figure 2.3 The compound error theory of history: The diagnosis

nature' and Adam Smith was aware of how the human economy used natural resources. After all, the word *economy* even shares the same linguistic root as *ecology*. *Eco* means house, and both are, in essence, about good housekeeping. Smith also wrote an earlier book (which he considered his best), *The Theory of Moral Sentiments* (1759), in which he wondered: 'to what purpose is all the toil and bustle of this world? What is the end of avarice and ambition, of the pursuit of wealth, of power, and pre-eminence.' Smith supposed the purpose to be the welfare of the common man, and wrote of the importance of an internal moral compass to our dealings with each other; 'we also need to meet the approval of our own inner judging self, which understands when we really are what we approve in other people: honest, trustworthy, generous, compassionate'. Smith argued it is this capacity for self-judgement that makes us 'really fit for society'.[11]

But, as we know, the disciplines of natural science and economics went their separate ways. I often wonder if, were he to reappear today, Adam Smith would agree that the common man had been served by the rigorous application of his edict 'let good emerge as the by-product of selfishness'. I rather think not, and imagine that, with the evidence before him, he would magic back his old friend James Hutton to help him reconnect their two truly great ideas into a much better way of serving the good of all people and the environment.

Because that is what we have to do.

Chapter 3

The treatment

It may seem a tall order to prescribe a wholesale rethink about the way we humans organize the way we go about our lives, conduct our business with each other, and think and plan for our future, but nothing less will do if we want to resolve the ecological crisis. Taking a business-as-usual approach to remedying the financial/economic collapse will not get the patient back on their feet for long, as the same conditions that caused all the symptoms and the physiological breakdown of the entire economic system will still be in place.

On the one hand that seems a tall order. But on the other, it is less than 250 years since Adam Smith sat by the parlour fire with James Hutton. In human evolutionary terms, that's but a nanosecond ago.

Figure 3.1 sums up the job we have to do. We will have to reconcile the way the human economy works with the natural workings of the world, so that in all our theories, models and practice the latter sets the rules for what we humans can do. At the same time, a much richer and rounder view of what it means to be a person, what makes us happy and how we form satisfactory relationships will have to be incorporated into how we define the purpose of our economy and therefore how we measure its success.

As anyone tangling with economics and finance appreciates, some words have more definitions than there are dollars in an ex-banker's pension. So, for readers new to all this and to provide a smooth-ish transition into what reconciliation economics might look like, I've concocted some reflections (from a sustainability perspective) on four words unavoidable when thinking about the human economy – capital, money, markets and growth. These reflections may be read as one might read a label on a medicine bottle to be sure we administer the contents correctly. Unless otherwise stated, definitions are taken from *The Penguin Dictionary of Economics* (Bannock et al, 2003)

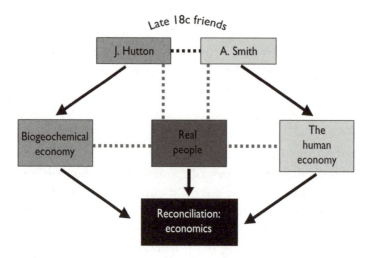

Key: Dotted lines show weak connections; thick arrows and lines, strong connections

Figure 3.1 The compound error theory of history: A grand reconciliation

Four reflections: Capital, money, markets, growth

> **Box 3.1 Reflection: Capital and capitalism**
>
> The dictionary defines capital as follows: 'In general usage capital is any asset or stock of assets – financial or physical – capable of generating income.' A link from this definition to one for 'wealth' finds that to be 'a stock of assets held by any economic unit that yields, or has the potential for yielding, income in some form'. Recognizing the Adam Smith differentiation between 'fixed' and 'circulating' capital, the wealth entry goes on to list 'diamonds, factories and houses as examples of <u>fixed</u> capital', and 'cash, bank deposits, loans or shares as financial assets' as examples of <u>circulating</u> capital. However, unqualified, the word 'capital' has become synonymous with financial capital.
>
> The word capital in fact means 'head' – in Latin *caput*. Its first use in an economic sense was in relation to livestock, as in head of cattle, and to this day the wealth of many families is counted in the very real number of livestock they have. Not just for the immediate lunch they represent, but for the potential flow of benefits from their fleece, milk or offspring. The term 'interest' is thought to arise from the natural growth of the size of the herd. Good husbandry meant using good years to build up a sufficient stock of animals to support the family or group in lean times (de Soto, 2000).

When circulating capital (finance) started masquerading as fixed capital and became traded as a commodity like corn or oil, it compromised its utility as a neutral mediator in our transactions with each other. The domination of money as the only capital that matters has also undermined the value of other capitals in wealth generation. Land, labour and the machines and buildings that make production possible are traditionally considered as capital in economic theory, but compared to the self-replicating powers of money their role even as collateral capitals has become greatly diminished.

As well as the misrepresentation of money/debt as capital, a second observation about capital is missing from the economists' definitions. Raw materials are varyingly under-represented, especially those once thought to be indefinitely renewable but now threatened, resources like fresh water, fish and soil fertility. Not included at all is the capital resource of the services provided by the environment, such as a reasonably stable climate and nutrient cycles. Also missing and unaccounted for are people beyond the contribution of their muscles and minds to producing goods and services (labour to economists). Unless it generates a taxable income, the human economy is not interested in whether people can write poetry, understand nutrition, play a musical instrument, build successful relationships or feel good about themselves. An original definition of wealth is 'being well', a state that owes to much more than *per capita* income. Indeed the evidence is that, over a certain level, there is no strong link between the economic definition of wealth and the purpose of life – to be happy.

The dictionary entry for *capitalism* describes it as 'a social and economic system in which individuals are free to own the means of production and maximize profits, and in which resource allocation is determined by the price system'. Further on, the price system is defined as the mechanism that determines a price in each market by balancing supply and demand. The intention of what became socialism was to favour a system in which the means of production were collectively owned and equality given a high priority. This would require collective (government) intervention in economic affairs, including markets. For well over a century political debate and factions have been about variations on the theme of capitalism and socialism. Both 'isms', however, including their respective extremes – fascism and communism – share the same fatal blind spots for natural capital and a full appreciation of people and their aspirations. Consequently the huge draw down on stocks of natural, human and social capital by all flavours of the human economic process has gone unchecked for decades. For a rollicking critique of modern capitalism try Reich (2007), and for more on the different sorts of capitals with a view to a more sustainable, reconciled, economy, see Chapter 8 on the Five Capitals Tool (page 200), and Porritt (2006).

Although the disproportionate power of financial capital is under the microscope, money has not returned to its vocation yet, which makes it safest always to qualify the word capital when you use it, and open the minds of others by quizzing them about what they mean when they use the word.

Box 3.2 Reflection: Money

When my children were small I belonged to a small babysitting group. On joining, each member was issued with a number of kidney beans (I forget how many but it doesn't matter). Each had the value of one hour. We took turns to keep the ledger in which each member's account was recorded. If you wanted a babysitter you phoned the holder of the ledger who gave you the names of the members with the fewest beans. The distribution of beans, the currency used by the group, was thus kept reasonably equal. If anyone accumulated too many beans, effectively taking them out of circulation, the book-holder redistributed the surplus. Cheating was rare as anyone tempted to introduce extra kidney beans could be spotted, and exceptions could be made for extenuating circumstances, such as illness.

Money is 'something that is widely accepted in payment for goods and services and in settling debts'. In the babysitting circle we could have used paperclips or pennies, but we chose beans and had some simple mechanisms to prevent accumulation and cheating. Our beans were worth one hour to us and no one else. Money, as a pound, euro or dollar (Zimbabwean or American) is worth what you can buy for it. Picasso famously paid his restaurant bills by drawing on the tablecloth. A London theatre ticket costs about £35, and £50 million has been paid for a famous painting by Titian. The price of a barrel of oil yo-yoes from over $140 to under $59, and China, Kuwait and Sweden are buying land in Africa to grow food and bio-fuels for themselves.[1] What is the price of that land relative, say, to a London theatre ticket? How many hectares to one Titian? Why does a big drop oil prices make wind energy 'too expensive'? What is valuing what?

The World Bank uses an indicator called 'purchasing power parity' (PPP) to arrive at a 'fair' way of comparing values of different currencies in terms of what you can buy. So, for example, US$1 would buy 0.65 dollars' worth of goods and services in the UK, 619 dollars' worth in Uganda or 3.45 dollars' worth in China.[2] *The Economist* magazine employs a Big Mac Index to plot the comparative cost of a burger in different countries. In the long run, so the theory goes, exchange rates determined by currency trading will equalize prices across countries. To me this seems optimistic. A London theatre ticket is of no value to a starving African, while access to a hectare of fertile land is worth the life of his or her whole family. The cost to our well-being of not building those wind farms *regardless* of the price of oil could be incalculable.

The idea of restoring money (of any denomination) to its original purpose is not new. The Islamic concept of *riba* for example reflects a belief that money should not be made through money. Money started its career locally, and despite the fact that it is easier to count than well-being, it has proved difficult to manage at national and international scales. Certainly, in times of recession or worse, money returns quite easily to its local habitat. An estimated 4000 local currencies operated in the US during the Great Depression, for example, and, famously, the mayor of Curitiba in Brazil provided a 1970s economic stimulus to the city by offering food and transport tokens in exchange for cleaning up slum quarters and a bay used as a rubbish dump. The environment improved, people got healthier and could commute to work. When the Argentinean government was forced to devalue the peso in 2001, regional currencies sprang up to keep public services going. In some places, Lima, Peru being just one example, an estimated 70 per cent of all economic activity is outside the formal national system (de Soto, 2000).

The same pattern is emerging in this recession. Hundreds of local currencies have appeared in the US and UK to add to established examples including 'time dollar' networks and Local Economic Trading Schemes, which support the exchange of good deeds, goods and services in a locality. London's Wedge Card, set up by John Bird ✱ is one example of a loyalty card that rewards 'buy local first' shopping in a particular street or community.[3]

Money, in other words, is what we want it to be. Its value lies only in its role as an intermediary to help us determine the comparative value of real things, be they goods or services, a well-functioning ecological system, a price for carbon. When its ability to be disinterested in that valuation is impaired because it is concerned more with its own replication, then money becomes useless – dangerous even – as we've found out the hard way. Money's proper job is to carry information.

Box 3.3 Reflection: Markets

'A market is created whenever potential sellers of a good or service are brought into contact with potential buyers and a means of exchange is available. The medium of exchange may be money or barter.' Markets are good places. What they are not are 'interested' actors in the way the economy works. There is no such thing as *The* Market. Markets do not possess hands, invisible or not. Markets are not sentient, they do not hold values, nor are they a value themselves. And, despite the puff it gets, a totally free market is an ugly place, as in Haiti or Nigeria or early post-Soviet Russia. It is people who set up a market, who buy and sell in it, who have values and interests, and who set rules. They may be honest or dishonest.

The size of any market matters. Getting the price right involves a fair way for the buyer and the seller to agree on it. Easier to do in a street market or small shop than in huge, more impersonal marketplaces for, say, mobile phones or insurance. One of the criticisms of globalization of marketplaces, particularly for finance and commodities, is that they are unfair, with the more powerful able to exploit the weaker participant. Most are controlled and manipulated in some way, not necessarily transparently. The rapid growth of fair and other ethically traded goods, like coffee, chocolate or bananas, and socially responsible investment, is evidence that plenty people find this unfairness unacceptable.[4]

When it comes to markets for money or shares in stock-exchange listed companies the complications multiply, one of the reasons that buying and selling is usually done by brokers. If you are on the inside track though, you can do all sorts of incredibly clever things. The money market is 'the financial institutions that deal in short-term securities and loans, gold and foreign exchange', its twin sister the [financial] capital market is 'for long-term loanable funds ... used by industry and commerce mainly for investment [although] there is no clear-cut distinction between the two'. It is in these markets that the extraordinary volumes of debt have been created, and then traded as assets via complex financial instruments. A 'transaction culture' developed where the size of personal and institutional commissions and bonuses depended on the acts of buying and selling, especially in the short term. As a consequence, frenzied trading of debt in fancy packages proliferated. So too did the myth that risk could be 'transformed' from liability to asset through an 'originate and distribute' alchemy that removed it from the immediate lender and borrower relationship and instead spread it widely across the whole financial system.

The 'transaction culture' made it quite legitimate, admired even, for investors to 'play' the financial markets, buying and selling currencies, stocks, debt and other financial products in order to make money. Border-crossing financial transactions massively outstrip those for real goods and services. It is not necessary for participants in this game to have any interest in or commitment to any company, commodity, country or currency involved. Betting on prices moving up and down to get a good return or 'profit' for that investment is perfectly legal – even the cruelty of 'short selling', where the bet is on the value of a share or currency dropping and the act of short selling helps that to happen. The big moneymakers in the financial sector got knighthoods and became the rock stars of commerce, yet compared to their gains, very little trickled down into the 'real' economy. Much of their activity is what Charles Handy calls 'a froth on the surface of enterprise', more boldly branded as 'socially useless' by the Chair of the UK Financial Services Authority.[5]

Marketplaces of all shapes and sizes will have to be salvaged from corrupt or inappropriate practices because they are too important as vital facilitation devices for human social and economic commerce. In most of the world (including where I live in London) they can be an enjoyable meeting place for human values that involve conviviality as much as fair trading. At that scale self-regulation is not difficult. A trader once responded to my question about whether a shirt would shrink or not with a hurt 'but I am here every week!' as evidence of his good faith. It cannot be impossible to imagine ways of restoring trust and fairness to larger marketplaces. eBay, for example, is a huge marketplace. Although it can't prevent skullduggery, its fully transparent policies discourage it and deal with fraud quickly and fairly should it occur.

Box 3.4 Reflection: Economic growth

Very regularly, Herman Daly points out the difference between the words 'growth' and 'development'. If something is growing, he says, it is getting physically bigger, if it is developing, it is realizing its potential, improving *qualitatively*.

The ecological systems on the Earth are into developing the potential of evolution within the physical laws described in Chapter 2. Consequently the biogeochemical economy works roughly in equilibrium, to all intents and purposes balancing the inflow of energy from the sun with the outflow of energy from an Earth that neither grows nor shrinks.[6] Within these physical constraints the natural world is in the business of growing quality, not volume. For example, a tree, doesn't grow forever. When it reaches maturity (is big *enough*) it starts to provide sustenance for others. By contrast, the human economy is all about *quantitative* growth manifest and measured in ever-increasing consumption of goods and services. There is no maturity. It acknowledges no limits to either environmental resources or services, and any regard to social and ethical constraints it gives (working conditions, equity) tend to be put aside should quantitative growth slow.

The now globally accepted method of judging economic growth is gross domestic product (GDP). GDP is calculated (in money terms) as the total output of goods and services from all the productive activities of the economy. It was never intended to become, as it has, a proxy for the general well-being of a country. If GDP is up, so the assumption goes, people are 'better off' than before. And of course some are. But many are not. And for GDP to grow, more throughput of resources is needed to keep the output rising. The mechanism for keep GDP (as the sovereign indicator of success) on the rise, involves a fairly straightforward cycle: demand is stimulated (more people borrow and consume more goods and services), which in turn prompts firms to (borrow and) produce more (resulting in more jobs, more consumers); and investors to (borrow and) invest more in innovation of new products (to stimulate more demand and consumption), and so on round it goes. Or may do in reverse, as recession is defined by negative GDP growth. All the effort that goes into pushing this cycle back into positive GDP growth through encouraging more consumption (e.g. new cars for old), borrowing (low interest rates), bailing out bust banks (£/$trillions) is clinching evidence of just how central this process is to governments. Quantitative economic growth must be restored – at any cost. There is no Plan B!

Attempts to break the relationship between increasing resource use and current notions of economic growth (i.e. obtain more outputs with less inputs) have met with mixed results (Jackson, 2009). Efficiency, in particular of energy use, has brought relative gains. For example, globally, the amount of CO_2 emitted per US dollar has improved from one kilogram in 1980 to 770 grams in 2006, though a slight increase has been evident since 2000 (IPCC, 2007, p4). Nevertheless, due to more people producing and consuming more stuff, over the same period the total emissions of CO_2 have more than doubled. Growth in other material throughputs has also increased in absolute terms over the same period. Neither of these trends, which are negative to the biogeochemical economy, is captured in GDP.

According to Adair Turner, the time has come to 'dethrone growth' as in quantitative growth of GDP.[7] Pioneering ecological economist Herman Daly has long pointed out that what he calls a 'steady-state' economy does not have to be seen as a 'failed growth economy'. Rather it is an economy with a constant human population and stock of environmental capital, maintained by a low rate of throughput that is within the regenerative and assimilative capacities of the ecosystem. 'This means low birth equal to low death rates, and low production equal to low depreciation rates. Low throughput means high life expectancy for people and high durability for goods.'[8] Economic growth, therefore, could be entirely qualitative – how much the environment is back in control of its own ecosystems, and how good we are getting at living longer, healthier, happier lives using vastly less volumes of natural resources.[9] Very different from the way it is now.

In the meantime, a good question to ask about economic growth is 'What is growing, where, for whom, and at what cost'?

A particularly helpful trick for opening minds to the possibility that radical change could happen to the way we run the human economy without total mayhem, is to imagine that money, in all its forms (cash, debt, stocks) disappeared overnight. The following day, absolutely nothing else would have changed. The environment, people, buildings, roads, houses, the washing-up and other unfinished work would still be there, just as they were the day before. Wave another wand, and a new currency comes into being, along with rules that say it can only be used to value and exchange things, and cannot itself be traded. Debt has disappeared (we swallow and cope with the moral hazard one last time), and credit is available but only to the creditworthy for socially useful activity. Life in the economy where real people live would continue.

Wands, sadly, are in short supply for even the most ambitious positive deviant so we are at the beginning of what James Galbraith calls 'a long, profound, painful and irreversible process of change [and] we need to start thinking and acting accordingly'.[10] Either we make the transition to an ecological economy in as planned and orderly a way as possible, or the environment and (increasingly likely) social disorder will do it for us – suddenly and probably brutally. The job of positive deviants, therefore, is to pre-empt this eventuality and convince others that doing right by the environment and people can be the motor of a perfectly satisfactory economy.

Reconciliation economics: What does good look like?

This section ends with a look at the possible ingredients of a reconciled economy. To convey not only a sense of what is possible, but to underline the urgency of having something like this in place as soon as possible, I've written it in the present tense. Here we are, with the patient flat out in the emergency room. How to form a judgement about different cardiac resuscitation techniques for the global or UK economy? Will these policies or that action raise the old Frankenstein of business as before to wreak havoc again, or will they create a new economy, with different values and goals – one that the sustainability-literate could do business with? Something like this, for example:

There is a plan: A Sustainability Consensus governs global economic and international relations

A Sustainability Consensus has replaced the Washington Consensus (see page 159) on how best to run the world economy. The debate around details is robust and creative, but the direction of travel is agreed. Signals, both political and economic are clear and consistent that a new type of economy is under construction, with qualitative growth in human and environmental well-being as its purpose. For example, the competitive advantage between nations for the cheapest production of this or that is replaced by collaboration around what is most advantageous for social and environmental resilience everywhere, and includes the lowering of birth rates to meet the lower UN projections.

Learning from the tactics of the economic theorists who fought a guerilla-type campaign to get the idea of a self-perfecting market into political power, an influencing strategy at international and national level, and amongst citizens, helps to promulgate understanding about what is happening, what the Sustainability Consensus means to them, and how they can contribute.[11] Thus a strong and attractive counterpoint to extremism fuelled by injustice and lack of hope is created. People see there is a positive way to take hold of their own destiny, and reformed national and international institutions and sustainability-focused diplomacy helps to built trust and a sense of common purpose amongst people and between nations.

A package of emergency measures is underway, making sure catastrophe management favours a forward transition to a Sustainability Consensus, rather than a patched up version of business as it used to be

The idea of a Green New Deal to 'tackle the "triple crunch" of credit, oil price and climate crises', was launched in the UK in July 2008. Within weeks, the UN had picked up the idea, spotlighting the Triple F crises in finance, fuel and food. At the launch of the Global Green New Deal, Pavan Sukdhev, head of global markets for Deutsch Bank, explained: 'Here you have some of the choices in a nutshell. If we are to lift 2.6 billion people living on less that $2 a day out of poverty, do we put them into making more and more motor cars, TVs and PCs, or do we invest in the network of protected areas [particularly forests] and develop its potential for green and decent new jobs?'[12]

The point of the emergency packages is to jump-start activities to prevent the worst consequences of environmental degradation (climate change, loss of biological resources) and pave the way to a future eco-logical economy. New money, credit, tax incentives, regulation are all geared to the infrastructure that will support a low-carbon economy: modernizing the electricity grid; energy efficiency and renewables; growing biological capital; civic renewal; securing water and food sup-plies; public transport; splicing sustainability literacy into all education and training; helping people feel secure where they are, and all the sorts of goods and services that enable people to live low-carbon/high-happiness lifestyles. At home and abroad. The urgency of activities to mitigate climate change is not underplayed, but people are confident their worries and sense of justice are not sidelined.

Capital has taken a broader meaning, one that is located in the real economy

Finance, as cash or credit, is no longer considered as a 'real' capital in economics, and money is returned to its primary role as a means of exchange and a way of valuing other types of capital. Natural capital, human and social capital join fixed capital like infrastructure, machines and buildings as the primary stocks of capital – resources to be managed so that flows of benefits may be secured while the stock itself is maintained and wherever possible increased. See Chapter 8 (page 200) for more on this.

Lessons from the past have been learnt and a new method for macro-ecological-economic management by national, local and international institutions is in place. Building on Adair Turner's idea for a macro-prudential analysis to see the big picture for finance, macro-ecological-economic analysis monitors the balance (and potential for imbalance) within and between the four different sorts of capital stocks in the short and long term, and manages the effectiveness of finance in facilitating that.[13] New regulations, the balance between public and private sector, investment in critical sectors, tax and other incentives, innovation for qualitative improvements in well-being of the environment and people (rather than novelty stuff to buy and sell, or 'useless' financial products) are all managed to provide some protection from the worst of the now inevitable damage of the ecological and economic crises, and to set direction for a more resilient way of running our affairs.

Simple monetary policy is replaced by multi-capital policy, and resilience and stability become central economic disciplines. This means stronger, more diverse local economies, but not an end to trade across national and regional borders. There are, however, different rules for that trade. For example, produce like bananas and chocolate are not only subject to fair trade rules, but also to rules that mean the economy they come from should be equally resilient on a local basis. This requirement has changed the nature of international relations and aid, and fostered place-to-place partnerships to secure livelihoods, commodities and access to land in future-proof and just ways. The purpose of globalization is about increasing collaboration and reconciling national interests, not competing over them.

New models of ownership are in place or under discussion. What should be held in trust for future generations (as the UK National Trust does for heritage sites) – forests, global commons, like the Arctic, wild spaces, the sea? What does sovereignty mean? Who owns shared vital infrastructure in local communities or internationally? What counts as vital infrastructure – banks, trains, electricity grids, social services?

Money has gone into service, slavery even

Money no longer masquerades as 'real' capital like a horse, a house or a well adjusted person, and is subordinated to its proper role of lubricating the real economy. Reform to national and international financial institutions means only a publically owned and accountable central bank can create money. The long-standing idea that 'new' money, free of debt, could replace 'old' money (over 90 per cent of which was created as interest-bearing debt by private banks) has been implemented (a long shot, this!). Money, as a public good, is now a 'value information unit' created *ex nihilo* (out of nothing, so interest free) at need and will of the central bank.[14] National currencies are in effect nationalized and serving the public interest. Money no longer makes the world go round as the song goes, but instead facilitates the movement of people, goods and services round the world.[15]

There are times when money is not the appropriate medium of exchange of value, as in love and trust or neighbourhood conviviality, but ecological economists are capable of presenting a balance sheet that mixes different types of calculi to draw a picture of the overall health of the capital stocks and flow of benefits of any economic unit. Because it is disinterested, 'new' money makes it easier to put some sort of value on carbon in the ground, or on ecological system services, or on social contentment, for example, to inform macro-ecological-economic decisions.

The idea of complementary currencies has taken hold. Local currencies, like those described in the essay on money above, help smooth the transition out of the crash and between old and new money by keeping activity on the go in communities.

Credit is cool – meaning it is reliable and responsible, boring even

Restoring trust in a system that offers credit and manages savings and deposits for individuals, businesses and governments means risks have been returned to sender. Instead of the 'originate and distribute' regime that took loans off the lender's balance sheet, an 'originate and hold' policy is in operation and properly regulated. Lender and borrower have a relationship and share ownership of any risk associated with the debt of any householder or enterprise. For example a bank and a wind power company might share the risk with the local community that will benefit.[16] The Ecology Building Society ✱ long a pioneer in lending for green build and renovation is joined by a suite of new financial services to channel money and credit to renewable energy and efficiency schemes in housing and more generally. Credit unions, and new community development finance institutions are examples of this happening now. Enterprises like ZOPA ✱, which facilitates person to person lending, hasn't got a sustainability category, but could.

Banks are social enterprises

Light dawned, and governments abandoned the lunacy of pouring good money after bad debts of terminally untrustworthy mega-banks. Instead, the prescription of economists like Nouriel Roubini and Paul Krugman is implemented. Bad banks are nationalized, with good and bad assets separated, the good ones and innocent bystanders surgically removed and grafted into good (limited purpose) banks (some new and some existing) and the baddies left to go bankrupt, in effect writing off the debt as part of the move from old to new money. Governments no longer rely for advice on the very bankers and academics that got the economy into difficulties in the first place. The people who anticipated the *un*sustainability of past practice, including ecological economists, are piecing together the various solutions they've been preparing for some time. The foundation of a new and – vital this – *trusted* financial sector is established, with money created and moderated by a central bank. Private banks are still able to take savings and supply credit but cannot create money as interest-bearing debt. They are brokers not creators of money. The third element of the reform of banking affects advisors to individuals and businesses. They are separate from both the central bank and retail banks and strictly independent. The perverse relationship that skewed highly leveraged borrowing in favour of real estate (including commercial real estate) is ended. There is a mandatory preference for investment in, and lending for, sustainability outcomes, locally, nationally and internationally.

At an international level, John Maynard Keynes' 1943 proposal for an international banking system that kept in balance the deficits *and* surpluses of countries has been dusted off and adapted to provide a macro-ecological overview. A *possible* new Organization for *Ecological Cooperation and Development* promotes and supports countries implementing the Sustainability Consensus, but with the best diplomatic effort going to establishing a new intercontinental security relationship around the financial services needed to build resilient local economies. The erstwhile richer countries are humble and keen to learn from the very poor about how economic resilience works. What is it that keeps (non-corrupt) economic wheels turning in desperate times?

At a national and local level, the richer world has taken another leaf out of the poor world book and started to model some of its banking services on micro-credit enterprises like the Grameen Bank ✳, recognizing that trusted 'peoples' banks' are the route to regaining confidence in the whole system. Long-standing examples, like the Co-operative Bank ✳ replicate, as do financial services like Climate Change Capital ✳ and Triodos Bank. The endangered but trusted UK community post offices become a network of 'peoples' banks'. As suggested in the section on capital above, different sorts of ownership of the banks and other financial institutions are used, including community ownership. All, however, is kept under careful regulatory control. Banking is a public utility and ownership models reflect this.[17]

The quest for resilience in the banking system recognizes that the national and international banks are only as strong as the local banking systems are, not vice versa. The financial system is, in the words of Adair Turner, 'a shock absorber in the economy, not a shock amplifier'.[18] The phrase 'you can bank on me' means something again.

Governance is exemplary: Everyone knows and plays by the rules

The state and democratic process is free of compromise from financial interests. The 'revolving' door of money, people, special access and privilege between government and private sector companies and lobbying bodies is over. Political parties (if they still exist) have public funds for elections. In the UK, parliament (both houses) and local government are independent of private sector or special interest seeking sponsorship or political party funding.

It is illegal to avoid tax, and the complex, loophole ridden system is reformed – along with the accountancy firms, lawyers and so on who help clients to exploit it. Corporate influence over governments is ended, though philanthropically minded wealthy companies and individuals may pay to an international fund to support global projects to mitigate or adapt to climate change, improve health, relieve poverty, for example, *over and above* paying proper national and local taxes. Paying taxes and contributing to the 'common good' becomes a matter of honour, as is taking responsibility for how public funds are spent (via democratic channels and personal engagement). To evade tax is seen as distasteful as blowing cigarette smoke in a baby's face, rather than something rather clever.

Governance of all public and private organizations (not only banks) is properly overhauled. It is no longer acceptable to claim only middle-aged men from the charmed and virtually closed circle of eligible board members are clever enough to run companies, banks, regulatory bodies or head government task forces. Systems are simplified and made more effective and attractive to women and other under-represented groups, not to mention more intelligible to politicians and journalists as well as to savers and lenders. International institutions (like the Bank of International Settlement, the International Monetary Fund (IMF)) and self-regulating processes (like the Basel agreements on minimum levels of reserves) are, in whatever form they may be continued, scrupulous and transparent about their governance processes. There is, as Chinese President Hu Jintao told the G20 in April 2009 on behalf of the 9–20 countries newly added to the old G8 group: 'a new international financial order that is fair, just, inclusive and orderly'.[19]

A new type of ethic, as part of something perhaps called a 'civic ethic', has been born. It includes the understanding that tax is not a burden on society, but actually the making of it, as is the importance of competent and trusted governance in using revenues wisely. What is taxed, where, when, how and why, and how the money is spent is under continual public discussion. Prompted by the financial meltdown and the fearsome damage done to people and the environment in the past, a debate about what sort of society we really want is underway to inform the detail of the Sustainability Consensus. This is done regardless of distortion by the media and naysayers, through an energetic nonpolitical, non-partisan, inclusive and carefully facilitated public conversation fronted by people who hold the public trust.

Markets are designed and managed for resilience

That we ever thought an automatic, uncontrolled mechanism was the best way to shape the good life is relegated to the library shelves marked Science Fiction. *Homo oeconomus*, the unreal and not very nice automaton styled to fit the idea of a sentient market balancing the emotionless supply and demand of his needs, is in a museum.

Instead real, mostly collegiate, predominately loving and charmingly unpredictable *homo sometimes sapiens* takes his place. Behavioural economists, neuro-biologists and social-psychologists join the ecological economists for many days in the sun.

As far as possible, marketplaces are repopulated with real people meeting to trade things and exchange pure information. For most 'going to the market' is a pleasurable event, and the exchange is a social interaction as well as sale or purchase of produce. Gossip as well as goods are traded, as is information.[20] Relationships are formed. Trust in the value of the item to be sold or bought is enshrined in mutual knowledge about quality, shortages or gluts, degree of need to either buy or sell, but also the personal relationship between the buyer ('Will these T-shirts shrink?') and the seller ('I'm here every week, bring them back if they do.'). Transactions on a larger scale are fewer and may take longer, but they support the shift of emphasis from maximizing cash returns to maximizing returns to the environment and society. Participants can keep track of the relationships involved. Profit can be made but *sufficient* and it must meets rules – similar to those governing Fairtrade or Islamic murabahah (agreed profit-sharing), and including transparency.

Participation in a market for shares in any company, large or small, carries a shareholder responsibility for that company's contribution to the stock of all types of capital. It is no longer possible to be a 'semi-detached' shareholder, or solely concerned with financial returns. Those of a high-risk, quick-buck disposition are directed to casinos and betting shops. Damaging short buying and selling needs special permission. True values of shares are judged over a longer, say five-year, period, perhaps with shareholders 'locked in' as mortgage holders are today.

Analysts consider the value of a successful firm to lie in its longer-term viability and its contribution to sustainable development.

Gross domestic happiness

Lots of evidence that human happiness and growth in orthodox GDP are not related, has boosted the search for new ways of defining success – in a country or a neighbourhood. (Robert Constanza and colleagues give a helpful overview of different methodologies, some complementing or 'angelizing' traditional GDP, but others seeking to evaluate how much a community is drawing down on its stock of natural, social, human and built capital, rather than living off its interest.[21]) In the 1980s Herman Daly and John Cobb proposed a new Index of Sustainable Economic Welfare (ISEW) and the UK new economics foundation (nef) went on to develop the methodology that brings together indicators of social and environmental well-being, adjusted for defensive expenditure on, for example, health, air pollution, loss of farm or wetland and so on, to give a proper picture of how we are faring.[22] The NEF also publishes a *Happy Planet Index*.[23] The government of Bhutan has become famous for its adoption of a national indicator called Gross Economic Happiness, and the Canadians have developed a Canada Index of Wellbeing.

A boost to the dethroning of GDP as the most perverse and destructive measure of human well-being came from the President of France, Nicholas Sarkozy's Commission on the Measurement of Economic Performance and Social Progress. In 2009 its co-leaders, Joseph Stiglitz and Amarta Sen published a report recommending new measures based on the well-being of the family and broader ideas of environmental and social goods (based on a broad definition of capital).[24] The report differentiated between well-being now, and the potential for well-being in the future, which is critical to being able to make judgements about the sustainability of any choices made by a relatively short-lived government, for example. Drawing down on all of this new, 'gross national well-being' measures now do what Robert Kennedy wanted to do 40 years ago:

> ... the gross national product does not allow for the health of our children, the quality of their education, or the joy of their play. It does not include the beauty of our poetry or the strength of our marriages;

the intelligence of our public debate or the integrity of our public
officials. It measures neither our wit nor our courage; neither our
wisdom nor our learning; neither our compassion nor our devotion to
our country; it measures everything, in short, except that which makes
life worthwhile … [25]

I could go on. It would be fun, for example, to query the obsession with
jobs as the only legitimate way for people to meet their needs and find
self-worth. There's lots of work to be done, for sure, but recessionary
times reveal more ways of getting it done and otherwise meeting our
needs than through formal employment. DIY, barter and time banks,
local currency groups, volunteering, for example, with more people than
ever setting up their own businesses. Perhaps there is a resilience lesson
to be had from thinking how we might be less vulnerable to sudden job
losses, if paid employment was mixed in with different types of activity
that may or may not be paid, but which nevertheless contribute to our
well-being.

Although it is perverse to avoid economics when talking about economics, I've tried to maintain ideological neutrality and to be nonpolitical, though I hope radical enough in my imagining of what
reconciliation economics might be like to stir you into critical reflection
mode! According to Charles Hampden-Turner, who describes himself
as a management philosopher, economics is about describing the creation of wealth *after* the event, and, unfortunately, the politics of wealth
retention tends to swamp the logic of wealth creation (Hampden-
Turner and Trompenaars, 1993). Ecological or reconciliation
economics is quite different. It is about creating *future* wealth that will
sustain the well-being and health of people and the environment into
the very, very long term. And that can only come from the flow of
benefits – the interest if you like – from healthy stocks of *real* capital well
husbanded. A lot of the intellectual groundwork has been done already,
some of it exposed here, and although there are examples of different
features of ecological economics in action, wholesale shifting of
mindsets and purses will not be without difficulties.

But shift them we must, because the physical regulations operated
by the biogeochemical economy are much more powerful that anything
the UK Financial Standards Authority or the US Security and Exchange
Commission could dream up.[26] Moreover, the rage of the innocent and

those most hurt by the financial sector's debacle, climate change and continuing injustice will not be assuaged by anything but big changes. From the most poor in Africa to low-income UK pensioners following government guidelines about investment, thrift has been punished and survival strategies shattered. The feeling of injustice was summed up by Luiz Inacio da Silva (Lula) the President of Brazil. Clearly furious on behalf of what rich countries tend to call 'emerging economies' that have followed the Washington-led economic prescription he said: 'Before the crisis they looked like they knew everything about economics, and they have demonstrated they know nothing... This crisis was caused by no black man or woman or by no indigenous person or by no poor person.'[27]

A once in a lifetime chance to get it right

In the three chapters of this first section, I've tried to give you a different way of thinking about the symptoms of *un*sustainable development and how we have, collectively and personally, lost sight of the laws of right behaviour that should govern our relationship with the rest of life on Earth. As a consequence, we have 'permitted' the way we go about our business to take a course that means its success depends on inflicting damage to the environment and to people. Now we have a once in a lifetime chance to put things right. While the misery it has caused to so many innocent people is deeply regrettable, the massive failure of our financial system removes one of the greatest obstacles to sustainable development – the lack of space and the opportunity to imagine how the human economy might work differently.

At various times in recent history, there have been national leaders who rose to the responsibility of being in power at critical times. Attlee and Roosevelt, for example, were credited with grasping the moment after the Second World War to put in bold economic reforms that brought stability and prosperity to Britain and America. There is hope that US President Barack Obama ✳ is of even stronger mettle at an unprecedentedly critical time. But even if he is, and others rise to join him at the head of international institutions and countries around the world, they won't succeed without battalions of sustainability-literate people not only imagining how it could be different, but showing how good it can be in practise – regardless of the perversity of the systems and the barriers they encounter.

Which is where you come in. From this section and its references you should have a *sufficient* grasp of the larger ecological and economic context in which you will be exercising your leadership. Just as importantly, I hope you will have gained a *good enough* view of what a sustainability-driven route out of the economic crash might look like. At the very least, I hope you will feel *sufficiently* confident to make decisions now that will help guarantee the direction of travel is towards the future and not the past. If much of it is already familiar, I hope you've gained a few new insights nevertheless, and perhaps some fresh ways of convincing others to join in.

Section Two

Lost Leadership

Once they lost sight of their goals, they redoubled their efforts.
Mark Twain

Section Two

Introduction

A dysfunctional system

Leadership is a vital ingredient for achieving sustainability. Without it, sustainability will never make it – in government, business or anywhere. In and out of organizations, what everyone does at every level matters enormously, of course. Widespread, often localized, innovation in *how* to live and work in low-carbon/high-happiness ways is where sustainability will be put into operation and made real, but only leadership will give sufficient direction, scale and pace to what works well. There is plenty of historical evidence that one without the other will not be sufficient.

Which makes it worrying that the volume of grumblings about the quality of leadership *in all sectors* has now reached shouting level. Dramatic failures in the finance sector are the iceberg tip of stories about mayhem and mediocrity in the public and private sector attributed to bad management or leadership failure. Who is to blame? The organizations themselves? Or does the fault lie with management education, currently a boom sector for universities and business schools? Stefano Harney thinks so. He has studied 2300 research papers in the field and accuses business and management researchers for focusing on solving 'small technical problems' such as product placement and supply chains, and failing to examine the larger social and political questions that could provide fundamental answers on how to create a better world.[1] *The Economist* magazine is scathing about the legions of management gurus. 'If management could indeed be reduced to a few simple principles, then we would have no need for management thinkers', it says, wondering why 'their failures only serve to stoke demand for their services'.[2]

In the UK the complaints about the quality of leadership and management became so rowdy that the government set up a Council for Excellence in Management and Leadership (CEML) to find out what was going on. CEML's report was damning of both public and private sector, finding leadership skills such as vision, commitment and organizational smartness to be 'in short supply from the top to the bottom of organizations', as were more routine skills such as strategy, communication and planning. The working group on management and leadership education concluded 'we are dealing with a dysfunctional system'. The report's conclusion was unequivocal:

> Good management and leadership is pivotal to investment, productivity, delivery of service and quality of performance across both the public and private sectors. But despite the growth in formal management education over the last 20 years, and despite the increase in the amount of training received by managers in both large and smaller establishments in the same period, management deficiencies continue to be cited as a cause of poor productivity and performance. (CEML, May 2002)

Is it any better in the US, the birthplace of modern management education? Evidently not. In 2002 the US Association to Advance Collegiate Schools of Business (AACSB) identified a 'global bazaar' of courses. Studies consistently find that alumni cite skills like communications, interpersonal skills, multicultural skills, negotiation as most needed but most deficient in their education, while some of the externalities that current students think will have the biggest impact on organizational success – such as costs of health care, environmental concerns and climate change, quality of public education – get next to zero emphasis in their courses.[3] According to Harvard Business school professor, Rakesh Khurana:

> it remains a question whether university business schools, even today, have succeeded in creating a coherent, systematic, clearly bounded body of knowledge – much less one that is firmly connected with management practice – out of the individual disciplines (principally economics, applied mathematics, psychology and sociology) in which business school curricula and research are currently grounded. (Khurana, 2007, p91)

My hunch is that many readers of this book will have been on some sort of management training course, and that, to varying degrees, it will have been useful in some way. Teasing out what is relevant for a sustainability-literate positive deviant is explored in Chapter 4, via some of the 'theories' from which leadership 'thinkers' have tried to distil practical models.

I won't say this has been easy, nor that great enlightening conclusions are possible. Not least because there is an impossibly vast, frustratingly contradictory number of books and journals on the subject. The British Library has 'something in excess of 50,000 books ... of which about 80 per cent have been published during the last 20 years' while the Library of Congress admits to 'at least 30,000 titles on the subjects of Business Management and Leadership'.[4]

Unlike purveyors of snake oil with one remedy for multiple malaises, it seems management training has many complex remedies for one comparatively straightforward problem. The very large number of courses, in and out of universities and at all levels, have no common view on essential components. It seems that by and large teachers teach what takes their fancy, and, until very recently in both the US and the UK, public sector leadership theory seems to have followed slavishly the private sector model.

Nevertheless, with persistence, it is possible see through the fog of fashion surrounding leadership education to identify some useful insights – the babies we want to nurture and grow in a new vision for sustainability-literate leadership.

There are two chapters in this section. The first concentrates on the various theories around management (mostly) and leadership and uses two reflections – on women and on power – to help illuminate some of the deepest problems in the practise of leadership today. The second gives a twist of the lens to focus on business schools, where most management and leadership development takes place, and suggests they have been detrimentally influenced by ideologies and corporate interests. I also argue that that the advent of 'corporate social responsibility' may well have slowed rather than accelerated the passage of firms to genuinely sustainable practices.

Whether you agree with me about any of this or not, readers should find in these two chapters sufficient stimulus for reflecting on their own education and experience to date. Deconstructing what you know into a sustainability-sensitive mindset is the first step to analysing what you need to add as you develop your own sustainability-literate leadership 'persona'.

The 'wiring' diagram on page 92 should help you keep some shape to your learning journey, which, ideally, will be a lifelong commitment

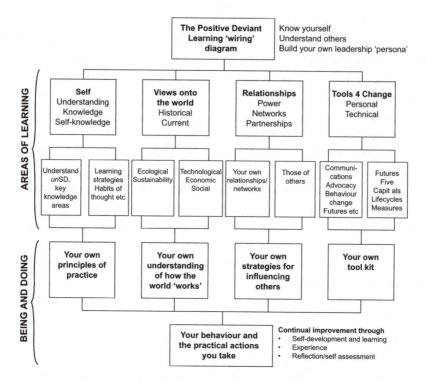

Figure 4.1 A personal learning wiring diagram

to always trying to do better, and to do more. To be most effective most quickly you need keep four wheels turning simultaneously: your self-knowledge and broad general knowledge; how views about how the world works shape what people believe and do; the quality of your relationships with others; and various tools to sustain your personal learning and to improve the capacity of sustainability-literate action in others. Ultimately, your learning should translate into your own distinct leadership model or 'persona' which guides your behaviour and the actions you take.

Chapter 4

The best and worst of it: Leadership today

I don't plan to cover the technical economic and financial aspects of leadership education, which usually make up the bulk of the syllabus. That is not because financial accounting, project management, marketing and other technical skills are unimportant; leaders do need to be *good enough* at all these things. But they are best considered as a subset of leadership, not a substitute for reflections on the larger matter of where leadership is heading – and why. Nor do I peer into the colourful kaleidoscope of fads peddled by legions of management gurus and consultants. Again that doesn't mean you shouldn't check them out. Once feeling comfortable with your own sustainability-literacy some of the more quirky approaches may be of use, but you do need to be a discerning consumer.[5]

So what follows is the fastest of tracks through the theories that attempt to distil some universal truth about leadership. But first, another dive into the world of definitions. As well as being strangely isolated from its own history, the world of leadership development is extraordinarily loose in its use of language. For example, as far as formal records are concerned, the words 'manager' and 'administrator' have, respectively, 16th century and 14th century Italian roots, while 'leader' and 'leadership' are Anglo-Saxon in origin, dating back to the 5–10th centuries period, though as a *practice* are much older. Cave dwellers organized their lives in order to survive, and many animals operate leadership systems, as in a migrating formation of geese for example. As an academic discipline, however, management and leadership only really emerged after the Second World War and then predominantly in the US.

The difference between *a leader* and *leadership* is as straightforward as it is little used and understood.

A leader is a post-holder and may be elected, chosen or appointed to lead something – an army, an organization, a government, a project team. The post-holder is viewed as the source of leadership. The holder may or may not be good at leadership.	**Leadership may be exercised by anyone**, from anywhere in an organization or group. Even when an appointed leader exists, others may exercise leadership.

It is on *leadership* that I focus, though I have to acknowledge that much writing and research on leadership is from an organizational *management* point of view, and principally a commercial organization at that.

In reality, the roles of leader and manager do overlap. Many leaders work their way up an organization before they take a top job, and many managers practise a lot of leadership – whether back-stopping poor performance from their official leaders or handling devolved responsibility. The following differentiation between 'leadership' and 'management' is helpful, though it is usually the source of more argument than agreement, and doesn't tell the whole story about sustainability-literate leadership behaviour.

Table 4.1 How leadership is different from management

	Leadership	Management
Creating agendas	Establishes direction	Plans and budgets
	Develops vision of the future	Establishes detailed steps/ timetables
	Develops change strategies	Allocates resources
Building networks	Aligns people	Establishes structures
	Inculcates vision in people	Staffs the structures
		Develops delegating and monitoring policies
Execution	Inspires	Controls
	Energizes others to overcome barriers	Organizes to solve problems
Outcomes	Potentially revolutionary change	Consistent key results

Source: Adapted with the permission of The Free Press, a Division of Simon & Schuster, Inc., *A Force for Change: How Leadership Differs from Management* by John P. Kotter. Copyright © 1990 by John P. Kotter, Inc. All rights reserved

For better or for worse, I have subdivided the various theories, mostly about management, into traditional and more contemporary ones, to make it as easy as possible to extract some useful learning. There is remarkable overlap and mix up between the various theories over time, and even a strand of academic endeavour that debates the best way to categorize everything.

Traditional leadership theories

The Great Man (and not so great woman) theory

Most of traditional leadership theory is concerned with the attributes and techniques of the person in the *leader* role. The heroic leader figure and analysing what it is that differentiates him (this is definitely a *Boys' Own Paper* story) from the rest (followers) has fascinated writers for a very long time (see Reflection: Followership, page 96).

The idea that some people are 'born to lead' still has resonance, with attendance at the right school or university, or belonging to the right family, giving disproportionate advantage to this day. So too does the power of money and force in securing leadership positions. Think of the US presidential elections for an example of the first, and look to Pakistan, Burma or any regime where the military have seized power for the second.

The Great Man theory is unquestionably a 'male' approach to leadership, with deep roots in military or aggressive solutions to problem solving and it is to be found in most cultures. Worldwide, mythologies and religions are dominated by 'great men' and comparatively few women. There are, of course, some rule-proving exceptions: Boadicea, Florence Nightingale, Margaret Thatcher, Marjorie Pearson or Mary Robinson, each active in very different areas and with different styles. And the US appointed its first five-star female general in 2008. But the principle holds. Leadership is, in reality as well as perception, for the boys. The heroic idea of leadership, where the Great Man bears all the burden, succeeding or failing on his own, remains attractive whether he is a polar explorer, military general or prime minister. Many leadership courses were started by ex-military or adventuring men and still use outward-bound type team building exercises. Great Men telling their stories are very popular on courses, in after-dinner speeches for business and political gatherings, or in books. The alpha male 'I did it my way' genre is exemplified in *On Leadership: Practical Wisdom From the People Who Know* by Allan Leighton, writing when Chairman of Royal Mail Group (Leighton, 2007).

But alongside the cult of the Great Man competing hard to win in a climate where losing is punished hard through loss of job or organizational takeover (though not always sacrifice of bonus), is a deeper analysis of leadership qualities that includes the ability to make decisions on sound evidence brought forward by high quality and trusted staff and advisors. Increasingly, the public persona of the Great Leader is analysed as being as good as the team around him or her. Supporting this counterpoint to the Great Man theory, anthropologists have noted that hunter-gatherer societies existing today are relatively egalitarian. 'The rank and file, watching leaders with special care, keep them from developing any serious degree of authority'.[6]

Box 4.1 Reflection: Followership

By and large, leadership theory pays scant attention to the study of the follower, even though history is thick with examples of how followers have supported or subverted the projects of bad leaders. I remember Vaclav Havel ✱ saying in 1990 that he found the ease with which the communist dictatorships were ultimately toppled rather embarrassing. Could we have done it sooner, he asked? Perhaps not, as it was some words Soviet leader Gorbachev used when he escaped his escort and walked into the crowds during the 40th anniversary of the German Democratic Republic (GDR) in East Berlin early in October 1989 that made the difference. 'If you want democracy, take it now' he repeated quietly and insistently as he wrung the outstretched hands. My friends who were there told me this was taken as a signal that, should GDR citizens seize the moment, Russia would not roll the tanks over them as it had done in the past. The revolutions were velvet, because the threat of very hard power had been removed.

Hitler, of course, and Stalin or Mao, are the most common examples of bad, hard, leadership, but not all their followers fell into the same camp. Close in were the inner circle (who truly believe in the project). Surrounding them were the loyal soldiers or henchman (who know on which side their bread is buttered). Beyond them were the majority (keeping their head down), and maybe a distant thin ring of the active dissenters and resisters. In a range of different situations followership patterns often appear in an approximate 10:80:10 ratio: collaborators:most citizens:resistance (France in World War II); gravely ill:ill:nearly well (hospital ward); achieving:average:in difficulty (school classroom, boardroom, any organization). Whether those in the 'middle majority' gravitate towards the 'good' end (resistance/nearly well/achieving) depends to a certain extent on self-motivation or serendipity, but mostly to the quality of a leadership that organizes towards a good outcome.

Barbara Kellerman brings more texture to the simple 'bell-curve' ratio by exploring the different theories for ranking follower behaviour (regardless of roles), for example as 'alienated, exemplary, conformist, passive or pragmatic', and shifting according to the issue in hand. In the end she categorizes followers according to their level of loyalty to a particular leader: 'isolates, bystanders, participants, activist, and diehards' (Kellerman, 2008, pp81–85).

Differentiating between different types of follower and paying a lot of attention to the middle majority is important to anyone exercising sustainability-literate leadership. Isolating yourself with the already passionately convinced is not leadership, and giving negative naysayers too much airtime can be unrewardingly exhausting.

Joseph Nye adapts various thinkers about followership to offer a helpful way to categorize good and bad followership:

	Low loyalty	High loyalty
Independent thinking	alienated	empowered
Compliant thinking	passive	conformist

Fostering the ideal – growing the number of very loyal independent thinkers able to maintain a fruitful relationship that benefits the objectives of the organization and helps leaders avoid mistakes – is not easy. It depends on 'the ability, benevolence and integrity' of the leader (Nye, 2008, p136).

But what of the ethics of followership? Research suggests that followers hanker after charismatic leaders who inspire more emotional responses – a feeling of significance, community and of excitement.[7] However, these feel pretty wobbly as a basis on which followers might judge the quality and direction of their leaders. As history warns, in times of fear and uncertainty, populist leaders excite followers by conjuring up demons and scapegoats and simple, often extreme, solutions, making this the very time discerning followers are needed most. The idea that wisdom resides in crowds is popular right now, but those tempted to think Gandhi got it quite right when he said: 'There go my people, I must follow them, for I am their leader', should read Charles Mackay's 1841 publication *Extraordinary Popular Delusions and the Madness of Crowds*, which describes crowds chasing everything from financial speculative bubbles to witchcraft. Barbara Kellerman recounts a story in which George Orwell shoots an elephant, against his better judgement, but because the expectation of the crowd that he should was so intense (Kellerman, 2008, pxv).

For anyone looking for a good way to judge *which* leader to follow, especially in difficult and confusing times, self-gratifying emotional responses or even the 'top five' leadership traits (self-confidence, empathy, ambition, self-control and curiosity) are not particularly helpful. Nor is the evidence that dissent in most organizations is discouraged and often punished. But help is at hand. In what may well become known as the 'positive deviant's defence', judge David Caddick ✱ ruled in September 2008 that the campaigning organization Greenpeace, accused of damaging the Kingsnorth power station in Kent during a protest, had a 'lawful excuse' as they were trying to prevent even greater damage caused by climate change.[8] This demonstrates there is a modern defence for defying orders on moral grounds.[9] Followers need to know this. Being a positive deviant is about doing the right thing *despite* the wrong institutions and so on in a (mostly!) legal context, but it is always comforting to know, as the Greenpeace case shows, that the law is making an effort to catch up.

So responsible followership may include mitigating poor or bad leadership, as an orchestra sometimes has to do with an ill-prepared conductor. It means being able to critically appraise the direction of any leaders from a sustainability perspective, and having the confidence to exercise the sort of loyal but independent challenges that good leadership depends upon. It means growing your own confidence about the right direction to take so you can dissent or deviate when appropriate.

Sustainability-literate followership thus begins to sound very similar to sustainability-literate leadership!

Traits (attributes, qualities, characteristics) theory

Whether working alone or in a team, the search for a set of 'universal' qualities or list of attributes (sometimes called 'unseen dispositions') as a hallmark of a Great Leader has been – still is – intense. Competing personality tests and psychological studies, some run over real live practising leaders, have generated a very large number of lists. Nevertheless, the universal slide rule of traits and skills that could predict leadership behaviours in different circumstances remains elusive. For what it is worth (not much), one of the most famous lists of 'natural' traits and 'learned' skills is given in Table 4.2.

Table 4.2 Leadership traits and skills

Traits	Skills
• Adaptable to situations	• Clever (intelligent)
• Alert to social environment	• Conceptually skilled
• Ambitious and achievement-oriented	• Creative
• Assertive	• Diplomatic and tactful
• Cooperative	• Fluent in speaking
• Decisive	• Knowledgeable about group task
• Dependable	• Organized (administrative ability)
• Dominant (desire to influence others)	• Persuasive
• Energetic (high activity level)	• Socially skilled
• Persistent	
• Self-confident	
• Tolerant of stress	
• Willing to assume responsibility	

Source: Adapted with the permission of The Free Press, a Division of Simon & Schuster, Inc., from *Handbook of Leadership: A Survey of Theory and Research* by Ralph M. Stogdill. Copyright © 1974 by The Free Press. All rights reserved

An extreme distillation of leadership traits to five key attributes – self-confidence, empathy, ambition, self-control and curiosity – is the foundation of many personality tests and competency lists. Amusingly, the first four are said to echo the analysis of the 'body humours' that affect personalities (blood, black bile, yellow bile, phlegm), described by possibly the first leadership guru, Hippocrates, 2400 years ago.

Box 4.2 Reflection: Charisma

Charisma: a gift of grace or of God (Chambers Dictionary); a certain quality of an individual personality by virtue of which he (*sic*) is considered extraordinary and treated as endowed with supernatural or exceptional forces or qualities (Max Weber, 1947)

Because charisma is in the eye of the beholder and not under the control of the possessor it is not strictly speaking a leadership attribute and, interestingly, is rarely cited as one. Exercised without integrity or competence, charisma can be downright dangerous.

Indeed, there's little research into whether charismatic people are more likely to be good at leadership than those without it, or whether they possess other specific leadership attributes or skills beyond those associated with inspiration. Peter Drucker insists effective leadership doesn't depend on charisma, comparing Dwight Eisenhower, Konrad Adenauer and Abe Lincoln as effective leaders with 'no more charisma than a dead mackerel', with John Kennedy, who, while super-charismatic, accomplished little (Drucker, 2001, p269).

Perhaps the most contentious aspect of charismatic leaders is that they seem to dampen the capacity of followers to question the direction or quality of the leadership provided. We know charismatic leaders, chosen or self-appointed, can lead others for good and for bad. Stalin, Hitler and Mao were charismatic and, arguably, effective leaders, but not for good. Particularly at times of trouble and distress there is a tendency for people to turn to charismatic individuals who seem to have simple solutions or a route out of the difficulty. Followers can also 'anoint or appoint' leaders to transfer responsibility for resolving a problem, as following is easier than leading. Max Weber noted that the charisma of inspirational leaders, by focusing authority in the individual, can be a powerful solvent of an institution's resilience (Nye, 2008, p128).

Charismatic leaders can be transformative in that they inspire followers, but it is not automatic that they do so for the good, nor that they are able to sustain their transformative inspiration over time.

Situational and contingency theory

A consistent theme about leadership, but a missing dimension for early theorists is that of the *context* or *setting* in which different leadership styles are exercised.

In what became known as situational or contingency models of leadership, the circumstances and processes by which leaders emerge (in a crisis, through careful succession planning, in a vacuum) joined the type of organization (companies, public sector, armed forces, political parties) and the power relationships within the organization or situation, to develop a more complex picture of an ideal leader: one who was fitted for or could adapt their style to a particular situation. Ideas about the *conditions* around the leader that would influence his or her success began to be developed too. This *contingency* approach draws (often unconsciously) from the great military writers on battlefield strategy and tactics like Sun Tzu[10] or, a more recent example, Field Marshal Montgomery.[11]

Joseph Nye calls the ability of a leader to tailor their leadership to different situations, 'contextual intelligence', meaning the ability to pick up and empathize with the context and culture of an organization. I know from my experience with the European Green movement that some colleagues managed to make a happy transition for their leadership from dissident or radical opposition into government (two prominent examples are Vaclav Havel ✱ in the former Czechoslovakia who became President, and Joschka Fischer, who became German Green Foreign Minister 1998–2005), while others were uncomfortable and did not succeed. Similarly, 'professional' leaders who move around companies or public sector organizations succeed or fail depending on whether their leadership persona fits into to the new context or not.

John Adair's action-centred leadership model (see Figure 4.2) was designed to help leaders align their leadership persona with the task in hand. Derived from the military leadership learning model of 'be, know, do' Adair's recipe is widely used in leadership training. He sees the circles as bigger or smaller, depending on the situation, with the leader's task to manage all of them.[12]

Essential to contextual intelligence is cultural sensitivity beyond the organizational boundary. It is easy to get lost in the complexity of running any sort of organization well, and to forget that the outside world may see things differently. HSBC illustrated contextual intelligence with its 'global, local bank' advertising campaign showing how similar gestures – like the thumbs up sign – can have different meanings to different cultures. And just as American and European ways of

Adair's three core management
(sic) responsibilities:

- achieving the task
- managing the team or group
- managing the individual

Source: Adair (1979)

Figure 4.2 The action-centred leadership model

embarking on relationships or doing business differ, so they do in Japan, Brazil or Africa too. Even close to home, unless they play it carefully, big organizations can encounter hostility to even a simple relocation from, say, an urban to rural setting.

Despite the opening up of leadership theory from dissecting the personal qualities of individual leaders to the external contexts and situations in which leaders find themselves, the territory for shaping leadership action is nevertheless still seen to be bounded largely by the team and the interests of the organization, not the state of the world or any feeling of responsibility towards it. Only the last of the traditional leadership theories tried to resolve that, and then with mixed success.

Transactional and transformational theory

Transformational leadership is considered by many to be the acceptable face of charismatic or Great Man leadership because it 'is closer to the prototype of leadership that people have in mind when they describe their ideal leaders, and it is more likely to provide a role model with which subordinates want to identify' (Bass and Avolio, 1994, p11). The principal contrast being made is with *transactional* leadership, which is more concerned with immediate and practical needs of the organization, including 'getting on with it'. Table 4.3 outlines the difference.

Table 4.3 The difference between Transactional and Transformational leadership

Transactional leadership	Transformational leadership
• builds on a man's (*sic*) need to get a job done and make a living	• builds on a man's (*sic*) need for meaning
• is preoccupied with power and position, politics and perks	• is preoccupied with purposes and values, morals and ethics
• is mired in daily affairs	• transcends daily affairs
• is short term and hard data oriented	• is oriented towards long-term goals without compromising human values and principles
• focuses on tactical issues	
• relies on human relations to lubricate human interactions	• releases human potential – identifying and developing new talent
• follows and fulfils role expectations by striving to work effectively within current systems	• designs and redesigns jobs to make them meaningful and challenging
• supports structures and systems that reinforce the bottom line, maximize efficiency, and guarantee short-term profits	• aligns internal structures and systems to reinforce overarching values and goals

Source: Covey (1992)

The good thing about transformational leadership is that it introduces the idea of the person in the leadership role being conscious of the need of other people (and therefore the organization as a collection of people) for a greater meaning in life than the daily round, and thus of the importance of ethics and values. To be a transformational leader differs from just being charismatic in that followers are informed as much as they are inspired, and are not passive but expected to provide leadership themselves. Ronald Heifetz called this 'adaptive' leadership – meaning the inspiration of the leader encourages the followers to adapt their own behaviour to tackle the shared challenge themselves, rather than waiting for the leader to tell them what to do (Heifitz, 1994). In theory an insurance against the hubris of charisma, transformational leadership seems to be getting close to the sort of leadership that a transition to a sustainable way of life might require. Sadly, Heifetz rather messed it up – for me at any rate – in a book co-authored with Marty Linsky called *Leadership on the Line: Staying Alive Through the Dangers of Leading* that resuscitated the image of the so-called 'adaptive' leader as paternalistic and heroic, risking their own life ('being 'taken out') when navigating the perilous straits of leadership (Heifetz and Linsky, 2002). No one is suggesting leadership is a cakewalk or without all sorts of risks, but really! I can't think of any better way to put off followers (and women), than getting lost in myths about your own supremacy.

Joseph Nye points out that successful leadership does mean possessing both the 'soft' skills implied by transformational leadership, and the 'hard' transactional ones more associated with a tightly run organization and sometimes Machiavellian political skills. He quotes Adam Smith who noted 'we see frequently the vices and follies of the powerful much less despised than the poverty and weakness of the innocent' and cites studies that show bullies are not always detrimental to an organization. 'Great intimidators' with a vision and a disdain for social constraints often succeed. According to former cabinet minister Chris Patten, John Major was the nicer, but Margaret Thatcher the more effective leader because of her bullying. One venture capitalist pointed out that 'almost all our [Silicon Valley] innovators are jerks', though Nye quotes Daniel Golman to remind us that 'in general, leaders who are jerks must reform or else their moods and actions will eventually catch up with them' (quotes in Nye, 2008, pp41 and 81). An Asian friend of mine described how one of her ambitious colleagues used people ruthlessly 'like a ladder' to get to the top, but when his career stalled and he wanted to come down again, he found all the rungs were broken.

Contemporary leadership theories

It is easy to get thoroughly lost in the bustle of more contemporary leadership theories. Many seem to be variations on past themes, in the quest, the more cynical amongst us might say, for book sales and student recruitment. Here are some of the more useful and/or amusing.

Dispersed (or distributed) and collective theory (featuring chaos and co-creation)

An extremist view of dispersed leadership applies chaos theory to that of management and leadership. While Arnold Schwarzenegger's open diary approach to canvassing views of constituents during his early weeks as Governor of California sounds sensible, the concept of 'messy leadership' where chaos creates 'flexibility, variation, inconsistency and the unexpected' does not. Moreover, no evidence is provided that followers like this sort of this leadership style (Abrahamson and Freeman, 2006). To me it all sounds like 'mushroom' management, so called because it involves keeping people in the dark and throwing s**t at them from time to time. It is a management technique demonized on leadership courses, but practised more often than is imagined, because chaos and lack of structure and information gives disproportionate power to the 'boss' as the only person who has a clue what is going on.

One step this side of total disorder is complexity theory and the idea that organizations should be structured on the 'edge of chaos', in an ultra-creative 'sweet spot' between over-structured inertia and under-structured chaos. This has been described as sailing between the rock of excessive control and the whirlpool of disaster (Hampden-Turner, 1994). Richard Florida argues that creativity thrives best in the context of a shared sense of purpose and a reasonably structured and stable framework (social or organizational). The ferment of trial and error that fosters creativity depends on boundaries being clearly set because creativity disappears if there is fear of reprisal for failure – or of being ignored (Florida, 2002).

One topical and more organized idea of how leadership can pursue the quest for creativity, is to be found in the rise of co-creation. Although it is more of a tool for involving a wide range of people than a management technique, collaborating with customers and clients in the design of new products or services for example does hold promise for constructing what NESTA (National Endowment for Science, Technology and the Arts – the UK government funded organization with a mission to stimulate creativity and innovation for the UK economy) calls 'coalitions of the willing'. NESTA promotes co-creation rules as a technique for engaging 'extreme collaboration – disrupting boundaries between disciplines, organization and places'.[13]

Devolved, distributed or 'federal' organizational structures take leadership roles down into smaller units. Charles Handy recommends that industrial federalism learn from what works best in federally organized states, like Germany or Switzerland (Handy, 1987, p264). With instant electronic communication, variations on the devolved or dispersed model have been adopted by many big companies and public sector organizations; for example: construction; computer software and hardware companies; health and education services. Paradoxically, although this is a model close to the hearts of sustainability-literate leadership (smaller units, nearer to the client and more intimate for the workforce, more resilience overall etc.), it can make the diffusion of whole organization objectives – like sustainability-literate practices – more difficult. A good example of an organization trying do both is The National College of School Leadership. It is growing a culture of *collective* leadership responsibility across all schools as a strategy for raising quality – and sustainability-literacy – in individual schools.[14] For an example of a company that exemplifies distributed leadership and seems to have hit the ultra-creative 'sweet spot' try W R Gore.✱

Emotional intelligence

The work by Daniel Goleman on 'emotional intelligence' has been so influential that it deserves a category of its own. His book and an article in the *Harvard Business Review*, from which Table 4.4 is taken, 'gave permission' to many stiff-lipped and -shirted corporate leaders to display their 'softer side'. Goleman identifies five 'soft' skills as the hallmark of truly effective leaders.

The use of psychology, anthropology and now neuroscience to bring insights into leadership theory is growing. So when Goleman addressed the question about whether emotional intelligence, like presumed 'natural' leadership qualities, are born or made, he answers 'both', citing neuroscientific evidence that emotional intelligence 'is born largely in the neurotransmitters of the brain's limbic system, which governs feelings, impulses, and drivers. Research reveals the limbic system learning best through motivation, extended practice, and feedback.' He concludes, however, that: 'One thing is certain: emotional intelligence increases with age. There is an old-fashioned word for the phenomenon: maturity' (Goleman,1998, *Harvard Business Review*, p4). So while management theory was starting to explore the complexity of relationships between leaders and teams and the various circumstances in which they find themselves, emotional literacy theory brings the focus back tight onto the individual leader.

Table 4.4 The soft skills of leadership

	Definitions	Hallmarks
Self-awareness	The ability to recognize and understand your moods, emotions, and drives, as well as their effect on others	Self-confidence Realistic self-assessment Self-deprecating sense of humour
Self-regulation	The ability to control or redirect disruptive impulses and moods The propensity to suspend judgement – to think before acting	Trustworthiness and integrity Comfort with ambiguity Openness to change
Motivation	A passion to work for reasons that go beyond money or status A propensity to pursue goals with energy and persistence	Strong drive to achieve Optimism, even in the face of failure Organizational commitment
Empathy	The ability to understand the emotional makeup of other people Skill in treating people according to their emotional reactions	Expertise in building and retaining talent Cross-cultural sensitivity Service to clients and customers
Social skill	Proficiency in managing relationships and building networks An ability to find common ground and build rapport	Effectiveness in leading change Persuasiveness Expertise in building and leading teams

Source: Goleman (1998, reprint January 2004) 'What makes a leader?', *Harvard Business Review*

However, in *Social Intelligence: The new science of human relationships*, Goleman takes forward the implications of neuroscientific research to understanding how people build and maintain good relationships, and what in turn this means to human purpose and organization (Goleman, 2007). The logic he follows in this book swerves away from the focus on the individual in *Emotional Intelligence* (Goleman, 1995), to the recognition that we are only the people we are through our relationships with others, and it is getting those relationships right that is the key to good leadership.

Strategic leadership theories

Probably as a reaction to the mess and chaos of management theories, and maybe even as a retreat from the self-exposure of the softer leadership skills, the idea of 'strategic leadership' emerged during the 1990s. Which is rather odd as strategy is hardly new to the toolbox of leadership skills. John Kay opined only partially in jest that the idea of strategic leadership (rather than a leader or manager who knew how to do strategic planning) developed in order to differentiate the more highly paid executive from one who 'deals with operations'. That is, the further the leader or manager gets away from actually doing what the business or organization was set up to do, the more important they are.[15]

One of the doyens of strategy theory, Henry Minzberg, tries to unpack the muddle of what he generously calls schools of thought to identify five different aspects of strategy. Irresistibly, they all begin with the letter P: plan, ploy, pattern, position, perspective.[16]

Many modern leadership theorists, however, leapt at an opportunity to hark back (again) to the Great Man theory. The idea of a strategic leader at the pinnacle of responsibility with a mind and a desk uncluttered save for key intelligence needed for high-level decision making, is very, very, appealing.[17] It conjures up an attractive vision for which the large business schools proposed to prepare their students, and in which apprentice Masters of the Universe happily saw themselves. In one case study, Rod Eddington described his experience as CEO of British Airways (BA) at the time of the terrorist attack on the World Trade buildings in New York in September 2001. His four strategic (common sense?) objectives: keep passengers and staff safe; get them home; get planes into right position; return to business as usual, are dissected alongside the contrasting strategies of George Bush (go into hiding) and New York Mayor Rudi Guilliani (go shoulder to shoulder with the firemen on the ground).

Researching what he calls greatness in leadership, Jim Collins considers 'Level 5' strategic leadership, something he sees as 'a paradoxical mix of personal humility and professional will' in the CEO, to be key in turning good companies into great ones. (Collins, 2001, p20) However, Phil Rosenzweig in *The Halo Effect* debunks Collins' theory by pointing out that the criteria used for selecting the companies on which Collins based his theory had experienced 15 years of steady, above average performance already. They had been selected for their stability, making consumer products like razor blades, and were not in higher risk more turbulent sectors like information technology (Rosenzweig, 2007, p158).

As many readers probably know already, strategy development and execution, plus the associated management of risk are big in most leadership development courses. But usually the teaching is about how to remove risk, using case studies from the past and strategies that are narrow, mostly relating to the organization more than the context (local or global) in which it is or will be operating. Rosenzweig's point is that in a highly risky and uncertain context, embracing risk and chance as *normal* should be part of any organizational strategy. It won't guarantee success, but it makes it more likely.

Rosenzweig is not alone in criticizing attempts to find the key to business success through leadership or management theories: 'stories of inspiration may give us comfort but have little more predictive power than a pair of coconut headsets on a tropical island' (Rosenzweig, 2007, p17) . He sees no reason to despair, however, as he believes leadership success lies with 'thoughtful managers who recognize that success comes about from a combination of shrewd judgment and hard work with a dose of good luck mixed in' (p159). His heroes are men (*sic*) who 'made risky strategic choices with eyes wide open and then pushed for great execution' (p159). It is *how* they did it, not the outcomes that interest him.

So far, the theories about strategic leadership are way behind the practical needs of organizations and governments, where the biggest problem is the firewall between high-level strategic policy and decision making and getting the desired outcomes on the ground. Rosenzweig is right about process, but wrong about the lesser importance of outcomes. Where your leadership is taking people has never mattered more. If they don't like the direction, they won't come along with you.

Public sector and not-for-profit leadership

I have given public sector and not-for-profit (NFP) leadership its own category as a contemporary leadership theory. Almost all of the public sector leadership development – and practice – is mesmerized by the ways of the private sector. Yet because running a not-for-profit organization with multiple non-financial measures of success is more difficult, it is here some of the most interesting innovation in theories about leadership is taking place.

For a remarkably short space of time, it was assumed that the same techniques used to obtain *private* value, could be applied to creating *public* value (CEML, 2002). Well before the auto-destruction of the financial sector, this strategy backfired. Patients don't like to be called customers, and it turned out that value is computed by citizens very differently to the productivity or monetized measures used in the private sector.

Part of the problem is a genuine citizen confusion about which services are provided by the public or the private sector. For example, most people think the utilities – water, gas, electricity, and the railways and buses – are public services, when in the UK at least they are not any more. Along with the companies that provide us with food, they are mostly privately owned, with shareholders. In fact, generally speaking, resources coming in to our households are controlled by the private sector, while stuff going out – like sewage and all domestic waste – is still the responsibility of the public sector, though often subcontracted to private companies. So in their homes, people are not sure what to 'expect' of services once unambiguously provided by government, national or local. The slipperiness of arriving at a definition of *public* value is compounded by confusion about who should do the defining.

To sidestep the considerable sound and fury around the debates about what *public* value is, Jake Chapman has a go at defining some characteristics that would indicate value is being added to what was there before:

- the level of service provision is improved;
- the quality of service is increased, particularly in treating all recipients with respect;
- the equity or fairness with which the service is delivered is increased;
- the service provision is more sustainable and takes into consideration the needs of future generations;
- the provision of the service is done in a way consistent with the expectations of a liberal civic society;
- the service provision enhances the level of trust between government and citizens.[18]

Table 4.5 Types of public sector management

	Traditional public management	**'New public management'**	**Public value**
Public interest	Defined by politicians/ experts	Aggregation of individual preferences, demonstrated by customer choice	Individual and public preferences (resulting from public deliberation)
Performance objective	Managing inputs	Managing inputs and outputs	Multiple objectives – Service outputs – Satisfaction – Outcomes – Maintaining trust/ legitimacy
Dominant model of accountability	Upwards through departments to politicians and through them to Parliament	Upwards through performace contracts; sometimes outwards to customers through market mechanisms	Multiple – citizens as overseers of govt – customers as users – taxpayers as funders
Preferred system for delivery	Hierarchial department or self-regulating profession	Private sector or tightly defined arms-length public agency	Menu of alternatives selected pragmatically (public sector agencies, private companies, JVCs, Community Interest Companies, community groups as well as increasing role for user choice)
Approach to public service ethos	Public sector has monopoly on service ethos, and all public bodies have it.	Sceptical of public sector ethos (leads to inefficiency and empire building) – favours customer service	No one sector has a monopoly on ethos, and no one ethos always appropriate. As a valuable resource it needs to be carefully managed
Role for public participation	Limited to voting in elections and pressure on elected representatives	Limited – apart from use of customer satisfaction surveys	Crucial – multi-faceted (customers, citizens, key stakeholders)
Goal of managers	Respind to political direction	Meet agreed performance targets	Respond to citizen/user preferences, renew mandate and trust through guaranteeing quality services

Source: Kelly et al (2002)

Despite the vague language (improved, increased) this is a pretty good template from which to derive leadership responsibilities in the public sector or a NFP organization – and it has sustainability built in! Moreover, with not a lot of tweaking it could serve for characterizing *private* value too.

A good summary of the evolution of thinking about public value, whether delivered by the government or through the private sector, comes from a widely used and quoted framework from the Cabinet Office (See Table 4.5, page 111).

Like Jake Chapman, Geoff Mulgan feels public sector leadership at its best is fully involved in the lived experience of people in the communities they serve. Hospitals, fire services, waste removal, water and energy, schools and social services are all part of the mix that makes local life livable, and while competition and choice may be seen as the bread and butter of commercial success, they are not always the best nourishers of equality of access or quality of service (Mulgan, 2006, p44).

Twenty-first century leadership theory

It may be a bit premature, but I've elevated a relatively new kid on the block of leadership theory to a section of its own. Paradoxically, it has arisen, not out of the challenges facing the mighty but ethically challenged corporate sector, but from the differently challenged public sector. Some of the impetus comes from the discussions about public value outlined above and from the fudging of the boundaries between public and private provision of services. The main reason though is a realization of the public sector's rather large role in sustaining a major part of our economic and social systems, not least through the number of people employed either directly or by contracted service providers. The importance of what happens in this sector is obviously magnified by economically wobbly times.

From the perspective of the leadership of public sector organizations like the National Health Service (NHS) (the largest employer in Europe) the need to allocate (and justify) expenditure against complex outcomes over which you may not even have that much control, demands very different behaviours to those we might call 'premillennial'. Ironically, it has taken the complexity around the causes of climate change for people to see the similar interconnectedness of what used to be treated as discrete decisions in the workplace. The consequences of segregating for so long policies on transport, energy, waste, environment, education and health, for example, means that solutions to problems in each are missed because all are inextricably linked in a way that surpasses the remit of each sector and of any organizational unit of government – national or local – and the competence of most organizational leadership.

Though his classification would probably have worked in the 20th century too, Keith Grint has characterized 21st century problems as tame, wicked or critical. Tame problems are the solvable ones. They will be complicated but may have precedents and not involve too much uncertainty. Wicked problems are more intractable, definitely complex, involving lots of uncertainty, and with no clear solutions that don't generate even more problems. There may not even be right or wrong answers, just better or worse alternatives that need to be worked out through a collaborative process. Critical problems are just so bad and urgent that a command and adjust strategy needs to be used. As with a sudden ambush or sea-level rise, a command to attack, defend or retreat is made, with refinements to get the best outcome done afterwards (Grint, 2005). As the 21st century progresses, however, the trend will certainly be towards critical problems, slowed or hastened by our ability to solve some of the wicked ones.

Although in its infancy, this development in ways of thinking about leadership is extremely welcome. Some protagonists are dusting off the concept of 'adaptive' leadership to deal with the necessary crossing of many boundaries, not only of policy but also of very different organizations and types of people, mostly at local level. John Bennington and Jean Hartley, for example, write about extending public leadership 'place-shaping' roles (still in their infancy) to include 'place-shielding' ones, and of the importance of systems thinking.[19]

This is very promising, though the concept of 'adaptive' leadership may not be robust enough to carry the load, unless it is made very clear what that leadership is *for*, and that it is much more than a problem-solving technique. It goes without saying that both leaders and followers must be involved in co-creating new ways of living and doing things, but unless the problems – whether tame, wicked or critical – are solved in a way that contributes to sustainability, it will be for nothing.

Evaluation

'Evaluation, like breathing, is not an option' (James and Burgoyne, 2001 p50). Nevertheless, evaluation of the outcome of applying various leadership theories to practice is conspicuous by its absence. Questionnaires after training sessions or graduations evaluate only an appreciation of the teaching; the learning has yet to be applied. Many graduates of leadership courses long and short return to their place of work full of enthusiasm to do this, but meet with lack of interest from line managers and colleagues and therefore no 'permission' to put what they have learnt into practice. Only in rare cases are the colleagues of graduates invited to feed back on any effect a course has had on the learner's behaviour.

Traditionally, workplace evaluation of staff development at all levels has centred on often crude (input) competencies and (output) standards. Compendiums of these are multiple and varied. The UK government's latest attempt to standardize standards, in the form of National Standards for Management and Leadership, updated in November 2008, can be found at www.management-standards.org.

Unfortunately, although leadership frameworks, lists of competencies and golden tick lists abound, they are usually not the outcome of any rigorous research as to their effectiveness in growing good leaders and managers, so carry little authority or meaning except perhaps to the organization that produced them. It takes time, and effort, but if done as part of an individual's or an organization's normal learning cycle, evaluation should more than pay for itself. Lack of proper self-analysis and evaluation of the outcomes of its efforts is the main reason the whole 'industry' of management and leadership development has fallen into such a sorry state, with trust in the private and public sector leaders it generates at an all-time low ebb.

Which means, of course, that the opportunity for change has never been better.

This chapter concludes with two reflections, one about women and leadership, and the other about power. They each hold insights into why things are the way they are now, and some thoughts as to how the future might be different.

Box 4.3 Reflection: Wild about women

> I believe that women will change the nature of power, rather than power change the nature of women. *US Congresswoman Bella Abzug, 1995*

Women as chips off the block of men and (therefore necessarily subservient to them) is embedded deep in the mythologies and psychologies of all recorded history. Eve owed her existence to Adam's rib, and caused nothing but bother thereafter. Although he was kind to women, Jesus's disciples were all male, and although Mohammad is thought to have secured some rights for women (property, education, inheritance, divorce) his instruction to men to 'treat your women well' reminds women they are possessions of men. Before he became pope, Cardinal Joseph Ratzinger issued a controversial statement on the 'collaboration of men and women in the Church and in the World' saying women's characteristic traits of 'listening, welcoming, humility, faithfulness, praise and waiting' meant 'women should be present in the world of work and in the organization of society' but that combining work and family has 'characteristics different from those in the case of men'. A call for a 'just valuing of the work of women within the family' was the punchline, a view similar to that of the extremer interpretations of Islam, and one Ratzinger has repeated since becoming pope.[20]

Why this should be, and at what point in our species' evolutionary past women lost the reins of power is a conundrum that would take another book to solve. Here I want to explore why, despite decades of reasonable equal opportunities legislation in Europe at least, women are still so far behind men in positions of power and leadership. And what might be done about it. Intriguingly the *inequality* of female opportunity in leadership roles is better researched than the *quality* of men in such roles.

The statistics are dreadful. Of the FTSE 100 company directors, only 7 per cent are women, only 2 per cent in executive positions.[21] Third sector organizations fare better with 46 per cent female CEOs, but in the NHS (38 per cent), top tier civil servants (27 per cent), local authorities (20 per cent) and parliament (19 per cent) there are still dismally few women in senior roles. Globally the story is no better. Under 3 per cent of the US Fortune 500 company CEOs are women. In 2009 the World Economic Forum published its latest Gender Gap Index covering political empowerment, health and educational attainment alongside economic participation and opportunity. The index puts the UK at 15th overall, the US at 31st and has a dismal tail ending with Yemen at 134th.[22] The G20 summits about the future of the world, feature two women heads of state out of 20.

I could go on, so I will for a bit if I may. Amusingly, the UK Equality and Human Rights Commission's 2008 Sex and Power survey extrapolated the current rate of change to conclude that it would take only slightly less time than a snail could creep the whole length of the Great Wall of China (212 years) for women to be equally represented in parliament. Snail travel equivalents for equal representation on FTSE 100 company boards are a mere 73 years (Lands End to John O'Groats), and the judiciary, a pacy 55 years (nine time rounds the M25).[23]

Moreover, in the UK and despite 40 years of equal pay legislation, women are still earning on average 75 per cent of the male wage. Hidden in that average: women earn 89 per cent of the male wage in administration and support roles; 82 per cent in education; 75 per cent in the arts and leisure sector; 65 per cent in health and social work; and (lo!) 36 per cent in finance and insurance.[24] A recent study of graduates three and a half years after qualification found women already earning around £1000 less than male graduates, even before the impact of childbearing kicks in. On top of that, men are significantly more likely to go into higher paid jobs, with 40 per cent earning more than £25,000, compared to 26 per cent of women who are more likely to take entry level jobs and work their way up.[25]

Why, after decades of awareness of these inequalities, has so little changed? One part of the answer is that men want to be like another 'great' man, more than they want to be like a woman, however great, and it is this truth that pervades all leadership and management education and practice.[26] Another is that women are simply not going for leadership jobs in sufficient numbers. The study of graduates found women more likely to be satisfied with their jobs, even though they may not be the best rewarded by bonuses or prestige. Most do not want to be male clones and have broader criteria for happiness and success than equality of income with the next man.

The self-fulfilling dynamic at work here means that the existing testosterone-biased locker room (US) or clubbable (UK) culture of men in leadership roles has led to a wide range of discriminatory practice in the workplace. The terms 'glass ceiling', for example, became synonymous for the 'invisible barriers' put in place by the male directors to stop women's progress in favour of more 'chaps like us'. The UK Chartered Institute of

Personnel Development identified a 'glass cliff' where women are intention-ally placed in more risky or precarious roles than men, or given tasks that are considered more likely to fail.[27] Another metaphor, that of a labyrinth, sums up the complexity of the challenges a woman faces, not only at the last lap to the most senior posts, but also at many points leading up to that stage:[28]

- *Prejudice*. Despite a woman's higher educational attainment, marriage and pregnancy are associated with higher wages for men but not for women. Paternity man 'needs' a promotion, while a mother has hers delayed. Also, psychometric testing used to identify personalities and potential for future leadership may be calibrated to favouring what are predominantly male approaches to problem solving or self-promotion.
- *Resistance to women's leadership*. Masculine traits such as assertion and control are associated in most people's minds with effective leadership – they have the power to get things done. Women are considered to be more soft-spoken and showing compassion and concern for others. Men are 'default' leaders, women 'atypical'. This creates a no-win situa-tion. By behaving like men, women are criticized for not being more feminine, but if they stick with more female behaviours they are accused of not acting powerfully enough. Hillary Clinton is often used as an example of someone trying to surmount the 'double bind dilemma: damned if you do, doomed if you don't'.[29]
- *Leadership style*. Generally, men are considered to be more transac-tional in their leadership style, while women are more transformational. But men are also more prone than women to *laissez-faire* behaviour, meaning a lazy, non-leadership style that reduces effectiveness. If iso-lated in a leadership group, women find it hard to practise more participative and collaborative techniques, so are forced into the more masculine behaviour. If, however, there are several women in the group (at least three apparently), a more participative style is legitimized.
- *Demands of family life*. No surprises here. Although men are increasing their contribution to domestic work and childcare (2.6 hours per week in 1965 to 6.5 in 2000), women have increased their contribution as well (10.6 hours to 12.9). However, there has been no let up on the assumption that working 'extra' hours in the office is normal for the ambitious employee while career breaks demonstrate lack of commit-ment. If a couple both have careers and a promotion means one partner has to move, it is usually the lower earner or principle carer who gives way – most often a woman.

- *Underinvestment in social capital.* Progress to more senior posts can depend heavily on time and effort spent in socializing with work colleagues or building up professional networks. One study revealed that fast-track managers 'spent relatively more time and effort socializing, politicking, and interacting with outsiders than did their less successful counterparts'. Family commitments mean women find it more difficult to engage with informal networking, or may find it mostly about essentially male activities, including late night drinking, golf or visits to nightclubs. Even middle management conferences often have male themes such as football. As a result, women tend to network separately from men, which hampers their promotion chances.

So what will make a difference in the future? Wal-Mart is involved in a significant sex discrimination litigation for systematic pay and promotion discrimination that has escalated from six plaintiffs to a class action representing two million female employees.[30] Whether this will mark a sustained change in the culture of boardrooms remains to be seen because, so far, legal remedies may provide financial restitution, but have not resolved the inequalities embedded in organizational culture and structure.

Unfortunately, most leadership stories by women tend to be about personal strategies for surviving and/or succeeding in a male-dominated environment, not about changing it. Indeed, a pretty constant theme is the assumption that it is women who have to shape up and develop techniques to manage in what remains a predominantly masculine world of leadership. A 2009 *Financial Times* article about the top 50 women in world business did acknowledge the serious discrimination women face in getting to the top, but missed the opportunity to ask how much of the journey the women were able to take on their own terms.[31]

With women forming 60 per cent of the EU graduate talent pool (54 per cent average across the Organisation for Economic Co-operation and Development (OECD)) and employers recognizing that having several women in senior positions translates into better financial and effectiveness outcomes, perhaps the tide is beginning to turn. Nevertheless, so deeply held is the belief in women as second stringers across different cultures – not least by women themselves – that radical changes will be needed to kick-start the process. Typically, the responsibility for making it happen is left with women. 'We can't make the future happen unless women help men to adjust', says Niall FitzGerald, chairman of Reuters and former CEO of Unilever.[32]

While comments like this can cause health-endangering teeth grinding amongst women, it reflects reality. A positive story of how women are getting serious about taking power *on their own terms* is beginning to emerge though. It is estimated that women now hold around 48 per cent of Britain's personal wealth, expected to rise to 60 per cent as women outnumber men at university and prosper in business and as entrepreneurs.[33] Moreover, companies with a 'critical mass' of women on boards (30 per cent or more) do better than those without it.[34] The international Food Policy Research Institute says that giving women equal access to land, fertilizer, credit and training raises crop yields by about 22 per cent.[35]

Without a doubt, women will have to lead if they are to regain their proper leadership role in all sorts of social institutions, ranging from the family to the workplace, government and, increasingly, their own enterprises. But at the very least, the male majority will have to be active in their support, and not at all *laissez-faire* about it. Change is beginning to happen, albeit shockingly slowly, in poor as well as rich countries. For example, Kenyan Wangari Maathai ✻ gained her Nobel Prize for Sustainable Development and Peace for political bravery and her massively influential Greenbelt movement that educated and empowered women as well as planted millions of trees. Both France and Spain have appointed women majority cabinets, and despite the odds, Iran has three women ministers. The UK business lobby group, the CBI, has appointed its first female President, Iceland has asked women to sort out its banking fiasco, and Norway's legislation for 40 per cent female board membership seems to have worked.[36] Mary Robinson, former President of Ireland and UN Commissioner for Human Rights has became Chair of the Council of Women, an organization that brings together 30 past and current women heads of state. www.womenworldleaders.org. In contrast to the Masters of the Universe's predilection for high altitude gatherings (Bretton Woods, Mont Pèlerin, Davos), women appear to favour sea-level venues. At the end of 2009, Sainab Salbi, founder of Women for Women International, told a meeting in Deauville, France 'in markets you gamble, if you invest in women you cannot lose. It will have a huge dividend now and in future generations. Women are the safest investment you can make.' And World Bank managing director, Ngozi Okonjo-Iweala, pointed out that attracting more women into the political system 'should also make it more attractive to intelligent men'.

How could I disagree? All of this raises hopes of more leadership from women already in leadership roles – all pushing for equality of all sorts of opportunity for women worldwide. Perhaps the best chance we've had for years to give that snail a run for its money.

Box 4.4 Reflection: Power

The absence of women from so many key leadership roles in the world – in government, business and public service – is bad news for the way power is exercised in the world today. It is, of course, power that appointed leaders hold, and no amount of speculation about desirable attributes or behaviours of people *en route* to or exercising power will substitute for a widely shared, healthy approach to what power is and how to handle it. Geoff Mulgan points out that 'power is part of life, not separate from it … Every relationship has power in it: the relationship of parent and child, friend and friend, employer and worker, lover and lover' (Mulgan, 2006, p10). In the 19th century, Lord Acton famously said 'power tends to corrupt, and absolute power corrupts absolutely', but I think he was wrong. It is not power that corrupts inevitably, but that some people are more likely to be corrupted than others – and women are not immune. David Owen has suggested it might be appropriate to consider what Bertrand Russell called 'the intoxication of power' as a medically recognized syndrome (Owen, 2009).

We shouldn't be surprised that people prone to becoming intoxicated by power are more likely to be attracted to positions of power. But we should be surprised at how even the most advanced democracies are extraordinarily casual in the way power is given to others without ceremony, never mind proper accountability or recall mechanisms if that power should be misused. Although a full psychological profiling of candidates for the top leadership roles in government is not with us yet, there is architectural awareness that it should be in the glass structures of the restored German Reichtstag and the new mayor's City Hall in London (both of which permit passers-by to see into the debating chamber from the street and the roof), the televising of local council meetings in California, and the open-sided council huts in Mali. All recognize that the citizen's ability to see and hear power in action is essential to its better functioning. Not so in many boardrooms where penthouses and personal jets serve to isolate the leadership, which Dr Owen suggests is causing a bunker mentality and other symptoms of power-damaged leaders.

Interestingly, and not entirely trivially, new research on (male) market traders has revealed that high testosterone levels may contribute to economic return, while risk-taking increases a trader's cortisol levels. Both hormones are known to have cognitive and behavioural effects, perhaps explaining herd behaviour rather than rational choice at times of market volatility. A former trader compares the physical and psychological state of being engaged in rapid transactions to that of a tennis player at the net.[37] I would draw parallels with the excitement of hunting down hairy mammoths, in recognition of how short a time it is since that is what most men did for a living. The culture of hard decision making and deal-chasing in boardrooms seems to parallel the culture of the trading floor, suggesting that power relationships within organizations and decisions made by men and women need a biological vetting as well as an ethical one.

The serious point is that power cannot be trusted, and may be dangerous, unless it is independent enough – of the military, of financial interests, of criminality, and of personal gain or hormonal bias. Fear of reprisal from power exercised under the influence of any of these shuts down healthy challenges to leadership and power, with women more likely to back off than men.

One solution, according to Geoff Mulgan, is to see good power as a 'co-creation: it is something done with the people, not done to them' (Mulgan, 2006, pp245–251). As a rule of thumb, I translate this to mean it should be the same people making the decision who both pay for it and live the consequences of it (i.e. the subsidiarity principle). That way, it is more likely the decision will be a carefully made and executed one. A principle that would more or less hold good in government, in a private company or in a charity. But of course real life is not like that yet. There are a lot of bad leaders out there.

To guide those trying to exercise good power and mitigate the worst of those around them who may be operating bad power, Joseph Nye offers two meanings of 'good' leadership – being ethical and being effective – with one being no use without the other. Unless you are both, you are a bad leader, and should not be in a position of power. He has a helpful table to explain what he means, and it is given here.

Table 4.6 Good leadership

'Good' =	Effective	Ethical
Goals	Balance of realism and risk in vision	Values of intentions, goals
Means	Efficiency of means to ends	Quality of means used
Consequences	Success in achieving group's goals	Good results for in-group and for outsiders

Source: Nye (2008, p112)

The lessons for positive deviants is that power matters. Like a football, if it is not at your feet then it is at the feet of someone else, and your role is either to help the ball into the net of sustainability or collaborate with others so the goodies gain possession. Standing on the sidelines is not an option. Wherever you can, try to make the location of power visible. Identify it and talk about it; what is it doing, what could it do better, especially about sustainable development.

Chapter 5

Business school betrayal

The place where most leadership development takes place is in business schools, mostly university based, but many private. Despite the heavy criticism of them quoted in the Introduction to this section, an MBA (Masters in Business Administration) or the new and rarer MPA (Masters in Public Administration) remains a very popular qualification that many consider essential for promotion to a senior management role in any organization.

Why should this be? If you have an MBA, you will be able to examine your own motives directly, and I am sure most students genuinely believe an MBA will make them better managers and leaders. When my cynical mode is switched on, however, I wonder if the real attraction is the promise of higher salaries and quicker promotion. The *Financial Times* (FT) 2009 ranking of the top 100 business schools, prioritizes criteria such as average salary of alumni today (weighted for sectoral differences), the percentage increase of salary from before taking the MBA, whether international experience is available and the number of publications of the faculty. Not a cheep about the quality of leadership provided by graduates. Quixotically, when surveyed, firms say they don't count MBAs above other qualifications (CEML, 2002). Perhaps this is because MBAs from even the most prestigious schools are no protection from leadership incompetence and corruption. As business journalist Simon Caulkin said: 'There seems to be no sense of history. How come we haven't learnt anything from Enron, the dotcoms and Long Term Capital Management?'[1] (I bring forward as part of the answer to that question the fact that only two of the FT's top 20 business schools in 2009, both in Spain, had at least 25 per cent women faculty.)

Top of the FT ranking is the Wharton School. It was founded in 1881 through an endowment to the University of Pennsylvania by

Joseph Wharton, a devout Quaker and successful businessman who made his fortune in steel and nickel. He wanted the 'business of business' to be as honourable a profession as that of a doctor, lawyer or clergyman. Although his vision for the school was elitist and sexist – to provide an education more appropriate for 'young men of inherited intellect, means and refinement' than working their way up from the 'counting house' of a business – Wharton was motivated by his religion's sense of social responsibility. It seemed self-evident that such young men would also want to dedicate themselves to the need of the community and to attacking 'social problems incident to our civilization'. Leadership in the business world brought with it, as it did in medicine and law, responsibilities to society at large (Khurana, 2007, p107).

According to Rankesh Khurana (Harvard), the original social mission of business schools to turn what the late Alfred Chandler called the 'visible hand of management' (Chandler, 1977) into a profession furnished (as are medicine and law) with ethics and standards of practice, has been diverted into an over-intimate relationship, first with corporations themselves and subsequently with economic ideology, specifically that based on the perfectability of the market. Students are more indoctrinated than educated with what Khurana dubs 'investor capitalism', to the point where good business practice has been corrupted by the nature of the relationship between the CEO and the investors, particularly in the reward packages tied to growth of shareholder value. 'The new logic of shareholder primacy absolved managers and corporate executives of responsibility for anything other than obtaining the desired financial result' and business school curricula came to be in full support of this new reality (Khurana, 2007, p303).

If the purpose of business schools is primarily to maximize the salary and career-enhancing networks of its graduates, then how, asks Khurana, do the schools justify the public funding many of them receive? Where is the 'basis of notions such as stewardship, stakeholder interests, or promotion of the common good – to any standard other than sheer self-interest'? (p323) The backbone of the system is no longer the executive or manager with a lifetime career, but rather a number of hired hands who buy and sell corporate assets' (p380). Srikumar Rao, Professor at Columbia University, New York, agrees: 'Our top business schools are really not education institutions, they are indoctrination institutions.'[2]

If the hallmarks of a profession are indeed a rigorously established body of knowledge, shared standards of practice and norms of professional conduct, then are there any signs at all that business schools are moving in this direction? Some argue that the rising interest in corporate responsibility and the growing popularity of courses on business ethics is evidence that time will prove the heart of business leadership to be in the right place. For others, immorality and greed has already rotted that heart from the inside out, so nothing less than a wholesale purge that returns both business and its educational institutions into service to society at large will do.

Whatever your view, from now on it is likely that those involved in leadership and management education will be judged on the adequacy (speed and comprehensiveness) of their response to the current co-joined crises – of financial markets and economics, of environmental degradation, and of poverty and inequality.

And as positive deviants have a vested interest in business schools generating sustainability-literate graduates instead of those who haven't a clue about either sustainability or socially responsible leadership, you might want to add to your To Do list chivvying for change in any school you know or deal with.

Corporate (social) responsibility compromised

Terminology note. The terms corporate responsibility (CR) and corporate social responsibility (CSR) tend to be used interchangeably. I prefer the first, as the second is sometime interpreted as being relevant only to people with a fairly direct relationship to the organization, such as its staff. CR covers the whole lot – global and local environment, governance, ethics, as well as people way beyond the end of a supply chain and maybe not even born yet. So, although CSR is more commonly used, I favour CR in this chapter.

Although the modern idea of corporate responsibility (CR) is little more than two decades old (Shell was the first major company to publish a CR report in 1989), the idea of business as a social enterprise with a flow of responsibilities to and from the society in which it operates is as old as the hills. Plato noted the damage commercial logging did to local climate, and the Dutch East India Company was the target of disgruntled shareholders who accused it of 'self-enrichment' in 1622. Models of business that operate as social enterprises as much as profit-seekers, range from the Co-operative Movement, founded in the early 19th century[3] to paternalistic but socially generous family companies like Robert Owens at New Lanark, Cadbury or Lever Brothers (later Unilever), and other modern staff-owned enterprises such as the John Lewis Partnership. There are business people who, like Joseph Wharton, feel 'responsibility' for the wider impact of their company on people and the environment, and share their profits through a sense of fairness as much as anything else. Few will have missed the rise of values-driven private enterprises, like The Body Shop, Ecover, Divine Chocolate ✱, and the increasing proportion of money looking for 'socially responsible investment' opportunities that has prompted larger traditional firms to, as one senior manager put it: 'chase some of that money for us'.

The growth of CR as a business function, however, is as much a product of the globalization of communication as anything else. The advent of the internet, and the immediacy of information and image transfer it made possible, means corporate watchers – benign or belligerent – expect copious and online information about all aspects of a company's activities, especially, but not only, if it is publically quoted. This means anything less than good environmental and social practice is a mobile phone camera's click away from newspaper editors and YouTube with immediate negative consequences to reputational and financial bottom lines. Though the value of reputation is difficult to assess, Christopher Satterthwaite, CEO of Chime Communications, a PR firm, thinks it is between 25 and 30 per cent of total value. Others think it might be more. Get it badly wrong and it is 100 per cent. Reputation is closely linked to trust, and in 2009 an Ipsos MORI poll found that only 25 per cent of people trusted business leaders to tell the truth, a score worsted only by journalists, ministers and politicians.[4]

Consequently CR is best seen as a fairly normal business response to anything that menaces any company's legal obligation to maximize the return to its shareholders. How it has been done, and how the concept has evolved, however, does have interesting lessons for sustainability-oriented leadership.

To help tease out these lessons, I've designated four types or 'stages' of modern CR: defensive, strategic, 'ambivalent supplication' and trans-

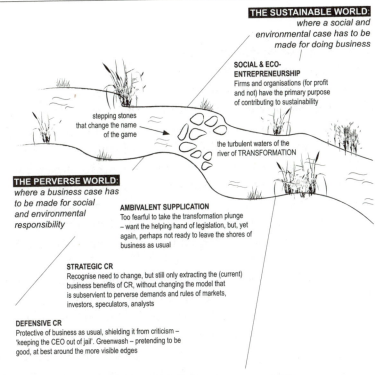

THE SUSTAINABLE WORLD:
where a social and environmental case has to be made for doing business

SOCIAL & ECO-ENTREPRENEURSHIP
Firms and organisations (for profit and not) have the primary purpose of contributing to sustainability

stepping stones that change the name of the game

the turbulent waters of the river of TRANSFORMATION

THE PERVERSE WORLD:
where a business case has to be made for social and environmental responsibility

AMBIVALENT SUPPLICATION
Too fearful to take the transformation plunge – want the helping hand of legislation, but, yet again, perhaps not ready to leave the shores of business as usual

STRATEGIC CR
Recognise need to change, but still only extracting the (current) business benefits of CR, without changing the model that is subservient to perverse demands and rules of markets, investors, speculators, analysts

DEFENSIVE CR
Protective of business as usual, shielding it from criticism – 'keeping the CEO out of jail'. Greenwash – pretending to be good, at best around the more visible edges

Figure 5.1 Different stages of CR

formational, which are illustrated in Figure 5.1. Although arranged roughly sequentially, like leadership theory they are really muddled up. Space is given to the case of CR detractors too, those who argue that the whole CR 'industry' has slowed the pace of corporate reform.

If you are in an organization that has a CR policy and function (maybe you even have a responsibility for it!) I hope what follows will provoke some constructive self-criticism. Where are you on the path to transformation, and are you going fast enough? That goes for anyone working in the not-for-profit and public sector as well. Even with public service as its primary purpose, because the public sector has been pushed into private sector behaviour, it too is taking up CR.

Defensive corporate responsibility

Corporate catastrophes like the 1978 Amoco Cadiz oil tanker spill off the coast of France and the 1984 Union Carbide pesticide plant gas release in Bhopal India, which killed and damaged 1000s of people, focused press, citizens and legislation on the responsibility of corporations for the safety of people and the environment in and around their operations. Compliance with legislation was no longer enough, corporate reputation depended on being seen to do the right thing as well.

Around the same time, the OECD and the UN Centre on Transnational Corporations began work on codes of conduct for companies operating in the rapidly globalizing marketplaces for goods and services. However, their codes were for governments to implement, not companies, which proved to be a mistake. Governments quickly became distracted by their own national interests in the new global arena for trade and development, while companies adopted sophisticated strategies to deflect any attempts at external regulation and lobbied to make voluntary self-regulation acceptable.

So, modern CR was born, as was the CR specialist in functional units of business and in academia. My job, the new specialists like to quip (without apparent irony) is to keep the CEO hands-free and out of jail. Campaigning organizations point to hypocrisy, with a favourite case study that of the Business Council for Sustainable Development (BCSD) at the 1992 Earth Summit. In an apparent mediation between a hard (no regulation) stance taken by the International Chamber of Commerce and a Nordic proposal for regulation of corporate behaviour, the BCSD won the day for 'the changing course of industry' – that is, voluntary self-regulation.

Gradually, and especially over the last decade, antagonism from campaigners towards private business mellowed into collaborations on a wide range of activities such as CO_2 emission reduction, ethical standards in the supply chain, and philanthropic ventures involving the company's own staff.

Governance systems came under the spotlight when, for example, Shell's leadership remained passive as Nigerian poet Ken Sarowiwa was jailed and eventually executed in 1995 for campaigning against the company's activities in the delta area of his country, and financial corruption was exposed at US energy company Enron and telecoms giant WorldCom. A raft of jointly established voluntary codes and standards like The Forest Stewardship Council and its Marine equivalent, Fairtrade, Business Principles for Countering Bribery and The Equator Principles have been joined by legislation on corporate governance, like the 2002 Sarbanes–Oxley bill in the US. Three quarters of the top 100 global corporations produce a CR report, and the idea of using CR to promote corporate 'hygiene' to a wide range of potential detractors has spread to non-business organizations, with government departments, local authorities and charities establishing their own policies and reporting regularly on progress in implementation. A sense of dizziness becomes unavoidable, not least when the Global Reporting Initiative (which sets a framework for reporting on CR activities) produces a report on itself running to 92 pages![5]

In almost all cases of the (still) minority of companies operating a CR policy, the function is usually to be found in the corporate affairs or marketing department. This has led to accusations that defensive CR is little more than an application of 'greenwash' to the company's real business of defending returns to shareholders, so as to camouflage it from the attention of campaigners and government.

Strategic corporate responsibility

Recently, *The Economist* started to question whether CR was still entirely *defensive*. Protecting reputation and financial bottom lines is surely part of good risk management, so is there something else going on behind the 'forest of figleaves'?[6] The magazine has a long track record of scepticism about CR,[7] but now admits that it is here and thriving, possibly to stay. If approached in a *strategic* way, could not CR become part of the firm's competitive advantage, meaning that through aligning social and environmental responsibilities with the *purpose* of the organization it can not only be in a leading position in the new economy, but also actually help shape it? CR is surely no more than simply enlightened self-interest.[8]

Forum for the Future is amongst the first to explore and promote the case that sustainability is not just good business practice, but good for business.[9] Its own list of potential benefits (given in Table 5.1) for making that case and measuring progress is relevant to both private and public sector, and influences the way Forum works with its partners on practical innovative solutions to their different sustainability challenges.

Forum for the Future's Dr Sally Uren has found a rapid rise in interest in sustainability in boardrooms in all sectors over the last few years, but notes 'the sustainability crown won't be won in a single sprint;

it's a contest of many stages, a kind of corporate Tour de France without Lycra'. Driving this change of heart are consumers she says. 'This isn't just the 'green watchdog' types ... this is a big chunk of the consuming public ... sustainability isn't a business distraction, it's a business must-have'.[10] Her argument is backed by the high percentage of people in the UK who feel it is fairly or very important that a company should show a high degree of environmental and social responsibility, and by the efforts of Forum's partners to meet those expectations.[11]

Table 5.1 The business benefits of sustainable development

The business benefits of sustainable development	
Eco-efficiency	1. Reduced costs 2. Costs avoided (design for the environment, eco-innovation) 3. Optimal investment strategies
Quality management	4. Better risk management 5. Greater responsiveness in volatile markets 6. Staff motivation/commitment 7. Enhanced intellectual capital
Licence to operate	8. Reduced costs of compliance/planning permits/licences 9. Enhanced reputation with all key stakeholders 10. Influence with regulators/government etc
Market advantage	11. Stronger brands 12. Customer preference/loyalty 13. Lower costs of capital 14. New products/processes/services 15. Attracting the right talent
Sustainable profits	16. Option creation 17. New business/increased market share 18. Enhanced stakeholder value

Source: Forum for the Future (2005)

In *Capitalism: As if the World Matters*, my colleague Jonathon Porritt takes a good swing at the shortcomings of 'greenwash' CR. He gives encouraging examples of big companies that do take a more strategic approach to embedding sustainability thinking into the way they plan, operate and appraise their business, like Marks and Spencer, but says most of it falls far short of full commitment to the imperative of sustainability (Porritt, 2006). To date, big company strategic CR is very dependent on a small number of people driving it internally and through the public position they take. Also to date, there is no evidence that an organization's public commitment will survive a change of leadership (e.g. BP) or that a big company taking over a successful social entrepreneur, as L'Oreal did The Body Shop, will be transformed as a result. All of which underlines the importance of the *individual* to sustainability-literate leadership in the all-important longer term. A few positive deviants here and there in an organization, even if one is the CEO, may not be sufficient to keep the organization on track for transformation.

'Ambivalent supplication'

To arrive at the point where sustainability is the *only* goal for business, government or indeed anyone else, there is the small matter of the way financial results trump the social and the environmental ones. Publically quoted business is shackled legally to growing the financial bottom line, and everyone else is constrained by accounting and reporting conventions from trading a lesser financial performance for a better social or environmental one. Consequently, the business sector in particular has got into the habit of sending different messages to different audiences. It is this habit of speaking out of both sides of its mouth that gets campaigners jumping up and down, and gives this section its rather awkward heading. Perhaps not unjustifiably corporate watchers smell a 'special relationship' conniving to cut out or dissemble to anyone outside the golden shareholder–business–government triangle.

On the one side, business is forming collaborations at CEO level, like the World Business Council for Sustainable Development (WBCSD) or the UN Global Compact, to shout about its own good practice and demand better regulation and legislation from government. To quote the WBCSD aim: 'be a leading business advocate on sustainable development and participate in policy development to create the right framework conditions for business to make an effective contribution to sustainable human progress'.[12] Grant Thornton, an accountancy firm, found over 70 per cent of the executives they surveyed 'believe government should regulate companies for their impact on the environment'.[13] The UK Corporate Leaders Group on Climate Change wrote to political leaders asking for 'a legally binding international framework ... to be agreed in Copenhagen in 2009, implying that the European Union should cut greenhouse gas emissions by 30% in 2020, not 20%'.[14]

On the other side, however, business is a very active supplicant *against* regulation and legislation, and *for* lower taxes on business, including special favours for offshoring profits and 'non-domiciled' staff. The WBCSD aim is to maintain the voluntary, self-regulating regime secured at the 1992 Earth Summit, and the otherwise admirable position of the Corporate Leaders Group is undermined by the fact few members would be affected by the admissions trading scheme for which they were lobbying. A *McKinsey Quarterly* survey points out that 'although lobbying – often behind closed doors – is as old as business itself, high-level and concerted corporate activism in the social and political arena has been conspicuous by its absence'. The same survey also found amongst CEOs 'a lack of familiarity with [sustainability] issues, and the sense that specialists in the public-affairs and legal departments handle this sort of things'.[15] This is depressingly at odds with reports of a growth in CR and ethics courses in business education – are they *still* not getting it right?

In a different survey of UN Global Compact members, McKinsey found that even the presumably more sustainability-committed CEOs confessed to a significant 'performance gap' between what they felt they should do, and what their companies were actually doing. The top four barriers to closing this gap were:

- competing strategic priorities (43 per cent) 'such as shareholders' demands for solid short-term performance';
- complexity of implementing strategy across various business functions (39 per cent);
- lack of recognition from the financial markets (25 per cent);
- differing definitions of CR across regions and cultures (22 per cent).[16]

Not surprising then that CEOs tend to back all horses – simultaneously lobbying for firmer regulation *and* for freedom to pursue the financial bottom line without constraint.

The investor George Soros says this is inevitable. As long as there is conflict between making money and social responsibility, CR has 'built in incentives for hypocrisy'.[17]

Transformational CR

But in good or in bad times where do we want the business sector to end up? Even the critics of CR are not always clear about that. In short, I reckon the best outcome would be a return of the private sector to the fold of Joseph Wharton's vision of social entrepreneurship, where financial gain for a few is substituted by *simultaneous* financial, social and environmental gain for the many. Instead of a business (i.e. financial) case having to be made for social and environmental benefit, the reverse would apply; a social and environmental case would have to be made for doing business. Several business models can do this, ranging from the purely philanthropically funded (like Bunker Roy's barefoot college ✱) to a global shareholder-owned-for-profit company like Unilever – in theory, that is. Currently, publically quoted companies will struggle as long as they are subject to rules governing maximizing short-term financial return to shareholders, and are permitted to behave on or over the edge of ethics in pursuit of shareholder gain. Some contrive to operate almost like 'a free roving alternative state' (Handy, 1997, p77).

Muhammad Yunus ✱, Nobel Prize winning founder of the Grameen group of businesses, is optimistic nevertheless. He says the more social enterprise 'moves in the direction of business, the better off we are – in the sense that we are free [of dependency on grants or philanthropy]. We have unlimited opportunities to expand and do more, and replication becomes so much easier. We can create a powerful alternative to the orthodoxy of capitalism – a socially-conscious-driven private sector, created by social entrepreneurs.'[18] Yunus also argues that for business to genuinely transform itself, new social stock exchanges are needed, with the back-up of rating agencies, standardization of terminology, definitions, impact measurement tools, reporting formats and new publications like 'The Social Wall Street Journal'.[19]

So will voluntary self-regulation get us to the point when businesses are transformed through their CR strategies? Almost certainly not in the timescales that matter. Certainly legislation around investor responsibility will be necessary. And, as yet, no country has a coherent, specific legal model for establishing social enterprises.[20] Positive deviants may wish to give some priority to arguing for both.

In the meantime, the idea that the growth of new businesses will creatively disrupt the way existing companies think and work has become popular. So much so that *The Economist* magazine has started a column named for Joseph Schumpeter, the economist who offered the notion of 'creative destruction' as a necessary process for refreshing capitalism. The difference from when Schumpeter was expounding his theory (1942) and today, however, is that these days disrupted companies are not necessarily being allowed to destruct (e.g. US motor industry, banks). Consequently (and remembering that in a low-carbon economy it is quality of consumption, not quantity, that will prevail), the market space for smaller new businesses driven by social and environmental values is constrained. When 'mature' social enterprises reach a scale that threatens to disrupt a market or when ongoing innovation becomes too expensive, they tend to be either taken over by big companies (as L'Oreal has done with The Body Shop), or find their ideas co-opted (e.g. Café Direct's fair-trade coffee by supermarkets). It is very hard for them to expand market share any other way. As one successful social entrepreneur put it: 'I feel a bit like bait, waiting for someone to gobble me up.'

In fact, bigger companies might be helped if smaller socially motivated, sustainability-innovative companies got together, not just to defend themselves against predators but to create a more powerful sector that can say to both government and society: 'We are the ones that are too important to fail. Help create a business climate in which we can thrive.' Creating a strong sustainability-motivated business sector is probably the only way to liberate the bigger publically quoted companies from the pursuit of relentless growth in returns to investors – regardless of the cost to everyone else.

Transformation means to be changed in an irreversible way, and it is hard to find that sort of ambition in CR as currently defined and practised, however well-intentioned it may be.

The anti-CR argument

Despite the theoretically possible progression of companies to the safe and sunny banks of transformed purpose and performance, CR has some pretty vociferous and influential detractors. They seek to skewer CR from two directions. One simply wants to protect the apparently unique right of business to be as socially irresponsible as it likes, while the other sees CR as a dangerous distraction from the need for urgent and radical action to meet mounting environmental and social problems. To be fair, the latter view does sort of make the case for transformation as outlined above, but it has no confidence business can do it on its own.

To start with the first argument: that CR is as huge an albatross around the neck of financial profitability as managerialism once was. One of the earliest cheerleaders for this point of view was an architect of free-market economics himself, Milton Friedman. As he said famously in 1970: 'The social responsibility of business is to increase its profits.'[21] It was the job of governments to worry about poverty and environmental degradation. It was the business of business to do business. The most recent version of that argument rejects the idea that the sequel to managerial and investor capitalism is socially responsible capitalism. While he admits that CR has 'caught on', David Henderson's conclusion is unequivocal: 'The *current doctrine* of CR, despite its general and growing support, is deeply flawed. It embodies a mistaken view of issues, events and economic relationships, and its general adoption by businesses would reduce welfare and undermine the market economy.'[22] The emphasis in this quote (mine) warns that although this particular anti-CR argument has probably been timed out by the recession, it is way too soon to call mission accomplished.

The precious-time-wasting case is made most powerfully by Robert Reich. He accuses consumers who clamour for low prices while paradoxically demanding high standards of social responsibility, as equally responsible for the excesses of capitalism. The root of the problem is not with corporate greed (this has been a constant over time Reich says) but with competition. Competition is the main reason for the 'race to the bottom' – cheapest goods with cheapest labour and minimum concern for resources or pollution. Firms compete to cut costs to perform for their shareholders (and avoid takeover) and to please customers. CR and other things, like political donations, participating in government committees and reviews and conspicuous philanthropy, are done *only* to maximize competitive advantage. Customers love it (but no more than they love the lowest prices), governments roll over and give in to corporate demands for low taxes and regulation. 'Most of this [CR] is in earnest. Much of it is sincere. Some of it has had a positive impact. But almost all has occurred outside the democratic process. Almost none has changed the rules of the game' (Reich, 2007, p168).

Reich's argument is that what he calls 'supercapitalism' has contributed indirectly and unwittingly, to a decline in democracy), an abdication of government from its responsibility and a concomitant disaffection of citizens, who, getting weak signals from governments that prioritize corporate interests, are ambivalent about changing their own behaviour. As the power of investor capitalism has grown and globalized, so democracy has weakened. It is misguided to think that corporate democracy and voluntary donations are any substitute for strong public policy, says Reich. CR is a pale substitute for effective laws against corporate misconduct. The solution? The only remedy, he concludes, is to purge corporate cash and influence from the political system: 'keeping supercapitalism from spilling over into democracy is the only constructive agenda for change. All else is frolic and detour' (p14).

Reich is not alone. For example, Harvard Professor John Ruggie, the UN Secretary General's special representative on business and human rights, points out that 'the debate about business and human rights would be far less pressing if all governments faithfully executed their own laws and fulfilled their international obligations'.[23]

Green shoots

Now that capitalism is no longer 'super' and the race to salvage the economy intensifies, it does seem that sustainability-focused companies might be outperforming their industry peers in returning value to investors. Over the six months May–November 2008 the stocks of 99 companies quoted in either the Dow Jones Sustainability Index or the Goldman Sachs SUSTAIN listing showed a 15 per cent better performance than their peers. Although it is not all over yet, the message coming through is that if you are genuinely working towards transforming your business practice, the more likely it is your company will emerge from the current financial crisis stronger than ever.[24] It is also too early to say whether the returns to the environment or society will be *sufficient*; certainly they should not be taken for granted as things are changing so fast.

Forum for the Future finds that, for many of its partners, particularly those quoted on the stock exchanges, its process for fast-tracking larger existing businesses along a *beginner – performer – leader – pioneer* pathway seems to be working. But even the best-performing amongst our partners are not as prepared as they should be for the scale of the changes the looming ecological crisis threatens to impose. Nor are they anywhere near the stage of the new sustainability entrepreneurs like Divine Chocolate * or Ecover, companies that have had sustainability outcomes as their goal from the outset. In a look at the next decade for business and sustainability, the Forum explores the challenges to the current way of doing business and concludes that 'sustainability is too important to be left to CR departments'.[25]

So what about business schools? According to *Business Week*, the recession has brought a flock of people into MBA programmes who have an interest in green business and social enterprise. They, more than employers, are pushing schools to allow what the magazine calls 'The Millennial Generation' born between 1980 and 2000 to customize their curriculum to their career ambitions. 'They are strong-willed, passionate, optimistic, and eager to work … there is so much potential for this generation. They are going to change the world.'[26] A profile that fits with the findings of a *Future Leader Survey* done by Forum for the Future with new entrants to the UK university system.

The US Aspen Institute Centre for Business Education 2009 Beyond Grey Pinstripes survey, found that 69 per cent (up from 34 per cent in 2001) of schools require students to take at least one course on business and society, evidently in response to business and student demand.[27] However, only 30 per cent of the 149 self-reporting schools have sustainability issues as part of their core content. Moreover, as far as I can gather, most are, at best, teaching at the boundaries of *defensive* CR and *strategic* CR. If any reader is aware of any business school teaching at the *transformation* end of CR please get in touch!

So, although most organizations and what is being taught in business schools are in either the pre-engagement or the defensive mode when it comes to embracing sustainability, and relatively few at the strategic stage, there is no reason why a rapid transit cannot be made by all to the shores of the admittedly turbulent waters of transformation. I would say that this is where events environmental and economic have brought us already. Either we wait for further crises or panicky government intervention to shove us unprepared into the water, or we become become positive deviants moving fast but thoughtfully across the water to the other side where our sole purpose is to contribute to sustainability.

In short, don't wait for the stepping stones of transformative change to appear before you; make your own.

Transformation means no going back

By the end of this section, I hope readers who are new to all this have some idea of the sort of leadership 'persona' they have already, or at least have worked out what they are not! I hope too that you have picked up that, although not everything about different leadership theories is worthless, it pays to cherry-pick the insights that help you understand yourself better. Above all, I hope to have convinced you that the sort of leaders the 21st century needs will be thinking more deeply about what the leadership is *for* (sustainable development) and about the interconnectedness of both the problems and the solutions involved. Perhaps you have started to use the wiring diagram on page 92 to build up your current sustainability-literate leadership persona, ready to complete the job as you read through the rest of this book. If not, I hope you have created a similar framework for yourself, not only to bring together your knowledge and understanding as you progress, but also as a habit to keep yourself on a lifelong learning journey.

Although I don't want to get into this in a major way (in this book at least!) some people are arguing that what is needed is a more feminine approach to leadership. Certainly the reasons so many women are repelled by today's dominant leadership behaviours, and that they seem to improve an organization's performance if on the board in sufficient numbers, or running it themselves, indicates a more rigorous (evidence based) investigation into what happens differently would be worthwhile. Not about why women are not there, but about what happens when they are.

When it comes to CR, you may have detected my lack of sympathy for the whole concept. In fact there is a third type of anti-CR to which I subscribe – that CR has critically delayed the whole process of company/

organization transformation to a fully sustainability-oriented position. My 1972 fret that setting up separate Environment Departments in government would ghettoize the problems of environmental degradation and give the finance and other departments an excuse not to get involved was, as it turned out, entirely justified. I feel much the same has happened to the corporate social responsibility 'community'. Both practically and academically it is a bit adrift in organizational and intellectual backwaters. How many organizations have an executive corporate sustainability officer sitting next to the CEO and chief finance officer? To be fair, CR is gaining much more resonance and attention now, and a handful of CEOs are taking leadership positions. Even though negative environmental and social trends are the main drivers, the 2006 Companies Act did help a bit, and the Climate Change Act in the UK and the designation of CO_2 as a pollutant in the US signpost a direction of travel for legislation. But so much more could be done to create structures and processes within an organization to make *it* unable to do anything except go forward in a way that makes sustainability the purpose of the organization. Transformation means there is no going back, even when the main sustainability champion leaves.

The next section of this book is devoted to the knowledge and skills you will need to practise the arts of sustainability-literate leadership and to be an effective positive deviant for that cause. From this section I hope you have garnered sufficient insights to your own knowledge and experiences so far, and perhaps embellished them through my reflections on different aspects of current approaches to leadership development, especially in business schools. Being aware and comfortable with who you are and what you know will enable you to sustain the 'authentic' you as you open your mind and develop your personal sustainability-literate behaviours.

Section Three

Sustainability-Literate Leadership

All of the great leaders have had one characteristic in common:
it was the willingness to confront unequivocally the major
anxiety of their people in their time. This, and not much else, is
the essence of leadership.

J. K. Galbraith, 1997, p330

Section Three

Introduction

Let thousands of positive deviants flourish

Previous sections provide the reasons for shifting to a more sustainable way of life and try to harvest some key lessons from existing leadership education. The section following this will give you some headlines about global solutions to *un*sustainability, to demonstrate the true scale of the effort needed, but also so you can see where your more local efforts and that of the people you influence are contributing. This section sticks with the thesis set out in the Introduction to the book – that there is no one model for sustainability-literate leadership for an individual or an organization (which is a collection of often very different individuals anyway). Here, therefore, we major on areas of thinking, learning and practice that will help you build your own, unique, brand of sustainability-literate leadership. A successful positive deviant can only persuade others to trust and believe in them if you are speaking from the heart, in your own way. Quoting and cribbing from others is fine – indeed essential – but won't be believable if it is parroted without reflection.

In truth, there are many blurred edges between different parts of this section, but I've tried to organize and write so the ideas will be accessible to someone tangling with leadership and/or sustainability for the first time, yet also offer the more experienced some new angles and insights. I've tried to minimize (though not eliminate) the amount of jumping backwards and forwards, and to offer all types of reader a variety of trails of interest to follow through the references.

Each item is prefaced with a learning outcome (what you should expect to be able to do if you are *sufficiently* up to speed on each component) to help you quiz yourself on your progress. The exceptions is the Four Habits of Thought, which start with questions you should be asking yourself all the time, ideally automatically, to keep your immediate decisions firmly in a longer-term and broader sustainability context.

Although my focus is the individual learner, if you are responsible for delivering leadership and management education or training that might be classed sustainability-*light,* I hope this section will help you transform your courses. If you are in a business school and looking for redemption for past sins of commission or omission, there is only one place to go – sustainability-literacy! By moving it from the wilderness of an optional module and mainstreaming into in all your courses, you can help bring battalions of allies in behind the positive deviants already out there in the field.

Chapter 6

Four habits of thought

Normally I am resistant to lists in management books citing the Top Ten This, or the Seven Essential Thats, especially if they all start with the same letter. So it is with some humility, not to say embarrassment, I offer four Rs as important concepts, or more accurately four habits of thinking – resilience, relationships, reflection and reverence. Summarized in the Introduction to the book, and recurring throughout all the chapters, they are described more fully here.

For me they provide a background thrum to all that I do. Have I conveyed their importance in a speech or lecture? In an analysis of a problem or the crafting of a solution are they all honoured? In the heat of the urgent, these are the cooling thoughts that ensure the general direction of travel towards sustainability is kept on course. If what I am doing or saying does not contribute towards a resilience for people as part of the ecology of the Earth; nor deepens and extends the sort of relationships that form part of that resilience; nor has reflected sufficiently on what was good or bad about the past to inform the best for the future; nor is cognizant of our dependence on a natural world with more power over our fate that we dare recognize, then perhaps I need to try a bit harder.

Resilience

Am I enhancing the capacity of any ecological or social system to stay strong or become stronger so as to absorb large shocks yet remain fundamentally unchanged?

Resilience is the capacity of a material, system or person to experience shocks while retaining essentially the same function, structure, feedbacks, and therefore identity. The more resilient is something, the

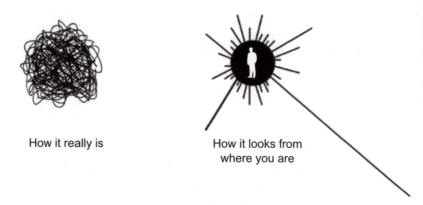

How it really is

How it looks from
where you are

Figure 6.1 Resilience

larger the disruption it can absorb without shifting to an alternative
regime. To an engineer, the resilience of a piece of steel is as good as its
capacity to be bent or heated without breaking or losing strength. Buildings and bridges are constructed to 'survive' things like fires, earthquakes
or flooding. To a psychologist, resilience is the level of stress a person (or
people) can undergo before breaking down. In an ecological system, it is
the point at which the diversity within a biological system is so weakened the environment transforms, as it did for the cod fishing grounds
of Newfoundland in the early 1990s. Using that example, the way the
ecological system (the biogeochemical economy) underpins the social
ones (which include the human economy) was epitomized by the excessive and destructive trawling practices that caught not just the cod, but
wiped out the ecosystem on which they depended, and with it the livelihoods of 40,000 people. '[The trawlers] dragged the ocean floor like a
paved floor.'[1] Damage to the complexity of the ecological system in
which the cod lived, did for the cod (which still haven't come back after
a moratorium on fishing 15 years ago) and for the local community. A
drop in fish stocks and sea birds in the North Sea suggest it is on track to
go the same way this decade (Clover, 2008).

So what is it that makes a system – ecological, social or economic –
resilient? At its most straightforward, it is the number and quality of
interconnected parts it has. Evolution aims to maximize resilience by

strengthening and making ever more numerous and complex the relationships between chemicals, plants and animals.[2] If it were possible to draw them, they would probably look something like the illustration on the left of Figure 6.1.

For most of us though, this degree of complexity is too difficult to cope with, and it is certainly troublesome to communicate. The other illustration in Figure 6.1, on the right, with you in the middle, may be more helpful. It illustrates how your personal resilience depends on the number of connections you have with other people. The majority of them will be with people near to you, family, friends, colleagues and so on, but others are more distant, some may be on the other side of the globe, an aunt or colleagues in Australia for example. Robert Lane's research shows that the more personal connections you have, and the more you nourish and increase them, the better you will weather the shocks life may bring (Lane, 2000).

Substitute your local community for yourself in the right-hand diagram and ask how resilient is it, in the holistic sense of the Newfoundland cod example. Is there a variety of opportunities for people to work, gather or otherwise interact with each other (cafes, clubs, shops) so a sense of community means people look out for each other? Do you party together, hold fetes, turn out at funerals? Is your local economy resilient in that it has a lot of different types of activities, and is not over-dependant on one industry, perhaps with decision makers in other countries, as happened with Coventry and car manufacturing?

Exactly the same reasoning may be followed if you substitute your organization in the middle of the right-hand diagram. How resilient is it, or will it be in the future? Do the multiplicity of interconnections it has – internally or externally – make it stronger or more vulnerable? Does the diversity of suppliers and customers, near and far, protect you from damage should one or two drop their relationship with you for any reason? Does your organization treat its social, environmental and economic responsibilities and risks separately? If so, it could be more vulnerable to crises in any one of them, like the developers who replaced mangroves with leisure resorts and lost everything to coastal storms.

It is very good news that one of the 2009 Nobel Prizes for Economics went to Elinor Ostrom. She has written about the usually complex systems of governance that give resilience to ways of conserving and sharing equitably scarce 'common' resources like water, and uses real-life case studies rather than abstract models to demonstrate her arguments (Ostrom, 1990). Her co-winner, Oliver Williamson, has similarly examined the more complex non-market relationships that influence how corporations behave, but which are rarely represented in the market price, though critical to its resilience when markets change or fail (Williamson, 1999).

True resilience, the resilience that reduces vulnerability to shocks for people and the environment, resides in fitting social resilience (concerning ourselves, our organizations and our economy) into that of the rest of the biogeochemical economy. The other way round doesn't work. We know, we've tried it.

Relationships

Am I creating and protecting the good and many relationships that underpin resilience in individuals and in systems?

Resilience is about masses of relationships. It is about strength gained from many interdependencies. As in sustainable development. And, of course, happiness. There are legions of studies that show successful intimate relationships and close friends to be the most important source of happiness and other positive emotions like good self-esteem and contentment (e.g. Argyle 2001). We know how the *absence* of satisfactory friendships make us less resilient when other things go wrong, with our jobs, our health, our love life. And we know that abuse of power can be very damaging in relationships.

Much has been made of the importance of good family relationships as a basis on which to found an economy. From prehistoric times, I would guess, dysfunctional families have cost society more than they contribute, so it is good news that Nicholas Sarkozy's review of measures of economic progress recommends the household be the favoured unit for measuring *real* well-being – for people and of a national economy.[3] Strangely though, given the new political reality that recognizes local government and communities are where implementation of policy takes place, the report underplays the African observation that 'it takes a village to raise a child'. Families are important, without a doubt, but if for some reason the family unit malfunctions, a child is more likely to grow up resilient if around her there are other models of success and nearby opportunities to learn about loving and effective personal and social relationships and behaviours. And while families can make a big contribution to a low-carbon future, it is only communities working together that will make possible the required radical shift to low-carbon energy generation and ultra-efficient consumption.

The importance of good relationships within the family and in 'the village' remains high in societies more concerned with survival than in those countries where many households have, as one South American finance minister puts it, 'more cars than children'.[4] A chief of an African village in Mali explained to me how the village provides the social services for all its people. As there is no state pension, it is the village that looks after its own old and frail members, and always has an open door for returning sons and daughters. Despite my scepticism, he assured me that, outside disaster, 'In Africa, even today, there is no such thing as homelessness.' However tough things may be, everyone has a village to go to – even if drought, migration or the scourge of diseases like AIDS means they have no family left.

Not so in countries now deemed to be economically 'fully' developed. In *Bowling Alone,* an influential exposé of the decline of social capital in the US, Robert Putnam describes how, over the past 25 years, people have become disconnected from family, friends, neighbours and social organizations like the church, Parent–Teacher Association (PTA), recreation clubs, political parties or bowling leagues. The social 'glue' of multiple quality relationships has dissolved in a more individualistic scamper for personal wealth and the opportunity it brings for solo activities, like watching TV or playing computer-based games. Putnam cites 'cold capitalism' as one culprit, but also blames 'big' government and the growth of the welfare state for 'crowding out' private initiative and undermining trust, the top ingredient of any relationship, personal, social or commercial. State intervention has subverted the relationships of give and take that made society civil. We no longer feel responsibility for the old, frail or even our neighbours (Putnam, 2000).

Righting the relationships that govern the way people rub along together will be quite a task, but ignoring the challenge is not an option. The primacy of trust in making society and the economy work is underlined by Partha Dasgupta, as are the dangers of taking it for granted: 'rather like background environment, present whenever called upon' (Dasgupta and Serageldin, 1999, p330). Gaining and maintaining trust is a high maintenance activity, and hard to recuperate if lost. In any relationship, be it in a marriage, with a bank, between governed and government, of a company or brand, or amongst international treaty signers or trade negotiators, loss of trust can have corrosive consequences.

The importance of getting relationships right extends beyond the social realm to the environment, something not well understood by most social scientists (including economists) who analyse human behaviour as if it took place in the ether rather than on Earth. However difficult it may be to get to grips with the detail, we know the natural world and its long evolution is a mass of continually dynamic and complex interrelationships at and between every possible level – between atoms and species, between air, land and sea. As we humans are intimately caught up in that, it is a strategic failure that so much scholarship ignores it instead of being informed by it.

Sustainability-literate leadership, therefore, means thinking and acting like a relationship counsellor, seeking to repair, strengthen and increase in number and quality the intellectual and practical relationships between people and institutions, and between each and their biological roots. The more numerous, and the better the quality of your relationships, the more resilient you, your communities, institutions and the environment of which everything is a part will be.

Reflection

Belongs to the Learning for Life family of understanding (see page 195 for explanation)

Am I taking time to think about things so as to learn from experience and apply the lessons to the future?

Do you consecrate time to reflection on a regular basis? Most people think over incidents and conversations, but do you consider formal reflection time as important as exercise or good nutrition? Very few yeses here I would guess. A busy life puts time at a premium so thinking through the next day is hard enough, never mind stopping and taking a serious pause to think things through systematically.

For sustainability-literate leadership, in particular those who count themselves as positive deviants, reflective practice is important for two reasons:

- To develop your own sustainability-literacy – it is simply good learning practice.
- To learn from past experience about what works and what doesn't in order to avoid repeating mistakes and take right behaviour forward – and to scale. Protects against hubris.

Professional reflective practitioners (and there are several) have a variety of definitions about what reflection is. My favourite is by John Biggs and Catherine Tate: 'A reflection in a mirror is an exact replica of what is in front of it. Reflection in professional practice, however, gives back not what it is, but what *might* be – an improvement on the original' (Biggs and Tate, 2007).

When it comes to making the sort of 'wicked' (complex) decisions intrinsic to good sustainability outcomes (believe it or not as he clearly didn't practice it!) Donald Rumsfeld makes the best case for reflection in his famous dissertation on 'unknowns' in decision making: 'As we know, there are known knowns. There are things we know we know. We also know there are known unknowns; that is to say, we know there are some things we do not know. But there are also unknown unknowns, the ones we don't know we don't know.'[5]

We've never 'done' sustainable development before, so success will depend on how well we are able to disassemble current knowledge and perceptions about how the world works, and put it all together again in a way that informs new practice. Rumsfeld, Biggs and Tate, and even the Socratic method of reflective learning through asking questions and getting feedback, are part of the diligence required when making decisions in the context of sustainable development.

Training yourself to be a reflective practitioner need not be complicated, and it can quickly become a habit. The process illustrated in Figure 6.2 is reasonably straightforward, and how you do it – in your mind when exercising, doodling in a notebook or in conversation with friends or colleagues, or all three – is up to you. But whether you are accruing knowledge and insights for yourself or an organization, sharing the learning is a must. One way positive deviants measure success is by the number of people and organizations they recruit to their way of thinking.

Purists in interpreting the Kolb cycle will note I have not included searching for useful theoretical models or frameworks to help understanding, when considering how to change or improve something. That is because so many are sustainability-illiterate, thus potentially time-wasting. Developing your own sustainability antennae *sufficiently* to be a critical consumer of other frameworks will help, but as I urge you to do throughout this chapter, designing your own or adapting those illustrated in this book is the quickest way positive deviants can make big, fast leaps from analysis to action.

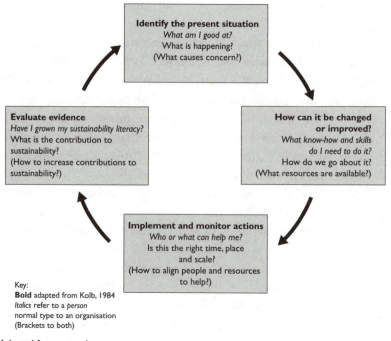

Key:
Bold adapted from Kolb, 1984
Italics refer to a *person*
normal type to an organisation
(Brackets to both)

Source: Adapted from several sources

Figure 6.2 The reflective learning process

Reverence

Am I demonstrating a 'respectful awe' for the power of the natural world and the intimacy of our biological relationship with it?

Respect is a good word and, especially in the world of racial and cultural diversity, preferable to the use of tolerance as a counter to discrimination. But although I use it a lot, it doesn't quite do the thing for me when it comes to describing the proper relationship between people and the rest of the environment. Reverence, not in a religious sense but meaning 'respectful awe' in a spiritual sense, seems more appropriate.

American biologist Edward Wilson reminds us we only know a fraction of the species alive today and next to nothing about the intricacies and interdependencies of how even a small ecological system works. In one patch of forest, for example:

> live legions of life forms: perhaps 300 species of birds, 500 butterflies, 200 ants, 50,000 beetles, 1,000 trees, 5,000 fungi, tens of thousands of bacteria and so on down a long roster of major groups. In many of the groups a large minority of the species are new to science, their properties wholly unknown. Each species occupies a precise niche, demanding a certain place, an exact microclimate, particular nutrients, and temperature and humidity cycles by which the sequential phases of the life cycles are timed. Many of the species are locked in symbiosis with other species, and cannot survive unless arrayed with their partners in the correct configurations. (Wilson, 1998, p331)

Even if we could sort and preserve them once disrupted we have no chance of putting communities like this back together again. 'Such a task anywhere in the world would be like unscrambling an egg with a pair of spoons', says Wilson, because

> for the present the biology of the microorganisms needed to reanimate the soil is mostly unknown, the pollinators of most of the flowers and the correct timing of their appearance can only be guessed at. The 'assembly rules' the sequence in which the species must be allowed to colonize in order to coexist indefinitely, are still largely in the realm of theory (Wilson, 1998, p331).

The same 'assembly rules' apply to us humans, and although a lot is known about the bits that make us up – from cells and genes to livers and brains – how it all is assembled and maintained in continuous exchange with the rest of the environment remains a bit of a mystery. The same goes for global ecological systems as catalogued by the 2005 Millennium Ecosystem Assessment. We know a lot, but to imagine we will ever know how it all fits and works together is, I would argue, dangerously hubristic.

Strategies for sustainability, therefore, need to accommodate the likelihood that the workings of nature may be beyond our understanding, possibly forever. So a position of reverence, a respectful awe of its power, beauty and complexity, and of our total interdependency with it, seems to be the only sensible position. Practically speaking, this means thinking continually about how best to give nature back control over its ecosystems, in our own backyards as well as globally. Even in the most densely built environment, many opportunities exist to liberate hectares of land from tarmac or industrial grass and give it over to plants and trees. We do know that the better the quality of the environment, the better our own biochemistry and spirits.

Chapter 7

New perspectives and broad knowledge

Everyone reading this book will come to it with a different perspective on the way the world works, and an entirely personal range of knowledge and experiences. This chapter tries to bring some of it together from a sustainability perspective – to help you fill gaps for yourself, and perhaps gain some helpful insights into why other people think and behave as they do. It might be because of what they do know and have experienced, but equally it may be because of what they do not know or understand. You may not agree with what I have considered important, and be cross that I have left out something you think is vital. But no matter. The objective is for you to mobilize your critical faculties and arrive at your own broad but sustainability-literate view of the world.

A sustainability-literate world view

You have a *sufficient* understanding of what constitutes a world view and can critically appraise different ones (and the values behind them). You can articulate an attractive sustainability-literate or ecological world view.

Welanschauung (German: *Welt,* meaning world; *Anschauung* meaning view or outlook)
A view onto the world, or a perception of a person or group of people. A set of pre-suppositions or assumptions we hold about the world, and through which we make judgements and choices. The assumptions may be true, partially true, or completely false, and we may hold them consciously or subconsciously and be consistent or inconsistent about how we apply them (Sire, 1997).

The inconstancy of the way we tailor world views to suit ourselves at different times, is summed up by Berthold Brecht. He said: 'world views are hypotheses under development'. As many of us aren't self-analytical enough to realize we possess such a thing as a world view in the first place, fully formed or not, it is no wonder we find it difficult to understand those of others. Like our personal values and ethics, we tend to leave unexamined the reason we interpret events in a particular way, often preferring to go along with the majority around us.[1] Positive deviants, wanting to shape the future in a different way, will need to examine and then shake off wrong assumptions that have shaped past ways of viewing the world.

Although we can only imagine it now, our earliest ancestors must have had a view onto the rest of the world that saw starkly and simply its dangers (bad weather, predators) and its beneficence (good weather, food). Rituals to fend off the first and conjure up the second, and the move to agriculture are evidence of the (understandable) human desire to remove some of the uncertainties of living with nature.

Later, but still in times when most people will have viewed the Earth as flat, organized religions took over the role of sacred (or otherwise)

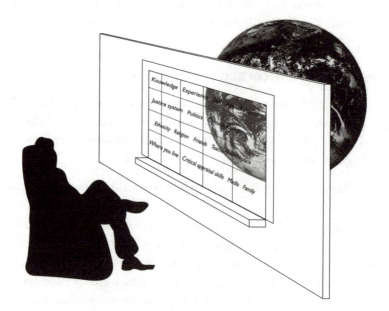

Figure 7.1 Views onto the world

rituals that helped people mediate their relationship with nature and each other. Christianity and Islam are two major examples. Others include Buddhist, Hindu and Jewish religions. All are a mixture of ways of interpreting the world to make sense of its unpredictability, and rules for getting along with it and each other. Buddhism (there are many Buddhas) or Confucianism (lessons from antiquity to guide living today) may be less world views and more guides to discovering 'enlightened truth' or values that matter, though both influence the way many people interact with the world and people around them.

In what became known as the Age of Reason in 17th century Europe (the precursor to the 18th century Enlightenment and the 19th century industrial revolution), science and human rational argument started to challenge religion or 'supernatural faith' as an interpreter and dictator of how humans understood the world and shaped their society. They were part inspired by Aristotle's view that human beings are rational people, and as such could reflect and make choices – including choosing 'the moral life' – and part rebellion against the tight grip the Church had on the state and all aspects of human life. Modern humanists continue the campaign for the separation of state and religion, including, for example, ending charitable status for religious schools. Leading humanist philosopher Tony Grayling argues that 'mankind's future needs the public domain to be a neutral territory where all can meet without prejudice as humans and equals: and that requires the wholesale privitisation of superstition' (Grayling, 2003, p237). A sustainability world view might accept the need for a moral and spiritual dimension to public life, beyond the liberal preference for neutrality, while agreeing that the public domain should not be captured by either religious, commercial or any other special interest.

Other philosophers with no particular truck with any organized religion argue the universality of a sense of the sacred with regards the Earth, whatever our world view might be. As Roger Scruton puts it: 'birth, copulation and death are the moments when time stands still, when we look on the world from a point at its edge, when we experience our dependence and contingency, and when we are apt to be filled with an entirely reasonable awe'.[2] Eco-philosophers and 'deep ecologists', like the late Arne Naess, have long argued that an 'Earth first' perspective is the only legitimate 'world view', and much of their writing adorns my shelves and informs the way I think about the world (Naess, 1990). In the end though, I stopped Save the Planet sloganeering as soon as I worked out that it was our own species that is imperilled. Consequently, my own world view is deeply rooted in our total dependence on the biogeochemical economy and love for its power and its beauty, but my motivation for action is my compassion for my fellow humans and our not yet fully realized potential for happiness.

Recently, and not always for the best of reasons, we have been forced to learn more about the world view resulting from particular interpretations of Christianity and Islam. The term 'Christian right' in America, for example, involves a muddle of conservative views about morality and political ideology and scientific naysaying about evolution. Islamic extremism, in much the same way, confounds distorted interpretations of the Koran with political ends. Gaining clarification is not helped by the use of the word 'fundamental' to describe extreme positions in both Christianity and Islam. Meaning 'serving as a foundation, essential, primary, important', the word fundamental has been co-opted to mean 'literal', as in a literal interpretation of the written Bible or the Koran, or 'extreme' as in intolerance or violence to those believing differently. Both extreme Christianity and extreme Islam claim to be repelled by the secular world and offended by modernity (everything after circa 1850), yet like other naysayers offer only solutions that step backwards. Hard though it is to see the world through eyes so different from your own, try we must, because it is only by doing so that dialogue and reconciliation, and thus forward movement, is possible.

Reconciliation here does not mean arriving at a uniformity of world view. One for all is neither possible nor desirable. It means a reasonable agreement around some shared purpose and values, yes, but is mostly about moderating the extremes. Remembering the quest for increased resilience, the richness of cultures and diversity of who we are as people is something for careful conservation, celebration and growth. Our individual world views and that of our communities are coloured by many things: the ideas we bump into or learn about; the experiences lived; and whether we are male/female, young/older, urban/rural, rich/poor, gay/straight, disabled/or not, optimistic/pessimistic, tall/small, fat/thin, the colour of our skin. All of these things, and much, much more, influences how we look out onto and interpret events locally and internationally. A sustainability world view would not be looking for consensus but for constructive coexistence.

Notwithstanding this mostly (but not always) glorious diversity of world views, trumping them all is a political and ideological assertion – that the post-1945 period of relative peace (known as Pax Americana thanks to the US role as 'global policeman') and prosperity (thanks to the Washington Consensus about best way to run the global economy) is the only possible view of how the world can ever work. International institutions like the World Bank and the North Atlantic Treaty Organization (NATO), for example, have been little influenced by either Buddhist economics or Gandhian principles for conflict resolution, and the OECD little exercised by Islamic culture, despite the membership of Turkey.

The price of decades of intellectual and political laziness is now due for payment in the form of dangerously degrading ecological systems and the disaffection of the 'rest of the world' (aka most of the world). Patronizingly labelled 'emerging economies' or 'underdeveloped', yet firmly kept in their place by the 'first' world, the so-called 'second' and 'third' worlds have bleeding sores of resentment going back for centuries. The stumbling of the 'first world' over its immature response to the suicide terrorist attacks on the New York World Trade Centre towers in 2001 and the US's serial failure to understand the leadership responsibility that goes with being the world's most powerful country (in military, economic and political terms), has joined devastatingly poor management of the global financial and economic systems, and unimaginative behaviour in international forums (such as the climate change negotiations) to liberate the 'second world' from its submission to the 'west knows best' world view.

Parag Khanna is one of several writers to reflect on emerging powers like Russia, China, Brazil, India and Saudi Arabia, Kazakhstan and the United Arab Emirates, which are forging multiple connections and relationships (Khanna, 2008). A new, potentially more resilient world economic and military arrangement may be developing that is not dependent on what the US or Europe does next. Interwoven with the geopolitical shifts in global power are other seekers of power for their ideas and influence, ranging from the religious crusaders, non-governmental activists and mega-philanthropists. The undertow in all these globally massive shifts in economic, social, political – and military – power, is access to resources in a world popping from the pressure of a huge human population with aspirations to lifestyles similar to the high-consuming US and EU. 'Resource nationalism' warned the International Energy Authority in relation to oil some time ago, is now a reality, undermining the ideology that trade was the ultimate international peacemaker because it aligned the interests of buyers and sellers on a global scale. Russia has (literally, by planting its flag on the sea floor) staked out its claim to the resources under the melting Arctic ice. As ever, the poorest of the poor – the so-called third world – with so much 'real' wealth in its natural resources, is coming off worst. Africa, for example, is selling off its raw materials (and in the case of Zimbabwe, eternal access to them) mainly to China, but also India, Russia and Korea. An sustainability-literate world view would be informed by justice and equity, not only with regard to resources, but also to international relations.

A surprising indication that a sustainability-inspired world view is a real contender in the geopolitical stakes comes in a 2008 report on global trends to 2025. Produced by the US National Intelligence Council (NIC) it landed conveniently on US President Obama's desk as he was designing his priorities and strategies for power. The report anticipates the 'end of American supremacy' and envisages a world of competing centres of power, scarce resources, and countless potential shocks to 'the system'. It's influence may be seen in his peri-election speeches, and his actions so far suggest he understands that the response of the US under his leadership may stand between peaceful cooperation and global anarchy. Above all, the NIC has told Obama that the hallmarks of tomorrow's world will be scarcity – of land, water, oil, food and, not least, 'air-space' for greenhouse gas emissions. The bluntness of the message, as refreshing as it is shocking, carries 'a cautionary tale' from the past century, and suggests where we are now resembles the 1920s, when 'few envisioned the lethal situation about to unfold, ushered in by the Great Depression' (NIC, 2008).

Three lessons are ours to be learnt from the 20th century, says the report:

- Leaders and their ideas matter.
- Economic volatility introduces a major risk factor.
- Geopolitical rivalries trigger discontinuities more than does technological change. (p5)

And the greatest of these is leadership: '... leadership matters, no trend is immutable, and ... timely and well-informed intervention can decrease the likelihood and severity of negative developments and increase the likelihood of positive ones'. The last paragraph of the report reminds us again that individual and collective leadership have been (for bad as well as good) the biggest 'game-changers' of the last century (p98).

Two other big reports on the threat to human well-being from a degraded environment, on the climate change (Stern, 2006) and ecosystems and biodiversity (www.teebweb.org), seek solutions through the language of economics; by putting a proper value on the resources and services of the environment, they argue, it will become too expensive to over-consume and damage. By contrast, the NIC report puts scarcity of natural resources and services at the heart of international geopolitics and diplomacy as an apparently deliberate challenge to a predominantly economic view of the world.

So, from an unexpected quarter, we have an influential proposal for a new perspective on the world and its woes – one informed by the evidence of unsustainable development and with the protection of the natural world's resources and services at its heart. The NIC report does not predict what will happen, nor propose an action plan, but is clear the task before us all is to bring leadership, new social and economic behaviours and diplomacy at all levels in behind the emerging world view the NIC has begun to articulate.

Beyond a few hints, some not very subtle, I have not been specific about what your sustainability-literate world view should be. Arne Naess thought that everyone should develop their own philosophy, and I agree. Only your reflections on your unique learning and experience can shape your personal philosophy and view onto the world. I just hope there is enough here to nudge you in the right direction!

A good enough knowledge base

You possess a *good enough* knowledge base of, and are able to make connections between: ethics and values, people and community, science and technology and economics

> Science without ethics is blind; ethics without science is empty. (Des Jardines, 2001, p11)

The design of Forum for the Future's Leadership for Sustainable Development Masters (LSDM) course was much influenced by the gaps in my own knowledge when I got started as a sustainability campaigner. Finding out about how the environment was being trashed was easy in the 1960s. What was missing, however, was help in understanding why people – the demand side of the *un*sustainability equation – behave the way they do.

Rummaging amongst my bookshelves in 1995, I found I'd had to bone up on four particular areas of knowledge: ethics and values; what made people and community tick; the science around sustainability and climate change (we were worried about CO_2 emissions in the 1960s!); and economics as the apparent villain of the piece. After canvassing some colleagues and finding their own experience mirrored mine, the LSDM course developed four 'knowledge themes' to underpin the leadership and sustainable development elements and complement the six learning placements students have in different sectors. Intentionally, the environment was not a separate theme, but integrated with and viewed through the prism of all the others.

Here is a brief outline of the basic knowledge syllabus covered by students who come to the course from a variety of backgrounds. It has been adapted for the purposes of this book, and my advice is to treat it as we do – more like a menu than a prescription. It is not necessary to know it all, just *enough* to make you effective – and aware of what you don't know so you can seek help when you need it. There is an introduction to each knowledge theme, followed by a table to illustrate the topics in each theme; the Bibliography suggests some starter reading. The syllabus for each theme is organized into three strands:

Foundations:	basic knowledge relating to each theme presented in lay terms, in *extremely rough* recommended order, not of importance, but for getting into the subject if you are new to it
Applications:	examples of how basic knowledge would be applied to assist your thinking, reading and reception of information via newspapers etc.
Issues:	Areas for debate and reflection that help show up the connections between the themes and sustainability

Ethics and values

You are confident enough in yourself and your own values to identify and critique the values of others, whether they are explicit or implicit. Philosophically, you are able to question modern assumptions about progress and articulate sustainability paths to living a 'good' life.

As philosophy is more of an activity than a subject, many people are probably doing it without knowing it. Meaning 'love of wisdom', philosophy is about the search for truth (without worrying too much if it exists or not – it is the search that matters), through logical thinking and questions. So to 'do' philosophy' is to ask the What, Why and How questions about big things (like What is the good life?) but also everyday concepts, ideas and practices that are usually taken for granted. One of my favourite pub-philosophy questions is why do different brands of car look so alike? Counter-intuitively, the follow on why and how questions often lead into sustainability relevant and deep considerations about the values and ethics that shape what people do. (Working definitions for values, ethics and morality are given in Chapter Eight under *Ubunto*, page 174.)

When choices and judgements are made about a wide range of things – choice of technology for example, or responses to climate change – different views will be backed by different values (and/or world views – see above) – sometimes regardless of what the facts might be. As Kate Rawles puts it, values are not like tastes, such as a preference for thick or thin cut marmalade, and they can be made explicit and sub-jected to rational debate – through using that philosophical questioning again.[3]

People and communities

You understand enough about human behaviour (as individuals or as members of communities large and small) to design successfully different courses of action (that contribute to sustainability) and to bring people along with you.

Psychology is usually next up after philosophy as a subject most people wish they had studied. The 'science of the mind' has been much pepped up as a subject by new neurological research that demonstrates how our brain responds to emotions. (Re)discovering that we empathize physi-cally as well as emotionally with each other, backs the view of evolutionary biologists who believe our brain, which commandeers over 20 per cent of the energy we take on board as food, has evolved to make us successful social animals. Which of course undermines the standard economic model of the individual as predominantly (rather than rarely) selfish and greedy. Although we like to think of ourselves as having a strong individual identity, we are actually much happier in a compli-cated knot of personal relationships.

The social sciences help us understand how people and groups relate to each other on a larger scale – in communities, between countries, in organizations. Inequality of all sorts of opportunity, or the inclusivity or exclusivity of different social groups, or different approaches to justice and democracy, cannot be explained away by economic theory alone. For example, democracy, the lodestone of a civil society, and a precious mechanism for making decisions collectively, is, as Freedom House records, in decline. In 2009, 'for the fourth consecutive year declines have trumped gains' it noted.[4] Why? The sheer size of the human popu-lation, and its anticipated trajectory of its growth over the next 50 years or so, will bring unprecedented pressures to bear not only on the envi-ronment but also on the way we humans live and work together. How can we adjust? Already, more than half the world's people live in urban areas. What does community mean in large cities? What will happen as environmental and resource constraints change transport and consumption options? Being able to explore and answer these sorts of questions, will call on you to have a *good enough* grasp of sociological enquiry (as well as philosophical questioning skills). A cautionary note is needed though; some fields of sociological research and writing have disappeared off the scale of any jargon-ometer. Steer well clear, unless you understand the lingo already.

Science and technology

As a discriminating user of scientific evidence you know where to get reliable and current information, have enough knowledge and confidence to interrogate it and other sources, and are able to communicate effectively with others about scientific evidence and technological choices from a sustainability perspective.

The word 'science', as a noun, means knowledge ascertained by observation and experiment, critically tested, systematized and brought under general principles. Thus scientific evidence is knowledge that has been obtained through a rigorous and recognizable process. Unfortunately the word 'science' has been annexed in the minds of consumers and producers of that knowledge (you and me, scientists) to refer only to the 'natural' or 'hard' sciences like physics, biology and chemistry. Humanities and social sciences are (very wrongly) seen as second class, 'soft' science. Even ecology, the science of how the whole system of life fits together, didn't take off until research into climate change got started in earnest.

As the sustainability solution-seeking pendulum swings away from an obsession with finding a 'silver bullet' type high-tech fix towards ways of changing human behaviour, we are paying the price for that neglect of a broader interpretation of science. For example, and as Amory Lovins points out regularly, one of the largest sources of energy (apart from the sun that is) is using less more efficiently. That we are shockingly wasteful is only partly a technological dilemma, because if we applied the technologies we have already we'd be well on the way to meeting greenhouse gas emission limits.[5] The laws of physics dictate that, on any scale, technology can never compensate for continued wrong human behaviour so why we don't do what we know we should is an urgent area of social scientific enquiry.

If you don't count yourself as 'scientifically literate' already please don't be daunted. The word scientist was only coined in 1833, before which 'men (*sic*) of science' were known as natural or moral philosophers, an appellation positive deviants might take up again to describe their quest to gain *sufficient* scientific knowledge, and sufficient insights to the way it is generated and applied (often under political or economic influence) to make *good enough* judgements about what will contribute best to sustainability.

Economics

You have sufficient understanding about the core ideas of economics and the new, emerging economic ideas to argue for, and to contribute to, the transition to sustainability as the arbiter of economic success.

Until very recently, most people found economics too difficult to fathom. Until, that is, the banks and the whole hinterland of the financial systems they fronted collapsed under the weight of their own criminally large accumulation of debt. Now everyone, whether they have a mortgage, savings, stashes of shares, are employed or employers or neither, has become a keen student of what is happening to the 'real' economy where we all live and work. As Pete Lunn points out: 'the difference between economics and economic life, between our theories of how the economy works and our experience of it, matters' (Lunn, 2008, p4).

As one of the most powerful forces that shapes the world and our lives today, sustainability-literate leadership will need to understand not only the basic principles of how the economy *has* worked (including the ideologies that have dominated in recent times) but also the parameters it must respect if we are to move onto a glide path that leads to sustainability. As there is much more about this in Chapter 3, I'll only flag here the importance of attending to the 'new economics': the theories, policy and practical solutions emerging from the work of ecological and behavioural economists, which, backed by neurophysiological evidence, demonstrates we are more collaborative and unpredictable than orthodox economic models permit. One newspaper editorial thinks 'the study of behaviour is disrupting the foundation stones of economics'.[6]

Thank goodness! My only (but significant) grump is why they didn't recognize the same earth quaking effect from the ecological economics that has been around for several decades.

For an ultra-quick introduction look at Herman Daly, one of my most revered mentors about economics, who has written a brief and *good enough* overview of what is going wrong, and why, and what to do about it.[7]

Table 7.1 Sustainability-literacy knowledge themes

		Foundations		Applications		Issues
Ethics and values *You understand your own values and are able to identify and critique the values of others, whether explicit or hidden. Philosophically, you are able to question modern assumptions about progress and articulate sustainability paths to living a 'good life'*	1	Morality, values and ethics, and their role in life	●	The use of philosophical tools in decision making	●	Hidden world views: ethics and values behind politics and the meaning of development, progress, success, quality of life
	2	Philosophical approaches to living a good life and critical thinking techniques	●	SD as a values-based endeavour to live the good life		
	3	Environmental ethics – anthropocentric, biocentric, ecocentric approaches	●	The psychology and sociology of changing values	●	SD ethics – the relationship between human and environmental values
			●	Ethics and values in science and politics		
	4	Conventional western ethical frameworks	●	Ethics and values in religions and spiritual traditions	●	Deep and shallow reasons for environmental concern and the value of the other-than-human world
	5	Perspectives from other cultures and countries	●	Ethics of climate change, acting now for future benefit		
	6	Ethics of intra- and intergenerational equity – needs, wants and rights	●	Role of ethics in technological choice	●	Implications to ethics and values of the latest neurophysiological science (nurture v. nature)

Table 7.1 Sustainability-literacy knowledge themes (cont)

		Foundations	Applications	Issues
People and community *You understand enough about human behaviour, as individuals or as members of communities large and small to design success-fully different courses of action that contribute to sustainability and bring people along with you*	1 2 3 4 5 6 7	Human identity and a sense of place (self, relation-ship to family, community, society at large, nature) Anthropology and psychology of what it means to be human Population and demographics Concepts of human and social capital Theories of the development of modern societies Systems of govern-ment, governance and political process (local to international) Limits to social scientific methods	• SD and ideas about society and human nature (including chang-ing behaviour) • Denial – magni-tude of response in relation to evi-dence of *un*SD • Relationship between SD and human and social capital (under-standing inequality, exclusion and inclusion) • Relationship between society and democracy, concepts of citi-zenship • How community has been debated in past 50 years, lessons for the future • SD and ideas about modernity (post-industrial society) • Different responses to SD (by government, business etc.)	• Impact of demographics and population on SD options • Current debates about social capital, cohesion and multi-culturalism and future meaning of community • Social impacts of industrialization, mass urbanization, unequal wealth • Diversity, rights and emancipation • Nutrition and food – why obesity and starvation co-exist • The social role and future of shopping in a low-carbon society

Table 7.1 Sustainability-literacy knowledge themes (cont)

		Foundations	Applications	Issues
Science and technology *As a discriminating user of scientific evidence you know where to get reliable and current information, have enough knowledge and confidence to interrogate it and other sources, and are able to communicate effectively with others about scientific evidence and technological choices*	1	Methods of assembling and interpreting data and evidence (physical and social sciences)	• The role of scientific evidence (and ethical issues) in policy and other decisions	• 'Post-normal' science – new developments like genetics, nanotechnology, robotics, artificial intelligence etc.
	2	Uncertainty, including use and misuse of statistics	• Assessing and managing risk in uncertainty	• Role of non-experts in science policy and evaluation
	3	Basic concepts of ecology and the interdependence of living things	• Energy and material life cycle assessment generally and for specific tasks (like policy and technology choices, product or process design)	• Sociology and democracy of science and technology (access to it)
	4	First two laws of thermodynamics, chemical change and conservation of matter	• Decision-making tools – e.g. The Five Capitals, The Natural Step	• Social and environmental impact of ICT
	5	Global material cycles, how the biogeochemical economy works	• Public health and epidemics, prevention, containment. Environment and human health links	• Development of low-carbon heat, power and light (energy services)
	6	Genetics and evolution	• Climate change, predictions and solutions	• Controversial technology choices: GM v. local variety; 'big' energy v. distributed generation
	7	Neurophysiology (relating to human behaviour)	• Water and food security	

Table 7.1 Sustainability-literacy knowledge themes (cont)

		Foundations	Applications	Issues
Economics *You have sufficient understanding about the core ideas of economics and the new, emerging economic ideas to argue for and contribute to the transition to sustainability as the arbiter of economic success*	1	Core ideas of economics though concept of maximizing human welfare; allocating of scarce resources; competing uses; consumption needs and wants	• The design of a 'new economics' theory and practice for organizations • The transition from a *linear* to a *circular* (resilient) economy (compatible with natural cycles and waste avoidance) • Valuation of environmental and social capital: techniques, problems and criticisms • Framework for indicators incorporating social, environmental, ethical and economic dimensions • Cost–benefit analysis; green accounting • Globalization and local economics – including trade	• Economic and non-economic value of natural, human and social capital • Economic man v. Sustainability man in economic modelling • Happiness as economic objective • Economic world views of international institutions (e.g. IMF, OECD) • Economics of climate change, MDG and MEA • Economic growth: of well-being or consumption? • Role of finance in reconstructing a sustainability supportive economy • Different business models
	2	Concept of capital – natural, human, social, manufactured and financial		
	3	Wealth creation, monetary and non-monetary		
	4	Roles of markets, the state and reciprocity		
	5	Concept of the total economy		
	6	Financial sector role in 'real' economy		
	7	Resource economics		
	8	Behavioural and other 'new' economics		
	9	Other economic traditions (e.g. Islamic, Buddhist)		

Note: ICT information and communication technologies; GM, genetically modified.

Chapter 8

Principles of practice and tools of the trade

There are many books about the practical nuts and bolts of leading and managing an organization such as creating effective boards and governance systems, managing finances and human resources, planning and working strategically, ways of organizing and running management teams and so on. One that I turned to when we set up Forum for the Future was Mike Hudson's excellent *Managing without Profit* (1995). From the business perspective (but with lots of transferability to public or not-for-profit enterprises) I am also a fan of Charles Handy and the late Peter Drucker (see Bibliography). They both have shone lights of common sense and wise reflection down several decades of gobbledygook.

I have learnt a lot from them, but I am not going to repeat or even précis what they say. This is not to say you don't need to be able to construct a budget, manage people well, and read a balance sheet and so on – you do. But in this chapter I want to concentrate on the other things you will need to think about if you are to become sustainability-literate and an effective positive deviant – some principles to guide your practice, a new way to think about evaluating the outcomes of your efforts, and a series of tools to help you get going without delay.

Principles of practice

You use these principles of practice to increase the effectiveness of your own leadership for sustainability, as well as to help others to do likewise.

In Chapter 5 I cited Rakesh Khurana's view that in order to regain trust and respect, managers should adopt a code of practice, what he calls a

Hippocratic Oath for Managers![1] I almost agreed with Khurana, and fell to wondering if something similar might work for sustainability-literate leadership. In the end I worried more that such a move would only provoke arguments about what was in and what was out, and so deflect time and energy from getting on with it. So I am proposing instead some principles of practice that are more about growing your own distinctive sustainability-literate leadership persona and therefore competence as a practitioner.

Ubunto, morality, values and ethics

You live in a way that recognizes the interdependence of people and the environment. Your own values and ethics give you courage, power and consistency, and you know how to make the values and ethics of others explicit.

There is an African phrase *umunto agumunto mgabanto* (*ubunto* for short) meaning 'a person is a person because of people'. Archbishop Desmond Tutu explains it like this:

> *Ubunto* really means that I am because you are. We belong together. Our humanity is bound up with one another. We say in our language, a person is a person through other persons. A solitary human being is a contradiction in terms. I learn how to become a human being through association with other human beings.[2]

The idea of *ubunto* lives strongly in countries and communities where life is lived more often in survival mode. In cultures informed by Islam the equivalent word would be *ummah*, meaning an individual can only exist in the context of a larger community (sharing values as *ubunto* does). Such ideas transcend tribalism but recognize that individual survival depends on group survival strategies. Elinor Ostrom describes complex self-governance systems used for shared irrigation systems in Spain, and Nelson Mandela ✱ says *ubunto* means a traveller should always find a welcome and hospitality, remembering that for most people in the world, the village remains their only source of support in old age. *Ubunto* is everything from a universal truth and way of life to a pension plan.

The culture of *ubunto*, or recognizing our interdependency one with another, has shrivelled in many of the richer countries, with the consequent personal and social impoverishment chronicled by writers like Robert Putnam and Robert Lane. As Benjamin Franklin pointed out, 'a man who is wrapped up in himself makes a very small package'.[3] Adopting *ubunto* as a principle for how you carry out your sustainability leadership means you can be honest about not being perfect at everything, and content to be dependent on others. Pretend to be good at what you are not, and it diminishes you. Be frank about your strengths and weaknesses and build teams to complement this, and you will gain respect and authority. Bring *ubunto* into the workplace.

Taking *ubunto* seriously is also good protection against the dangers of 'getting above yourself', or becoming hubristic (arrogant to the point of inviting disaster) in a leadership role. Some people may simply be unsuited or unskilled enough for leadership roles, so cope by becoming an 'island', sometimes out of arrogance, but more often to hide lack of confidence. Extreme cases come to believe in their own myth; the flattering image reflected by colleagues, followers or newspaper profiles becomes what they believe themselves to be. The three heads of the Detroit car manufacturers flying in their individual personal jets to Washington to request multi-billion dollar bail outs from the US government is a non-banking example that springs to mind. As a general rule, the more powerful you are the more dangerous this self-deception can be, as those around you are unlikely to challenge any utterance or behaviour if they fear the consequence, and so the myth is reinforced. They become what Lynn Offerman calls 'toxic followers' who 'fool ... with flattery'.[4]

Behind what makes *ubunto* work is either a shared set of values, or at least finding in the values of others something you can respect. And like *ubunto,* values and ethics govern *how* we do something – including how we live. They form part of our personal politics, and, as such, need to be made explicit in our dealings with others. Fiona Reynolds, Director General of the National Trust UK and one of the most sustainability-literate leaders I know, says cut her in half and you'd find her values written through her, like a stick of Blackpool rock. She uses them to guide her through tough decisions and help provide a consistency in her leadership. People trust those whose values they know and respect.

It is common to be bamboozleded by the difference between morals, values and ethics. Here is my attempt to distil the multiple, sometimes confused, explanations around.

Morality involves a basic understanding of good and bad. There may be arguments about what perfect morality – or virtue – may be, but the attempt to find out is, in itself, virtuous. Which is what makes a moral life worth living. Aristotle said that 'moral virtue comes about as the result of habit'.

Values are based on beliefs (or norms) of a person or social group. Family values or Christian values are examples. Values draw on an interpretation of morality that help shape attitudes to others and events around you. Shared values are important for the cohesiveness of the group and its members. Even when implicit, they help set the boundary conditions for what is acceptable behaviour and so form the social 'glue' that enables us to live and work together reasonably harmoniously.

Ethics are, in a sense, applied morality. They codify morality into rules of behaviour of, for example, doctors or lawyers. However, particular values, like racism or misogyny, can be disguised within codes of ethics, even though other moral considerations, such as the wrongness of killing or stealing, are explicit. Aristotle thought ethics and politics were continuous. Ethics are the 'operational' front for a set of values, if you like, so understanding the values behind any code of ethics (or political manifesto!) is important.

Fortunately, an interest in ethics and morality is re-emerging as political and financial sector leaders strive to regain respect, and (helpfully from a sustainability perspective) Daniel Goleman cites research that shows that the more empathetic people are – the more *ubunto* is at work – the more agreement there is around the moral principle that resources should be allocated according to people's need.[5]

I am frequently asked if there are any 'off-the-peg' values or ethical codes relevant to sustainability, but my answer is no. Values and codes of ethics are only made real by the people or organization hoping to live by them, with the process of generating them and forever refreshing them as important as the outcome. The only non-negotiable value, I would argue, is one that recognizes the indivisibility of life on Earth, and our total dependence on it. Mandela asks us to remember too that we are part of other people's *ubunto*, which brings with it responsibilities we need to reflect in the values we choose to live by.

To generate a set of values, or a code of ethics with sustainability as a destiny for yourself or for an organization you could use as a template either the habits of thought in Chapter 6, or the twelve features of a sustainable society cited later in this chapter (page 206). They work equally well as a framework within which to design questions for quizzing the sustainability relevance of the values and ethical codes of others. But most of all don't forget to dig deeper to explore what living a virtuous life – doing the right thing – might look like from a sustainability perspective.

You and positive deviance

You know how to do the right things *despite* unfavourable circumstances and you can do them in a way that removes barriers and bring others along with you.

The title of this book comes from this section, and by now there should be little doubt about how much I see positive deviance as the main strategy for anyone actively practising sustainability-literate leadership! To delay action until the 'time is ripe', or this bit of legislation has been passed, or that balance sheet looks better, or those workmates agree, is no longer defensible. Because the timescales for getting it right are so short – measured in a few decades – and because the pace of institutional change is so slow – measured in one or more generations – everyone needs to practice positive deviance from now on.

Positive deviance means doing the right thing *despite* being surrounded by the wrong institutional structures, faulty policy processes or operational mechanisms, or uncomprehending and *ubunto*-free colleagues. But it also means doing it in a way that helps guide others around or over barriers too. It means exercising all your leadership skills to help them see the perversities that stand in the way of a more sustainable way of life. As the later discussion about evaluating outcomes suggests, your success is not only about what you do yourself, but also how much you are able to influence others to come along with you.

The term, positive deviance, is not new. It is used by others in a sense similar to, but not quite the same as, mine. Bizarrely, I first came across it in conversation with an official in the UK Treasury. He was on the lookout for examples of efficient (i.e. cost-effective) policy delivery in the public sector *despite* the policy chaos, structural inertia and bureaucracy; searching for examples of good practice to 'encourage others'. There is also a Positive Deviance Initiative (PDI) based at Tufts University on much the same quest. The PDI was started by development specialists who noticed that even in areas of widespread illness and poor nutrition some women managed to keep their children nourished and healthy. What were they doing differently, and how could others learn from it? The same idea has been used to tackle hospital-induced infections and school attendance.

So in the sense that taking examples of good practice from the locality and sharing it tends to have a better outcome than importing ideas from outside, positive deviance is good practice in policy development and implementation. Wanted are role models and case studies of people deviating past the unsatisfactory norm in a positive sense, and we could do with a lot more of them.

But to be a positive deviant involves much more than a quest for examples of good practice. It is a strategic commitment – by you and (ideally) your organization – to rebellion against the perversity of living with so many anti-sustainability policies and practices. It is not a strike or a campaign against what is wrong that I'm recruiting for, but a manifestation for what is right. Of, it is my fervent hope, such a scale and speed, that sustainability-literate behaviour quickly becomes the norm.

Anyone who is complacent that change will cascade down from national or EU policy without such a rebellion, need only recall that even after 40 years of equal pay legislation, women still get paid, on average, 30 per cent less than the chaps! Stephen Hale has dubbed the leadership impasse on climate change in the UK as an 'I will, once you have' impasse, with everyone trapped in dysfunctional relationships (Figure 8.1).

Even if it could move fast enough, legislation on its own won't right the institutional stand-offs within and between government, business and citizens illustrated in Figure 8.1. And although policy coherence

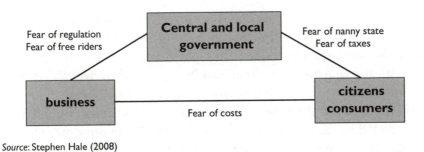

Source: Stephen Hale (2008)

Figure 8.1 The new politics of climate change

and uncomplicated steers for all sectors are extremely important, they won't, in themselves, drive the quick and radical action that is needed on a very large number of fronts at the same time. More than anything else, deviating off our current trajectory and onto one directed at achieving sustainability will depend on how fast people and organizations everywhere just defy the perversities and get on and do the right thing.

Some examples of positive deviants, selected for the different ways they have chosen to buck the trend are in the appendix. And, although they couldn't be more different one from another, all share one important feature – they learnt by getting on and doing it.

Social intelligence and compassion

You care enough about the condition of humanity to intervene to improve its lot. In doing so, you are able to demonstrate you understand the way people are, as individuals or in communities and under different circumstances.

Emotional literacy was until comparatively recently a no-no for leadership. The clinical, dispassionate decision maker was the most admired model. Yet when Daniel Goleman published his book *Emotional Intelligence* in 1995 floodgates of gratitude opened. It became legitimate to use the evidence of the damage done by emotional ineptitude in other parts of our lives to analyse its impact in the workplace. Not that much seems to have changed, the alpha male culture still seems to be everywhere! Even Goleman's now iconic list is mostly about control of yourself and situations. (The list appears in full in Chapter 4, page 106.)

In his most recent book, *Social Intelligence*, Goleman has graduated from his managerial approach to taming our own emotions and describes the emotions gained through satisfactory human contacts, especially loving ones, as 'that raw buzz of fellow feeling', which neuroscience proves contributes to our health and well-being. '[This is] well and good for our personal lives', Goleman continues. 'But all of us are buffeted by the vast social and political currents of our time. The last century highlighted what divides us, confronting us with the limits to our collective empathy and compassion.' What is needed, he concludes, is a collective reawakening, reminding us 'we need not accept the divisions that hatred breeds, but rather extend our empathy to understand one another despite our differences, and to bridge those divides. The social brain's wiring connects us all at our common human core' (Goleman, 2007, p318). Goleman has discovered *ubunto* and the central importance of human relationships in our lives.

It is hardly a surprise that science confirms we have a neurophysiological response to emotions like love and fear. We've all felt a fluttering heart on behalf of both of them. But compassion is probably the only emotion that has an inbuilt *obligation* to intervene on behalf of others. So out of fashion is it, sustainability-literate leadership will mean drumming it up in ourselves and in others.

Compassion is different from the much promoted leadership attribute of empathy. Empathy means you can put yourself in the shoes of others and see the situation from their perspective. You are able to enter into another's feelings and experiences, the better to understand them. But it doesn't mean you have to do anything about their situation, or even like them. Compassion is much bigger. It means you have sorrow for the sufferings of others, and are inclined to pity or mercy, regardless of your feelings about them, or anything they may have done to you. Like love, compassion is unconditional, and it demands intervention.

The difference between compassion and empathy matters in two ways. First in what I call the Mandela way. Never mind how you have suffered or been wronged, neither vengeance nor walking away will put things right. Mandela understood – and learnt in the hardest of ways – that compassion for the condition of both the victims and perpetrators of the crimes of the South African regime was the only foundation on which future justice could be built in his country. His policy of peace and reconciliation was cooked up in his claustrophobic Robben Island cell and then developed in 'co-creation' with his fellow prisoners and African National Congress (ANC) colleagues. Without being sure he was ever going to be able to implement his ideas, Mandela patiently prepared for leadership of his country, by extending his compassion for the exploited and oppressed black population to that of the white ruling class.

Secondly, compassion is a powerful motivator for action. Compassionate people do not stand by while others suffer. Compassion for other people near and far is what fuels sustainability-literate leadership. Caring for the larger human condition motivates you to be active in the relief of suffering and helps widen the field in which you search for sustainability solutions. The route to solving your own local problem may well be through solving the problems of others, but you have to care enough to look for it. And you have to understand how people tick, how they feel about their own identity and how they relate to others, in order to mobilize others around the solution. You will not be able to sell the primacy of caring for the environment if it is not wrapped up in a genuine compassion about the lot of people.

Everything is connected: Systems and resilience

You are able to analyse human problems and design strategies, projects and solutions in the context of the whole system – all life on Earth, which includes us: you can think of the connections within and between different subsystems.

A major reason we are locked into *un*sustainable development is the way we have disaggregated how we think and do things into what is horribly called 'bite sized chunks'. As a consequence we have a lot of specialists but collectively remain short on practical wisdom because we subdivide things that should be interconnected; human welfare, environmental protection and wealth creation, for example, are separated into different government or organizational departments, onto separate pages of the newspaper, into different classes in school and so on. UK research funding is allocated through 67 different subjects.

Encouragingly, according to the *Harvard Business Review*, corporate recruiters are starting to look for what they call 'T' shaped talent –

people who possess a broad understanding of other disciplines as well as a deep technical knowledge, as opposed to 'I' shaped employees competent in only one discipline.[6]

But what does that mean for someone trying to exercise sustainability-literate leadership here and now? How can we think, plan and work, not just systematically (methodically) but within one big hugely interconnected system (the Earth and everything on it)?

In *Science for All Americans*, the American Association for the Advancement of Science defines a 'system' as

> any collection of things that have some influence on each other. The things can be almost anything, including objects, organisms, machines, processes, ideas, numbers, or organizations. Thinking of a collection of things as a system draws our attention to what needs to be included among the parts to make sense of it, to how its parts interact with one another, and to how the system as a whole relates to other systems.[7]

The specialist discipline of systems theory has a long history in natural ecological and technical systems. But it was only in the second half of the 20th century that it attracted some serious multidisciplinary attention, largely through the work of people thinking about reconciliation between human and natural systems (see for example Capra, 1982, 1996; Wilson, 1998). More recently, systems thinking has informed analyses of the life cycles of products and the modelling of climate change (see for example Azapagic et al, 2004; IPCC, 2007). An engineer by original discipline, Peter Senge has applied systems thinking to organizational change and now promotes ways of creating 'the learning organization', which he calls 'the fifth discipline' (Senge, 1990).

For me, though, the most attractive thinker and writer about systems thinking is the late Donella (Dana) Meadows. A scientist and the lead author of the 1972 *Limits to Growth* and its sequels, Dana makes systems theory transparently understandable to even the most stubbornly linear thinker. She died suddenly before the book was completed – but some friends and colleagues edited her various manuscripts into a primer that includes practical illustrations of applied systems thinking to everything from an ecosystem to a company sales strategy or how best to position an electric meter (Meadows, 2009). Dana, an energetic campaigner, also designed a famous list of 'places to intervene

in a system' – a sort of positive deviant plumbers map to possible lever-
age points for spannering sustainability into an organization's policies
and practice. Here it is (Table 8.1), in order of impact from the least
(10) to the most (1) transformative (very slightly amended by me for
clarity).

Table 8.1 Places to intervene in a system

10	constants, parameters, numbers (such as subsidies, taxes, standards, targets, meas-urements)
9	material stocks and flows (in and out – resource management, could include people)
8	the strength of negative feedback loops (making things worse) relative to the impacts they are trying to correct against
7	the gain around driving positive feedback loops (that make things better)
6	the structure of information flows (who does and does not have access to what kinds of information
5	the rules of the system (such as incentives, punishments, constraints)
4	the power of self-organization (to add, change, evolve, or self-organize system structures)
3	the goals of the system
2	the mindset, paradigm, or world view out of which the system (its goals, structure, rules, parameters etc.) arise
1	transcending paradigms (making evidence-based judgement, independent of world views or conventional wisdoms)

Source: Adapted from Meadows (2009)

Given that most of us are working (and therefore having to think) in
structures and with processes that are far from interconnected, positive
deviants will need to provide leadership and examples that overcome
barriers to getting good sustainability outcomes. Figure 8.2 illustrates
how an organization (or a government's foreign policy for which this
model was developed) could be thinking about where good or negative
impacts might have systemic impacts across different geographical
dimensions, as well as across policy or departmental divisions – not
forgetting time dimensions.

As Figure 8.2 tries to illustrate, a national decision (say, on biofuels)
can have a negative impact on the environment at global level (black
arrow). Similarly, a sub-national region strategy for economic development, say, will only have a positive outcome if people living in
neighbourhoods are confident it will not damage their local environ-

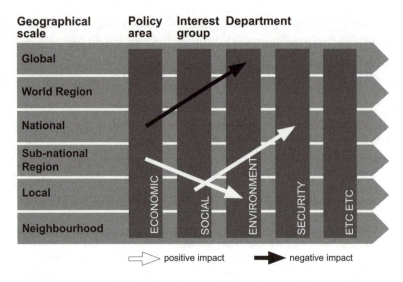

Source: Adapted from Parkin, S. (2006) Royal College of Defence Studies, 26 January 2006

Figure 8.2 A sustainability approach to organization or policy: Increasing resilience and security through multi-level and mult-sector/policy/interest group/department engagement

ment and quality of life; and national security is only as good as how secure people feel in their localities – not just safe from terrorists, war and crime, but safe from extreme weather events, disruption of services or shortage of food (white arrows).

Ecologists working on subregional ecosystem regeneration (for a river system for example) find success for their biological mission depends on getting right the relationships with local people living there. That can mean brokering quite sophisticated interactions within a multi-level coalition of organizations – local groups, national governments and international humanitarian organizations – which is beyond the capacity of my simple diagram to depict. However, a third positive example comes from former UN Ambassador Jeremy Greenstock, who finds people disillusioned by the nation state's ability to deal with the major issues of our times. 'Culture, identity and politics are going local', he says, not least because it is only there the global challenges of terrorism, crime or climate change can be addressed effectively. Moreover, a resilient and fair global economy can only be realized if it stands on a multitude of locally resilient ones. Leadership of any nation state will be judged on whether it understands that the success of the human enterprise on a global scale depends on decentralization of sensibly regulated power to its localities.[8]

This same view is echoed by the US National Intelligence Council on trends to 2025. It sees what it calls the 'institutional deficit' left by the aging post-World War II institutions, possibly leading to further fragmentation and incapacitation of international cooperation. Like Greenstock, it wonders if the arrival of new non-state actors and networks, such as businesses, tribes, religious organizations, non-governmental organizations (NGOs), might eventually strengthen a more complex international system, one that will have to be inclusive of what are currently viewed by the conventional wisdom to be second or third world countries (NIC, 2008). While this may feel like an excursion into geopolitics (it is, see 'A sustainability-literate world view' in Chapter 7) it is in the domain of human relationships and actions across all sorts of boundaries that success or failure of sustainable development will be decided.

In a nutshell, systems theory helps thinking about horizontal, vertical and diagonal relationships with people, organizations and the environment at every level and across policy and special interest boundaries. The home territory of positive deviants. Thinking of particular choices in a whole systems way means exploring consequences, intended or otherwise. Theoretically a bit mind-boggling, but in practice just another way of thinking about building more resilience through better relationships.

Thinking in outcomes and strategies

Belongs to the Learning for Life family of understanding (see page 195 for explanation)

You know where you want to end up (in life, in a project, for sustainability) and can produce a well enough considered and structured strategy for getting there. You approach opportunities, risk and changing circumstances in a creative way.

Apart from fascination with charismatic or 'hero' leader figures, probably no aspect of leadership and management education attracts more articles, books or sessions in MBA courses than strategy. Yet as the previous section suggests it remains one of the most misunderstood.

So best to start here with some definitions before thinking about a straightforward way to understand how to design and execute a successful strategy.

Strategy: 'generalship'; the art of conducting a (whole) campaign

Tactics: 'purposeful procedure'

The root of the word strategy is military. As in Figure 8.3 a general will first identify a military objective – a town to be occupied, a target to be bombed, a bridge to be secured – and then design a strategy according to the variables to be taken into consideration – time, territory, resources and so on. Crucially, strategies do not start from where you are, but from where you want to be. Visions and missions are fine, but unless the real-life destination towards which they point is convincing, it may prove difficult to marshal people and resources. Uncertainty over destination is behind the failure of many strategies. The rage (to the brink of mutiny we are told) of military leaders involved in the Iraq invasion and occupation was due to politicians failing to provide clear real-life objectives.[9] The same goes for corporate or other organizational strategies. If it is unclear what the outcome is meant to be, and appropriate resources are not in place, staff and others become disaffected.

Until I was nearly 30 I imagined everyone thought as I did – in outcomes. Whether in my home or work life I worked out what I wanted to happen by when and organized accordingly. Eventually, after many frustrating experiences in meetings and on projects, it dawned on me that most people were what I call 'next-steppers'; they do not think very far forward and struggle with the idea that the route to the objective might even be indirect. Three decades of observation and experience has convinced me that only about 20 per cent of people are natural strategic thinkers and leaders. I've found no research to contradict or prove this, but know several first-class strategic thinkers who think I am overgenerous.

Fortunately, strategic thinking is something that can be learnt. A few people can manage with a back of an envelope, many have favourite tools to help them think and plan strategies for their whole organization,

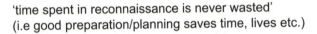

'time spent in reconnaissance is never wasted'
(i.e good preparation/planning saves time, lives etc.)

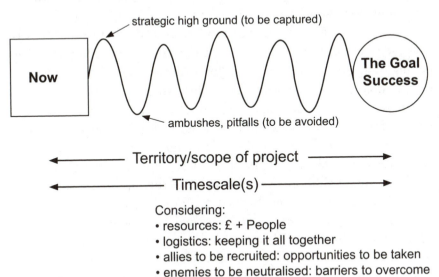

Figure 8.3 Strategic planning made simple

a project, or their personal life already, but some will be coming at this for the first time. I hesitate to recommend any particular recent book on strategy formulation, though from the stable of business strategy Henry Mintzberg (1994) describes it in a jolly guru-like way. From the stable of books with sustainability in their title, Wirtenberg et al (2009) has a helpful chapter, though it is written from within the conventional wisdom of business where finance is firmly in control of the bottom line. Writing about not-for-profit organizations, Mike Hudson (1995) has a very practical chapter too. For a fascinating read about how strategies could and should be designed from the perspective of government, try Geoff Mulgan (2009).

A word about risk, as both risk and opportunity identification are important features of strategic planning, futures thinking or specific change programmes. Risk can be loosely defined as the probability that something undesirable will happen, and risk assessment is the quantification of this probability (Rowe, 1977). Opportunity, therefore, must be the probability that something desirable will happen. This may include something new (innovation) or may be the amplification of something good going on already.

Conventionally, risk management is about domesticating negative risk – identifying and trying to reduce the risk of something nasty happening to as near zero as possible. John Adams, one of the best writers on the subject, points out most of the literature on risk is 'inhabited by *homo pruden* – zero-risk man. He personifies prudence, rationality and responsibility. Large corporations such as Shell Oil hold [prudent man] up as an example for all employees to emulate in their campaigns to eliminate all accidents' (Adams, 1995, p16). But so impossible is it to eliminate all likelihood of accidents that this approach to risk has stopped school outings and banned pantomime dames from throwing sweets into the audience. It certainly failed to prevent the massive collapse of the global financial system. A shocked member of the board of a large bank now mostly in government hands said that no one expected all the risks to go red at once: 'We didn't realized that everything was so interconnected – like a piece of knitting.'

So how can risk contribute to a strategy for creating a resilient, stable and sustainable future? Isn't there a contradiction here?

Not really, if instead of trying to stifle risk, it is 'outed' and used creatively to identify where the opportunities lie. Good leadership will allow scope for imagination and innovation to flourish uninhibited and create a culture that accepts some failure as an inevitable by-product of having a go; one CEO said he aims to be right 70 per cent of the time over his lifetime. The same 'percentage' risk/opportunity strategy is used by top tennis players. They calibrate in nanoseconds the percentage of safe shots against risky but possibly winning ones, and then choose according to how the game is going. When it comes to taking risks on the way to sustainability, getting decisions 70 per cent right would be a vast improvement on what has gone before!

However, a key element in calculations around risk is not just the likelihood of something happening, but the magnitude of the consequences if it does. As the evidence described in Chapter 1 suggests, living with uncertainty and the possibility of extreme events is now inevitable. While the government and others (particularly the insurance industry) are calling for more precise predictions from climate scientists,

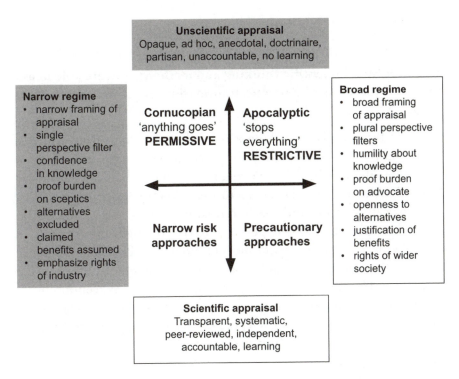

The figure contains the following text elements:

Unscientific appraisal
Opaque, ad hoc, anecdotal, doctrinaire, partisan, unaccountable, no learning

Narrow regime
- narrow framing of appraisal
- single perspective filter
- confidence in knowledge
- proof burden on sceptics
- alternatives excluded
- claimed benefits assumed
- emphasize rights of industry

Cornucopian 'anything goes' **PERMISSIVE**

Apocalyptic 'stops everything' **RESTRICTIVE**

Narrow risk approaches

Precautionary approaches

Broad regime
- broad framing of appraisal
- plural perspective filters
- humility about knowledge
- proof burden on advocate
- openness to alternatives
- justification of benefits
- rights of wider society

Scientific appraisal
Transparent, systematic, peer-reviewed, independent, accountable, learning

Source: Andrew Stirling (1999).

Figure 8.4 The relationship between risk, science and precaution

Alan Thorpe, Chief Executive of the Natural Environment Research Council (NERC) points out that 'scientific uncertainty could be seen by policy makers as a difficult thing to deal with … but perhaps its value is in opening up a range of options for action with various degrees of risk and consequences'.[10]

Andy Stirling has produced an extremely helpful way of thinking about the relationship between risk, science and precaution. Figure 8.4 (above) shows that by steering your strategy into the bottom right-hand corner, the worst risks may be avoided, and opportunities for different technologies or human behaviours identified and tried out.

Turning data into wisdom

Belongs to the Learning for Life family of understanding (see page 195 for explanation)

You understand scientific thinking and methods, and are able to ask the right questions of data and information to get the answers you need.

Evidence-based decision making is quite the thing these days, which is good. But the task of evaluating the evidence has almost certainly been made more difficult by the sheer volume available in hard and electronic form. The rhetoric of today uses terms like 'knowledge management', a 'knowledge economy' and the 'information age' as if these were 21st century phenomena. But the power of having the right information, in the right place and at the right time is far from new. The main difference between the Middle Ages and now is the magnitude of change in the volumes and form of the knowledge being transferred. Sixteenth century kings had to await the arrival of the information by horseback, and, until telegraphs (1844) and telephones (1876), it still came by post. Today, deluges of data and information can be on your desk at the click of a computer key.

Now as then, however, data and information are not the same as knowledge. We certainly live in an information age, but do we really live in a knowledge society? The knowledge pyramid illustrated in Figure 8.5 doesn't do justice to the enormous amount of effort that goes into processing vast seas of data into rivers of information that then must be manipulated into the streams of knowledge which, with great effort, can become the pools of understanding that, once a bit of experience is added, can take us to the well head of practical wisdom where good judgement and sound decisions are, or should be, made. Nor does it illustrate the proportions. Practical wisdom, (meaning knowing how to act as opposed to just knowing lots of stuff) is in short supply compared to data, which, like CO_2, is intrinsically good, but damaging if over-abundant or of poor quality.

Positive deviants are a bit like wild salmon, searching for and then swimming up the right rivers of knowledge to find pools of understanding in which to swim around gaining the necessary experience that eventually leads to practical wisdom, and (here's where the metaphor goes a bit wobbly!) the opportunity to replicate themselves by inspiring

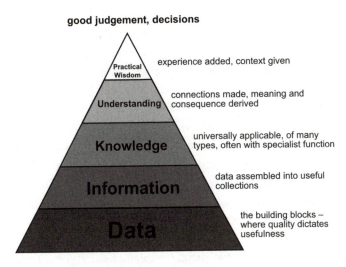

good judgement, decisions

Practical Wisdom — experience added, context given

Understanding — connections made, meaning and consequence derived

Knowledge — universally applicable, of many types, often with specialist function

Information — data assembled into useful collections

Data — the building blocks – where quality dictates usefulness

Source: Sara Parkin teaching tool

Figure 8.5 The knowledge pyramid

and enabling others through their leadership. There is a purpose to your learning and accruing of knowledge. You know what you want it for.

The importance of interconnectivity to sustainability-literacy underlines how difficult it is to process information across topics, sector or policy silos – despite technological advances. Witness the mess made over biofuel policy and the failure of the energy policy wonks to realize that crops are also food, and that land is needed for both food and ecosystem functioning. Even what is called 'second generation' biofuels (agricultural waste) are future soil fertility. Clearly, economic policy makers, energy specialists, agronomists, land-use scientists and bio-chemists weren't mixing far enough up the knowledge pyramid.

There is an expectation that, eventually, information technology will do this mixing for us, and already a new industry has grown up to specialize in processing data and information to extract knowledge in a form most salient to an individual's or organization's needs. But because of the garbage-in–garbage-out rule, while technology may bring speed and volume to the process, the non-linear computing capacity of the human brain still defines the quality standards for enquiry into, or synthesis of, information. As spy-thriller writer John Le Carré (once a spy himself) observes, there is no substitute for real life human-to-human intelligence gathering.

One of the surest ways to avoid drowning is to take a leaf out of John le Carré's book and start any quest for knowledge with people and organizations you already trust. If they don't have what you want, ask them where they would go. That way a personal network of 'recommended' and trusted sources of information can be built up, rather like salmon leaps. In addition, an occasional eye cast on unconventional sources, including contrarians and the more reputable, *named* bloggeristas, will check the information 'noise' for any worthwhile new trends. With the honourable exception of alerts about major breaches of environmental or human justice – as in dumping toxic waste or monks demonstrating in Burma – I have found anonymous bloggers tend to be trend followers rather than setters.

As it always has been, living in a knowledge society means organizing for yourself a system that prioritizes *enough* of the right information, at the right time and in the right place.

Imagining with others

You are able to imagine a believable future (one that is not only possible, but also desirable) and, with others, co-evolve ways of getting there.

It may seem odd to include imagination as a sustainability-relevant principle for the way you practise your leadership. But if you can't imagine what a sustainable future might look like, and explain how it would be achievable as well as attractive, then how to encourage people to join you in pursuit of it? I'm with Keith Grint, who says 'leadership is primarily rooted in, and a product of, the imagination' and 'to imagine what has not been experienced is to relay to one's followers the hope of a better future …' I agree too that it is wrong to label such imagining as *utopian* (meaning 'no place') in a critical sense. The original purpose of utopian thought was to transcend the present rigidities (conventional wisdoms) and construct a better future. That which is 'no place' now, may be somewhere in the future (Grint, 2000 pp13 and 14).

Making a leap, or even a small step, of imagination does not come easily to everyone however. For example, I've seen several attempts to identify future skills needs in the UK founder on the (mostly) employers' inability to imagine the future as anything but a continuum of the past. As a consequence we are facing the end game of *un*sustainable development deeply unprepared. By imagining what *might* or *could* be, it is much easier to identify ways of getting there that are ideally co-evolved with others. President Barack Obama ✳ obviously has a personal set of outcomes and a strategy for his time in office. In public (check out his inaugural speech) he has used imagination (the audacity of hope) and co-evolution (together we can) to try to make his followers active rather than passive participants in a shared journey.

In the world of business, co-evolution, or co-creation, means both the company and the customer are involved in new product development. Instead of keeping the car under wraps until its launch, for example, it is conceptualized (imagined), designed, developed and trialled by future drivers and the manufacturer together. Some rock stars prefer to co-create an album with other band members and technical staff in the studio, rather than write fully scored music.[11] On the sustainability front, Forum for the Future has helped co-evolve a water-based paint and is working with local government, innovative financiers and energy efficiency and renewable experts to imagine, co-create and pilot financial models to transit localities onto low-carbon strategies.

If you are starting from scratch, the tools at the end of this chapter will provide ways to make a quick start on imagining a sustainable future. They can also help you construct an engaging story about both the destination and the journey. If a strategy is already in place, the same processes may be used to design an inspiring and mobilizing narrative about it for people outside and inside the organization. The task of imagining and creating paths to the future is not, however, a solo activity, though it is an excellent way of stretching your own imagination and practising the interconnected thinking that is so important to sustainability-literate leadership. The more people active in co-evolving routes towards it, the more likely the imagined future will come true.

Evaluating outcomes

You use sustainability outcomes to judge progress and measure success.

In Chapter 4, I was pretty excoriating about the state of evaluation processes used by the world of leadership and management. I may be showing my age, but I have got more and more irritated when people talk about lessons learned from this or that mistake, when the same lessons were there to be learnt ten or more years ago. Biofuels is just one example. Another is the 'new' realization that chemicals made in Europe and Asia are to be found in the snows at both poles. Rachel Carson alerted us to the dangers of chemicals in the environment in a book in 1967, a book that help fire up a global environment movement. Since then things have got worse, not better.[12]

So when it comes to evaluating leadership for sustainability, it is outcomes that matter. *How* you exercise your leadership is extremely important, but pointless if you don't know if you are contributing to making things better or worse. Three areas where indicators should be assembled are proposed here: real contributions to sustainability, ubiquity of practice in an organization, influence on others.

Contribution to sustainability

What contributions have you made to the social challenge of sustainability?

It doesn't matter from where you start. As an individual or as an organization, everyone can adopt immediately a commitment to grow contributions over time as much as possible. It is not enough to behave as if your contribution stops at the boundary of your home or organization. Only by thinking beyond those boundaries and asking questions about what you can contribute to sustainability in the largest sense, will change happen fast enough.

It may be that what is called 'hard' evidence is difficult to get. In some cases it is worth striving to do that, for example in CO_2 emissions or carbon consumed. But sometimes the view of local fishermen or birdwatchers about whether a stretch of river is improving in quality can bring more useful information than a chemical analysis of the water. Similarly, measuring social outcomes is not easy, nor is judging how much of someone else's changed behaviour is down to *your* influence? Here the notion of *good enough* comes into play. A sustainability-literate leader will use a *good enough* suite of outcome-oriented indicators to ensure the direction of travel is right and the pace of change is accelerating.

There is more about this in 'sustainability measures' (page 220), and the 'Five Capitals Tool' (page 200) can help you design measures that fit with your priorities. It is not enough to restrict yourself to one or two areas, though. Broadening as well as deepening your contribution is what good looks like here. The measure of successful sustainability-literate leadership and how adept you are at positive deviance is not a series of ticks in a competency framework, however golden. It is in how many ticks you can offer the Global Sustainability To Do List (see Section Four), and how fast you are closing the gap between where you and your organization are now and where you know you could, and should, be.

Ubiquity of practice

How much has good sustainability-oriented practice soaked into the minds and activities of every part of your organization – or into your own life?

The second area for evaluation is to judge how deeply and widely is sustainability-outcome oriented activity embedded in your organization or in your own life. It is tough to 'walk the talk' in unpromising environments, especially when other things are going wrong too – like shrinking budgets. But an important success criterion for a positive deviant is how well you can push sustainability practice out of a specialist unit and around all the psychological and institutional barriers until it becomes normal practice for the whole organization.

Corporate responsibility functions, like functions labelled Environment or Sustainability, tend to be in their own department or attached to another department, such as marketing, communications or health and safety. Even if standing alone, they are likely to report (if they report at all) to the board via one executive, or one board member. As sustainability is about progressing environmental, social and economic goals *simultaneously* it should be the chief executive leading, with all other executives and board members having responsibilities written into their job description and appraisals. So any corporate responsibility or similar function not working to the CEO to make this happen would suggest a low ubiquity score. Very recently, a piece of research by Egon Zehnder International, an executive search firm, has suggested that the role of chief sustainability officer will soon be joining that of the chief executive officer and the chief financial officer at the pinnacle of an organization where the strategic decisions are taken.[13] Whatever influence you have in an organization and whatever its size, positive deviants will evaluate how well they have done in driving sustainability responsibilities, policies and actions throughout the systems of governance, administration and operations.

When it comes to your personal life, a word of caution is needed. There is a lot we can do to transform the way we live and contribute directly to a sustainable way of life as individuals. And no positive deviant can neglect the influence they can gain from being seen to 'walk the talk'. But the perversity of the way the world is means making a really big commitment in your personal life can involve a lot of time and money, at the moment only possible for the better off or through making it your sole activity! So be reasonable. Use your sustainability-literate skills to work out how to do the very best you can now, and design a strategy that means you are on track for continual improvement, in your personal life while remembering your mission is to make sustainability a realistic option for everyone. By definition, as a positive deviant, you have chosen not to 'opt-out' of the perverse world we live in, but to 'opt-in' and transform it – which leads into the third area where careful evaluation is terrifically important.

Influencing others

What influence have you or your organization brought to bear on the practice of other people and other organizations?

However progressive you are in delivering sustainability outcomes, and reshaping and redirecting your own organization, you cannot do everything on your own. So part of your own strategy will be a priority list of other people and organizations to bring alongside. Boastful headlines in the local paper may not always be the best way to do it, whereas inviting key people to an informal, off-the-record discussion to help you imagine your organization's own future from a sustainability perspective might get them interested in imagining theirs.

The extent to which you have been able to influence changed behaviour in other people and other organizations is not an easy one to evaluate. Policies and statements of intent are not as good as evidence of changed behaviour and therefore real sustainability gains. But 'soft' survey techniques, even simple questionnaires, can help until that firmer evidence emerges.

Tools for change

You are comfortable with some tools that support sustainability-literate decision making.

You may have some favourite management tools already that will either work for sustainability outcomes or could do if amended appropriately. Here are a small number of 'must haves' for positive deviants that may be completely new to you, or are twists to tools you use already – for change management or life cycle analysis for example. All are relatively easy to use straight away, making them the best way of learning about sustainability as you go.

Learning for life

You know about good ways to learn how to implement sustainability-literate leadership – for yourself and for others – in varying circumstances.

In the ideal organization, its structure and culture would be geared to learning from experience through continual reflection and improvement of practice. Organization objectives and strategies would be constantly aligned with this learning and against thoughtful consideration of current knowledge and possible futures. So continual change would be seen as normal and beneficial. As consilience of these six aspects of learning and working out what to do next is still a dream in most organizations, I've treated each separately. Positive deviants will think hard about how to bring them together wherever they can, as this makes it easier to integrate sustainability literacy into all choices and decisions.

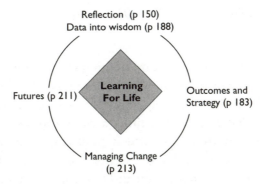

The Learning for Life family of understanding

To keep things as as straightforward as possible, I include here some ideas about personal and organizational learning, and share some of Forum's experience in integrating sustainability into courses for others. There is a daunting amount of theory out there about learning and teaching, so I propose to cut the story short, leaving you to investigate more if you choose.[14] Because it is so new, when it comes to personal learning about sustainability-literate leadership, self-help will be the situation for many people whether designing a plan for themselves or selecting from available courses. A possible learning 'wiring diagram' for you to use and adapt as you plot your own lifelong learning journey is provided in Chapter 4, page 92.

First, personal learning habits. Being aware of your own preferred learning methods is the starting point. If you are lucky enough to have access to professional coaches or learning professionals then they should help you. If not, you can self-analyse by listing the ways you *like* to learn. Some examples of different learning styles and techniques are given in Table 8.2. Only reflection is non-negotiable.

Table 8.2 Learning styles and techniques

By experimenting, experience	Through facts
Through logical arguments	In groups, discussing with others
On your own	Visually: diagrams, demonstrations
By relating it to other knowledge	Verbally: written, spoken
By repetitions – of facts or experience	Intuitively: emotion, deduction
By analysing ideas, concepts	Through stories, narratives
Through reflective practice	By understanding theory behind it
Formally, in a classroom	Imaginative problem solving
Through teaching others	Electronically

Source: Various sources

Unfortunately much education and training gives more credit for information 'banked' than understanding demonstrated, which takes time and help to achieve. You can help yourself to develop reflective practice and grow understanding by recruiting a small number of people who will challenge you to look more widely than you might otherwise. Ask them to prompt you to think more strategically, to introduce ideas and actions that might not occur to you and to recommend good courses for you to take.

You may be lucky and able to influence your organization's staff development programme to include sustainability-literacy and have the skills to do it yourself. For those not trained in the art of teaching (pedagogy), however, there are some tips (in no particular order) to use should you find yourself building the sustainability-literacy of others – in a seminar room, on the shop floor or in a bar.

- Aim for the interface between knowledge and understanding. Volumes of information is discouraging. Well marshalled and illustrated it becomes useful and memorable knowledge that can be presented in a way that encourages understanding. Use examples whenever possible. Margaret Thatcher, for example, didn't understand climate change until someone remembered she was a chemist and prepared a paper explaining the chemistry of what was happening in the upper atmosphere.

- Craft your course, lecture or conversation to your audience. Which means knowing where they come from, their world view, what worries them or what other pressures they have. Sometimes asking questions to find these things out can be the method of conveying what you want to say. As a couple of Forum graduates working in large businesses said, 'once you have found out what presses their buttons it is so much easier'. Your objectives for a more sustainable way of doing things can often be presented as a solution to their problem.

- Learners as teachers. The Forum for the Future Leadership for Sustainable Development mixes fairly traditional seminars with learning placements with different sectors, and practises a high level of reflective and group learning. Students from different backgrounds are encouraged to share their existing learning and take responsibility for different areas on behalf of the group, so enhancing the overall learning of everyone. This is the learning strategy Nelson Mandela and his co-prisoners used on Robben Island. Well led and kept forward looking, a 'learning circle' like this will generate good ideas about ways of deviating around obstacles.

- Play to your strengths. Not everyone can be on the Barack Obama scale of oratorical effectiveness, but most of us can learn to be *good enough* speakers and writers. What matters most is that we are believed and trusted. So best to be true to yourself – self-deprecating humour about your addiction to bullet points or a dead pan delivery can make it charming. It is said that audiences retain only a third of what is said to them in a lesson or a speech. Above all practise. Teaching is a good way of learning. There's nothing better than having to give a talk or write an article about something to force up your knowledge levels.

- Make your best points stick. Banish jargon and again learn from President Obama's inaugural speech about how to say the same thing three times but in different ways (to make sure the key messages are in that one third different people retain). The rest was about making his audience feel good – about themselves more than about him.

Just as there are no off-the-peg sets of ethics or values, there are none for courses on leadership for sustainability. Which makes it hard to decide what knowledge to include for different groups learning over different time periods and in different circumstances When Forum was involved in a project with universities, we tried to resolve this dilemma by innovating a tool that could be used by teachers of any subject either for a new course or for retrofitting an existing one.[15] It also works for designing your own learning plan.

The first step is to design a sustainability learner relationship profile. Draw about four nested circles and map onto them the relationships you have – with other people, with other organizations and social groups, and with the environment. The closer or more important the relationship the nearer it goes to the centre. Figure 8.6 is a generic version of a relationship profile to illustrate what I mean. You'll get a better result if you do this with other people. If, for example, you are retrofitting an existing course, it is a good idea to invite back graduates, and their employers, to find out what they would have liked to learn about, but didn't. Mixing them with current students will keep the course forward looking. For yourself you might like to include colleagues and friends. In both cases invite some real outsiders – they often ask the most mind-opening and useful questions, and make observations that those very familiar with the job might forget.

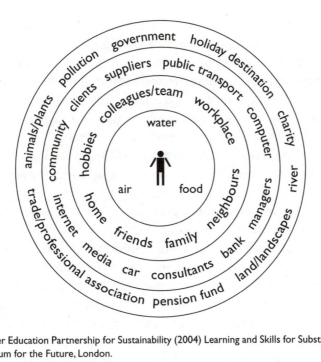

Source: Higher Education Partnership for Sustainability (2004) Learning and Skills for Substantive Development. Forum for the Future, London.

Figure 8.6 Sustainability learner relationship profile (example)

The next task is to identify what you need to know to sustain all those relationships in a way that contributes to sustainability. Again this is best done with others. Then comes a bit of pedagogy that turns everything into learning outcomes, and designs appropriate contents and learning methods. The outcome is either a new course or a refurbished one that can honestly say it develops sustainability-literate engineers, musicians, linguists, leaders or managers – whatever the special subject might be. We use the Five Capitals Tool to check back from a sustainability perspective that everything has been covered.

Decision-making tools for sustainability outcomes

You are comfortable with and use tools that support sustainability-literate decision making.

The most commonly used tool for deciding whether to do something or not, is cost–benefit analysis. A cash 'value' for various elements of the up and downside of a project is calculated and the decision based on whether the bottom line is positive or negative. This supposes two things: that a monetary value can be put on everything, and that everything is comparable. Questions around the morality of this approach are illustrated by tobacco industry calculations that the total of the taxes received from the industry and smokers, plus the savings on pensions from early deaths, equals a net benefit to the treasury. Just what is the 'market' or social value of a human life used here? And is it comparable to any consequent reduction in the public sector borrowing requirement?

The debate around setting a cost for 'carbon' in the greenhouse gas emission trading schemes is another example where clinical separation of monetary calculations from moral considerations is difficult. Calculations for setting the price for carbon – either through taxing it at source or as an emission – usually incorporate benefits from investment in efficiency and renewable generation, but not always those to human well-being. Speed limits on roads and less burning of fossil fuels by industry results in fewer accidents, less local pollution (less grimy buildings, less respiratory disease) and fewer greenhouse gases, all of which bring benefits in ways hard to compare with a monetary or other common denominator

Establishing monetary values is only part of the answer to making wise judgements as far as sustainability is concerned. The 'wicked' – meaning complex and interconnected – nature of the problems we face require more complex and interconnecting (but not wicked!) tools.

Here are three that we use in Forum for the Future – the Five Capitals Tool, The Natural Step and Futures.

The Five Capitals Tool

A bit of background

I'd be surprised if you haven't picked up by now that this is my favourite decision-making, analytical and planning tool! It marshals the difficult to integrate environment, social and economic aspects of sustainable development in a way that makes it easier to see the interconnections and, critically, where there are negative trade-offs happening or where useful synergies could be made. It visualizes the current separateness of the way things are done now, but in a holistic manner that illuminates the path towards sustainability. Using the Five Capitals Tool is also one of the best ways of learning about sustainability as you go!

I will try to give you enough background, insights and practical guidance on how to use it so you can get started straight away.

Many readers will be familiar with either the triple bottom line, favoured by business, or the Venn diagram of three overlapping circles favoured by the more technically minded, as ways of illustrating sustainability (see Figure 8.7).

Although conceptually neat, neither is particularly good at guiding us towards ways of implementing sustainability. Nor are they accurate, as in reality there is no equivalence or balance between the social, environmental and economic elements. Indeed, as Herman Daly points out: 'the natural world is the envelope that contains, sustains and provisions the economy, not the other way round' (Daly, 2008, p160), so the pecking order is better conceptualized as three nested circles (see Figure 8.8).

But even this way of thinking about the different elements of sustainability does not easily translate into actions that will end *un*sustainable human behaviours. The environment may be the real bottom line, and we humans might theoretically be in control of the design, values and operation of our economy, but manifestly this is not the case. It is the economy that wags the tail of both us and the rest of life on Earth.

When we set up Forum for the Future, we were already convinced by our colleague Paul Ekins' explanation that thinking about the interactions between *four* types of capital (natural, human, social and manufactured) was a more accurate reflection of the stocks of resources available to economy than the economists' traditional three capitals (land, labour, manufactured) (Ekins et al, 1992). Because the scale of natural and human capital degradation was making a critical reappraisal of what constituted capital long overdue, we decided to adopt a *five* capitals model of the economy as a framework within which to think about future sustainability.[16] The fifth capital – finance – was introduced by Jonathon Porritt. He argued, quite rightly, that for most people the word capital only meant finance. To ignore this reality made talking about other sorts of capital more difficult.

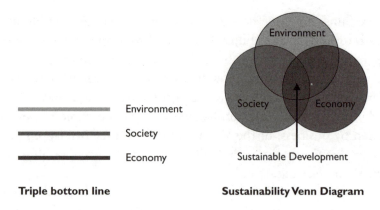

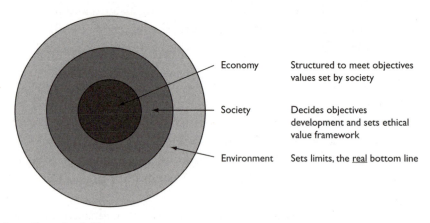

Source: Forum for the Future

Figure 8.7 Triple bottom line and the Sustainability Venn Diagram

Source: Forum for the Future

Figure 8.8 Nested circles: the real bottom line

A simple explanation of each of the five capitals is given in Table 8.3, with more reflection on capital from a sustainability perspective in Chapter 3 (page 61). As you study Table 8.3 try to imagine that you rule the world, elected on a sustainability ticket. These five types of capital stock are what you have to work with – no more, no less. All life on Earth, plus the minds and muscle of people, are your primary resources – the real bottom line. Everything else – all social institutions, the existing infrastructure, our economic systems – has been created by us. Consequently, and not just theoretically, they can be changed by us.

Table 8.3 The five capital stocks explained

Capital	Stocks of resources described
Financial	Comprises shares, bonds or banknotes, and its utility is as a means of valuing or exchanging natural, human, social or manufactured capital, either directly or through the goods and services generated by the economy. Strictly speaking, financial capital has no intrinsic value. By becoming a commodity itself, and through its accumulation via debt, it has lost the capacity to provide this service. If reformed it could help drive and support the repair and growth of the four other capital stocks.
Manufactured	Comprises all human fabricated 'infrastructure' that is already in existence. The tools, machines, buildings etc. where people live and work, and the infrastructure (roads, electricity grid that support modern society). It does not include the goods and services that are produced however. In some cases manufactured capital may be viewed as source of materials (e.g. building waste used as aggregate for road building or repair).
Social	Comprises the multitude of organizations and associations that people use to live and work together, such as families, communities, governments, businesses, health and education systems, trade unions, voluntary groups etc. Although they involve different types of relationships and organizations they are all structures, associations or institutions that add value to human capital. They tend to be successful in doing so if based on mutual trust and shared purpose (Putnam, 2000). Success in social groups is an important contributory factor to individual human well-being.
Human	Consists of the health, knowledge, skills, motivation and spiritual ease of individuals. All the things that enable people to feel good about themselves, each other, and to participate in society and contribute productively towards their own and other people's well-being (health, wealth and happiness).
Natural	Also referred to as environmental or ecological capital, natural capital represents the stock of environmentally provided assets and falls into two categories: Resources, some of which are renewable (trees, vegetation, fish, water), some non-renewable (fossil fuels, minerals). In some places ostensibly renewable resources (like fertile soil) have become non-renewable (desert). Services, such as climate regulation; the powerful waste processing cycles that breakdown, absorb, and recycle emissions and waste from all species; hydrological cycles etc.

Source: Adapted from Parkin (2000)

A word about stocks and flows

The next step is to understand the concept of stocks and flows, which is at the heart of any economic process, and is key to understanding the five capitals, whether as a decision-making tool for immediate use or as a potential model for a future sustainable economy. Table 8.3 describes briefly the five types of capital stocks that are available to any economy, organization or individual. If the stock of each capital resource was restored and maintained in good shape, we could expect benefits to flow, to all intents and purposes, forever. Neglect the condition of the stock, and the flow of benefits will diminish or stop. *Un*sustainable development is, in effect, the result of neglecting to invest in maintaining the health of all the stocks of capital. For example, we know only too well that low investment in the railways (manufactured capital) reduces the flow of regular, clean trains. Failure to invest properly in education and good systems of governance has resulted in poorly skilled people, and disengagement with democratic processes. Rapid erosion of the stock of natural capital – such as soil fertility, trees, fresh water, chemical cycles – is now dangerously imperilling flows of food, water, reliable climate. And so on.

The importance of stocks and flows to thinking about sustainability, and about how to make good decisions about what is the right thing to do, is that traditionally we judge success of our organizations and economies by the flow of things – interest, products, jobs, reliable weather, food. We assume that if the flow is OK, then the stocks must be OK too. But never before has it been more evident that our eye is on the wrong ball. A large part of the stock of financial capital has proved to be non-existent, for example, and a drop in the stock of soil fertility and water has compromised the flow of crops in Africa and Australia. In a world governed by sustainability thinking, we would be measuring growth in the stocks of capitals, assuming that if they are OK, it is very likely the flows of benefits will be OK too.

Twelve features of a sustainable society

The final bit of background before we get onto the tool itself is the result of a piece of research we carried out in 1997. Because thinking in outcomes is essential to good strategy design we wanted to use the Five

Capitals Tool framework to establish some 'destination statements' that would characterize what a sustainable society might look like. What would be the features of a sustainable society if all the stocks of capital were in good shape? Where would the flow of benefits take us? We wanted a rough idea to use, either as it is, or as a template for outcomes more tailored to particular organizational or geographic circumstances. To be 'universally' useful the statements needed to meet some criteria. They would have to be:

- comprehensive in that they incorporate ecological, ethical, social and economic dimensions of sustainable development;
- consistent internally (amongst themselves) and externally, with scientific laws, and other respected methods of conceptualizing and understanding sustainability (e.g. The Natural Step – see below);
- culturally neutral so they are relevant and widely applicable in any part of the world, thus facilitating learning from and between different cultures;
- non-prescriptive so they remain *characteristic* of a sustainable society and do not prescribe what the precise ingredients may be, leaving detail to the varied contributions;
- congruent with the general aspirations of people and communities (reflecting that few people *want* an *un*sustainable way of life);
- straightforward and as few in number as possible without losing clarity or causing too much overlap.

The outcome of the research project was 12 statements that would be true if we were standing in a sustainable world. They've worked for me in Europe and Africa, and in innumerable project designs and assessments and in writing assignments. They are the nearest I will get to a general statement of what sustainability is!

Table 8.4 shows them set beside the stocks of the five capitals. The statements were derived in partnership with Keele University in a 1997 project involving over 60 academics and practitioners, including government, with a grant from the Economic and Social Research Council (Global Environmental Change Programme, No L320263059).

Table 8.4 The twelve features of a sustainable society

Capital stock	Twelve features of a sustainable society
	Statements that would be true if we were standing in a sustainable society – of any culture in any country. They would be evidence the stocks of capital are in good shape and producing the expected flow of benefits
Financial Shares, bonds, banknotes etc.	1. Financial capital accurately represents the value of natural, human, social and manufactured capital
Manufactured All human fabricated 'infrastructure'	2. All infrastructure, technologies and processes make minimum use of natural resources and maximum use of human innovation and skills
Social Organizations and associations that add value to human capital	3. There are trusted and accessible systems of governance and justice 4. Communities and society at large share key positive values and a sense of purpose 5. The structures and institutions of society promote stewardship of natural resources and the happiness of people 6. Homes, communities and society at large provide safe, supportive living and working environments
Human Health, knowledge, well-being and happiness of individuals	7. At all ages, individuals enjoy a high standard of health 8. Individuals are adept at relationships and social participation, and throughout life set and achieve high personal standards for their own well-being and learning (+ sustainability literacy) 9. There is access to varied and satisfying opportunities for work, personal creativity, and recreation
Natural The resources and services of the environment	10. In their extraction and use, substances taken from the Earth do not exceed the environment's capacity to disperse, absorb, recycle or otherwise neutralize their harmful effects (to humans and/or the environment) 11. In their manufacture and use, artificial substances do not exceed the environment's capacity to disperse, absorb, recycle or otherwise neutralize their harmful effects (to humans and/or the environment) 12. The capacity of the environment to provide ecological system integrity, biological diversity and productivity is protected or enhanced

Source: Forum for the Future

Now to the tool itself, and how to use it. The next table shows the five capitals on the vertical axis and three ways of thinking about a company or organization on the horizontal:

- as a corporate entity, with buildings, staff, supply chains, governance systems and so on;
- doing what it was established to do – e.g. make a product or deliver a service;
- as an influencer of others – in the locality; through associations and sectors; of stakeholders, consumers; in society (education, government) etc.

Table 8.5 The Five Capitals Tool analysis grid

Capital	What an organization contributes		
Stock of resources	In its business practice	In the products or services it provides	In the communities where it has influence
Finance	I	6	1 I
Manufactured	2	7	12
Social	3	8	13
Human	4	9	14
Natural	5	10	15

Source: Forum for the Future

Disentangling the efforts an organization makes on recycling, energy efficiency, staff training and so on, from the purpose of the organization (the goods and services it produces), and its opportunities to influence others, makes it easier to analyse what is happening already (often more than people think) and encourages ambition about what more could be done in future. Numbering the squares helps capture and move information. For example, a management team or stakeholder group might be asked to map onto the grid what they know an organization is contributing to sustainability *now*. Some contributions may fit into more than one square, but forcing participants to choose a 'dominant' square and note which other squares are also relevant leads to better understanding of how things are interrelated. The 12 statements may be used to design some organization-relevant questions as a prompt. Using the same process, a second round with a fresh table can ask participants to let their imaginations fly and identify what their organization *could* contribute if time and money were not a constraint.

Once the before and after tables are complete, participants may be brought together to discuss what they have noticed from the exercise. Are some squares more populated than others? Why might that be? What have you learnt (about the interconnectedness of sustainability, for example)? A strategy may then be devised with priorities and time-tables for actions to take the organization from where it is now through a continual improvement plan, to its maximum contribution.

The horizontal axis may be changed to suit the organization or exercise, using instead, for example, an Internal and an External column, or more columns to cover the range of internal divisions (when you get into more operational detail). The Five Capitals Tool fits in with most other organizational processes, like strategic planning and existing quality management systems such as Investors in People, or standards like ISO 4001 (environment), or 18001 (health and safety).

Not everyone finds the five capitals an ideal way of communicating their contribution however, though some do use it unabridged.[17] One of Forum's graduates working in the oil industry simply shifted the contents out of the table cells she'd worked on with staff and rearranged them under the company's Values in order to communicate them more effectively.[18]

This is definitely something to try at home.

The Natural Step (TNS)

Forum for the Future is the UK licensee for The Natural Step, a methodology for learning about and changing business practices onto a more sustainable path. The organization (of the same name) was founded by Dr Karl-Henrik Robèrt in 1989, with headquarters in Sweden and offices in 11 countries. Like Forum for the Future, The Natural Step has also influenced a Masters programme, for Strategic Leadership towards Sustainability (MSLS) and run by the Blekinge Institute of Technology, in southern Sweden.[19]

The starting point for TNS is the fact that the world operates in systems, which, if disrupted, will be damaging not only to the Earth but to us too. It designed (after some high profile consultation amongst scientists) four 'systems conditions' that must be met if a sustainable society is to be achieved. The first three are similar to the three features of a sustainable society relating to natural capital in the Five Capitals Tool; the fourth covers the remaining nine features.

The Natural Step: Four systems conditions

In a sustainable society, nature is not subject to systematically increasing

- concentrations of substances extracted from the Earth's crust;
- concentrations of substances produced by society;
- degradation by physical means.

And, in that society ...

- people are not subject to conditions that systematically undermine their capacity to meet their needs.

The principle advantage of TNS is its major focus on the most important bottom line – the natural world. As a science-based tool, TNS's starting point is that lack of general understanding about the physical laws that govern the natural world leads people and organizations to decisions and actions that are harmful.

As well as the basic science and the systems conditions, TNS uses the metaphor of a funnel to help visualize the increasing constraints on business as usual, and what it calls an ABCD approach to helping an organization position itself so that is has a future in the new world for business where goods and services are geared to supporting sustainability (see Figure 8.9).

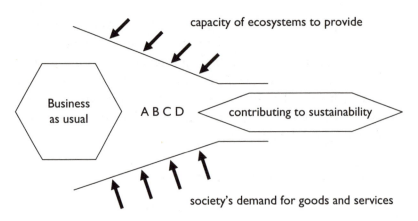

Source: Chambers T et al (2007)

Figure 8.9 The Natural Step: The resource funnel and the ABCD route to sustainable practice

TNS's ABCD approach to implementation more or less follows the basic model for changing behaviour (understand the need to change, have the knowledge and skills to behave differently, recognize right behaviour):

A Awareness
B Baseline mapping. What does your business look like today?
C Creating a vision: What does your business look like in a sustainable society?
D Down to action. Supporting effective, step-by-step implementation, including systems thinking and setting stretch goals

Long time users of TNS include IKEA, Nike, Electrolux, Interface, Scandic Hotels. TNS also works with municipalities. Whistler Resort in the US is an early example – Saskatoon in Canada, and Dublin in Eire, two more recent recruits.

Forum for the Future has produced a very good brochure on how TNS works in practice, which includes the vital process of 'backcasting' from step C (creating a vision of what good looks like) to work out the steps needed (and in which order) to get there.[20]

Futures

Belongs to the Learning for Life family of understanding (see page 195 for explanation)

You are able to use a range of structured ways to help other people take a longer-term perspective on what the future might be like and what it might mean to them, or their organization.

Being able to imagine and visualize what good might look like in the future is critical to the successful design of any strategy or implementation plan. But many people have difficulty in thinking about the longer-term future, mostly because of habit and short-term pressures, but sometimes for fear of what might be discovered. The relief of those who have made the effort confirms that having a view of the future – however complex and fraught – can really build confidence that decisions made now can help shape that future for the better.

As well as the five capitals model and The Natural Step, Forum for the Future uses other tools to help organizations think about the future in order to 'future-proof' strategies and decisions as best they can:

- Visioning.
- Trend watching (or horizon scanning).
- Scenario designing.

As I am one of those pesky people who see *everything* in terms of outcomes, I am comfortable with visioning or imagining what good might look like and working back from that. But not everyone is. James Goodman, Head of Futures at the Forum, likes scenario designing because it is a way of thinking about 'what the future might hold' that is broad and varied enough to prevent participants feeling cornered. Options are broadened not narrowed. He finds the sustainability 'aha' moments tend to come when participants' ideas are presented back in a number of well-researched and plausible – but different – scenarios. Seeing the different relationships between, say, future constraints on a natural resource and a facility in need of modernization can turn a major risk into a significant opportunity.

As a background for any particular scenario development project, my colleagues are regular trend watchers, holding an always-live list that is used in concert with a similar list generated by the organization doing the visioning and scenario planning process. As Goodman puts it, 'the objective is to flatten (metaphorically!) the walls of the organization so it's mind can be opened up to thinking about its own future on a broader canvas. We can stimulate, but a lot has to come from them.'

As with all futures work, the process counts a lot. In the example process in Table 8.6, it was a 'viral' engagement of many staff in the research that generated wide interest and ownership within the company; which in turn gave the leadership a mandate for what change or redirection of strategy might come next. A set of scenarios may be the outcome of the process, but are just the starting point. What the organization or sector has learnt about thinking differently while they were constructed and how it puts that learning into action is what really matters.[21]

Table 8.6 Example of the scenario planning process

Research	
Long list of factors affecting the company over next 15 years (PESTLE)[22]	Research done separately by staff in Forum and company, using a 'snowball' or viral technique – i.e. getting recommendation from interviewee for others to interview
Prioritization of key factors	Creates a strong participant list and wide ownership of priorities
Scenarios	
Use factors to create four credible future based scenarios in which the company might find itself 15 years hence	Again working on versions with staff from company brings understanding of thinking behind the scenarios Identify factors common to all scenarios
Vision	
Vision and commitments structured using Five capitals model of sustainability	'Sustainability-proofing' of vision and commitments increases understanding of sustainability
Outcomes tested and developed using scenarios in workshop(s)	Testing against scenarios ensures resilience in context of future challenges
Strategy	
A sustainability-based business strategy allows the company to meet its ambitions set out in the vision (no matter what future context)	Identify risks and opportunities Action plan to achieving vision Check for robustness against scenarios
Embedding	
Embedding strategy into various business planning processes	Merge wherever possible processes concerned with planning and continual improvement and base them on structured thinking about the future

Source: Forum for the Future

Forecasts are fine, the saying goes, as long as you do them very often. Futures thinking and other techniques for thinking about what happens next that are proposed in this book are not intended to predict or forecast the future. Their purpose is to help keep your mind and options open and your imagination alert to what could be, so you are ready to make the best of frequently changing opportunities and risks.

All change for sustainability

Belongs to the Learning for Life family of understanding (see page 195 for explanation)

The way you handle the potentially rapid and radical change sustainability requires, reflects your understanding that, although change is normal in life and organizations, many people feel threatened by it.

According to top change management guru John Kotter, 90 per cent of organizational change programmes fail. Even for those that start off well, Kotter finds 'the improvements have been disappointing and the carnage has been appalling, with wasted resources and burned-out, scared or frustrated employees' (Kotter, 1996, p4).

This doesn't bode well for positive deviants who are bent on changing a great deal about the way we do things – fast and far-reachingly. However, understanding the three major wrong assumptions behind this disheartening failure rate can give sustainability-bent leadership ideas about how to succeed.

First up is the baseline fact that most people, unless in a *very* miserable or dangerous situation, are resistant to change (O'Toole, 1995, pp153–189). Machiavelli observed that 'change has no constituency', meaning those who prosper in the old order resist change more energetically than those who champion it. But probably no less powerful is the emotional undertow of preferences for stability as the natural order of things – inertia, fear (including of failure), laziness, cynicism, lack of trust and so on.

Second, as well as underestimating the pull of the 'no change' option, many projects to change the way people behave forget some fundamental steps. Whether applied to small children, adults or an organization they are the same:

- The reason change is necessary is understood.
- The necessary knowledge and skills for changing behaviour are there.
- Systems are in place so that right behaviour is recognized and rewarded (reinforced).

I learnt these basics when bringing up my own children well before they were formalized for me by a top organizational change consultant. She had used them for years, confessing she dressed them up in different jargon from time to time.

Setting her prescription for successful change against that of Kotter's is instructive. Table 8.7 shows how my friend is thinking more from the perspective of those being subjected to change, while Kotter is thinking principally from the perspective of the leadership driving it.

Table 8.7 Contrasting views on managing change

Three processes for effective change	John Kotter's eight-stage process
The need for change is understood and accepted	Increase urgency Build the guiding team Get the vision right Communicate to get buy-in
Knowledge and skills to do things/behave differently are developed	Empower action
Right behaviour is recognized and, if appropriate, rewarded	Generate short-term wins Don't let up Make change stick

Sources: anon, personal communication and adapted from John Kotter (1996, p21)

There are other models for changing behaviour, including one adapted from Dana Meadow's list of places to intervene in a system (page 181), which is well worth a look (Doppelt, 2003, p89).

The third perverse assumption about change management is that it is a 'stand-alone' process, separate from the 'culture' of the organization and its current habits regarding strategy setting and learning. In an ideal world, learning, strategy setting, and actioning change should be part of the one organizational process. But usually they are not, and may even be led from different parts of the organization, which fosters amongst staff disdain ('Head office's right hand doesn't know what its left is doing!') and then disaffection ('We've been here before. If we sit tight, it will pass!').

So what are the key lessons for sustainability-literate leadership in the next, crucial couple of decades? How do positive deviants engage others in change on a historical scale?

- Align yourself with the people whose behaviour you want to change, whether it is staff, customers, neighbours, suppliers so they are confident you are on their side, and are to be trusted. If you use *ubunto* and compassion, you will be. Use social intelligence to convince others. Explore their values and what they care most about and connect these to sustainability outcomes. The most difficult thing you will have to overcome is the (not unsurprising) perception that human well-being is not the most important thing to environmentalists.

- Create a culture that acknowledges perpetual change is the default state of the world, not stasis. Evolution involves constant change, albeit in tiny steps and very slow. Children grow, buildings crumble, trees decay. How were things five years ago? What will they be like 5, 20 or 50 years from now? Use different tools to help people imagine attractive futures for themselves or their organizations. Whatever you do, connect the near future to the long term, ideally stitching it into one process for learning, organizational strategy and change.

- Sustainability-directed change cannot be about *incremental* change. It is too late for that, unless the increments are large and quickly gained. Nor should it be about intentionally induced *disruptive* change. This is to mistakenly translate theories about how commercial innovation works into human psychology. There is more than enough disruptive change coming down the line already, caused by ecological, economic and, possibly, social breakdown. Prescribing *disruptive* change as a solution is to court fear and resistance. Sustainability-directed change is more about *preventing, protecting and redirecting*. That means preventing the worst from happening while preparing for the inevitable change already in the pipeline, and, *at the same time*, setting a new direction away from *un*sustainable behaviours.

The importance of being *sufficiently* in tune with the hopes and fears of people cannot be underestimated. So I thought the most useful thing I could give you here is a short overview of the gamut of emotions someone might feel as they come to terms with the implications of *un*sustainable development and the consequent magnitude of change. Figure 8.10 is consistent with the cycle of grieving made famous by psychiatrist Elisabeth Kübler-Ross – denial, anger, bargaining, depression, acceptance – which I can confirm from my own experience as a nurse, and indeed in working with people and organizations broaching the implications of sustainability (Kübler-Ross, 1969).

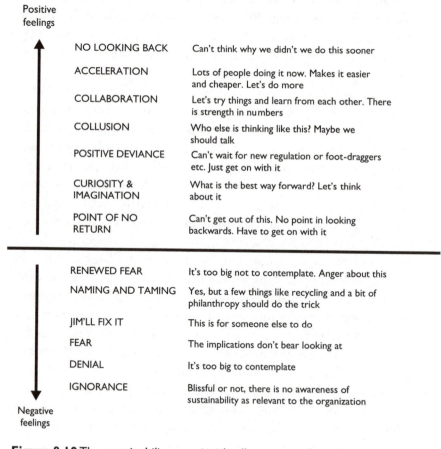

Figure 8.10 The sustainability emotional roller-coaster: From low ignorance to high engagement

Individuals (including yourself probably!) will move up and down this roller-coaster and may go round the loop or parts of it more than once. Sustainability-literate leadership is about moving people through to the positive deviance stage as fast as possible. Both sides of the figure may be annotated and amended to fit with your own observations and experience.

Cradle to cradle: Modern life cycle analysis

Belongs to the Climate Change family of understanding (see page 26 for explanation)

You are able to adapt and use concepts and tools like life cycle analysis to help close the gap between the way human economies and biogeochemical ones work.

For a long time the information and communications technology (ICT) sector puffed about its net contribution to sustainable development. The conceit was that using the phone, video-conferencing, sending emails instead of letters and so on scarcely used any energy at all. Not so. Today, it is estimated that the ICT sector is responsible for around 2 per cent of UK emissions, on a par with aviation.[23]

An ancient piece of research Forum for the Future did with the Post Office (from the wobbly data available at the time) concluded that a letter in a brown envelope, posted second class (and therefore going by train not air) was the least environmentally damaging way of communicating. What Forum did, which the ICT industry has not done until recently, was take the whole lifecycle of the communication medium into consideration. On the one side is the environmental cost of taking a tree, turning it into paper and envelopes, the fabrication of my pen (a refillable one that is with me all my life is best), the ink, the stamp, the contribution of the postal system (boxes, vans, sorting, transporting, delivering etc.), and the fate of my communication once read (stored for ever, burnt, recycled, sent to landfill). On the other is the fabrication of my computer and its software, its packaging and transportation, the energy consumed in use, and its relatively short life (compared to my pen) before its treatment prior to recycling and ultimate disposal (which includes hazardous waste). Also to be counted is the infrastructure that handles my email when I hit that send button: the telephone; the data lines and exchanges; the server farms and satellites that steer my message to the computer(s) that receive my email. That represents a lot of energy-intensive kit.

This is not to make an anti high technology case. Simply to illustrate the sort of whole-life thinking about energy and resources that should go into the choices we make – about sending an email, buying a lettuce or designing a new product.

What is called modern life cycle analysis (LCA) has been around for 15 or more years in waste management circles. But it has only recently entered the minds of policy makers. Consequently, their poor understanding of how different types of material affect the environment (e.g. paper, plastic or aluminium) has resulted in policies with perverse consequences. For example, it is physically more efficient (and therefore less polluting) to take a tree through the human economy as high grade paper, followed by alternative uses such as packaging or insulation, then, say, as animal bedding, before recuperating the energy via composting or burning in an ultra-efficient combined heat and power or district heating plant. Only recycling graphics-quality office paper makes environmental sense. Same with a metal like aluminum as it is environmentally costly to make in the first place, although the use of reusable bottles instead of cans for fizzy drinks would be better. However, the EU policy that requires the fraction of the waste stream recovered for recycling to be calculated by weight, means paper and bottles tend to be in (they are heavy) and aluminum may often be out (it is very light).[24] A double perversity means that a high market value for recyclates can block the movement of materials up the waste hierarchy.

All these problems could have been avoided through analysing the biogeochemical life cycle of different resource streams coming into the human economy, and structuring markets and policy and financial incentives to fit with the sort of 'factor ten' reductions in use and/or inefficiency that scientists say is entirely possible. Experts in energy and material use like Ernst von Weizsäcker (Weizsäcker et al, 1993, 2009) point out that money can not only be saved through efficiency, but made through the innovation of new low-carbon products and processes that reduce the use of resources in the first place. However, the example of the ICT industry is replicated across many industries: as the economy grows (as growth is currently measured) it sucks in resources and energy at a rate that outstrips efficiency gains.

Chemical engineer Michael Braungart and architect Bill McDonough say the proper way to think about the life cycle of anything is from 'cradle to cradle' and they have written a book with that title to explain what they mean. Their argument is that people can become beneficial to the planet, not just less destructive of it, if we 'make nutrients' as well as use them, like the rest of life on Earth. In other words, everything is designed so it goes into one of two cycles in volumes that overwhelms neither: either the biogeochemical one, or a 'technical' one that keeps non-biodegradable resources moving round the human economy. A process called by some industrial ecology, a closed loop economy or a green industrial revolution. As *Cradle to Cradle* points out, energy from the sun is not in short supply – we are just not very intelligent about harnessing it – while many natural materials are (McDonough and Braungart, 2002).

The key to thinking and deciding like Braungart and McDonough is to imagine the *services* we want from this or that resource (including energy) and work back from there on ways to get them that fit with the biogeochemical and technical cycles. Some leading examples include Interface, the carpet company that has used The Natural Step (see above) to develop floor coverings it can take back and reuse to make new carpets. As the company says, people don't necessarily want to *own* a carpet, but do want to enjoy the services it provides – warm, attractive floor covering. The same goes for cleaning products. Ecover tries to 'borrow' ingredients from nature, so once they have provided the service of cleaning our clothes and homes, they are returned benignly to the environment.

The big learning from a LCA lies with the process more than the outcome. For example, Walkers Crisps did a LCA on a packet of crisps, to make the 75g CO_2e per packet visible and find where reductions could be made. Walkers discovered the most CO_2e intensive part was not the transport (9 per cent) but the ingredients (44 per cent), and learnt that farmers keep the potatoes humid to soften the skins, and that meant extra heat was needed for frying. So by moving to bonuses for dry-weight potatoes the company, the farmers and the environment all did better. In a similar exercise, this time with tea, a company discovered that 60–80 per cent of the CO_2 emissions came not from the processing and transport of the tea leaves, but from boiling the kettle to brew a cuppa.

You may already be involved in quite technical ways of doing LCA. But as with cost–benefit analysis and environmental management systems (EMS), the need for action is overtaking detail and time-heavy processes. Systematic and sensible thinking about the cycle – from service desired back round to a benign return to the biosphere or the technological pool of materials used – can set the direction of travel very well. In the two examples given above, the organizations worked with Forum for the Future and their Streamlined LCA, which helps cut swiftly to the place where the biggest and quickest improvements can be made.[25] More detailed analysis and innovation may be drawn in to support and improve along the way. But establishing and keeping hold of the bigger picture as you do, is where the real learning and the big sustainability gains lie.[26]

Sustainability measures (including accounting for carbon)

Belongs to the Climate Change family of understanding (see page 26 for explanation)

You understand enough about ways of measuring progress towards sustainability to support your objectives and strategies.

In the part of this chapter on evaluating outcomes I said judging personal or organizational progress means measuring progress in three areas: contributions to the larger shared challenge of achieving a sustainable way of life; the ubiquity of those contributions (e.g. not only on Fridays but all year; in every department not just CSR); and how much of an influence has been made on the behaviour of others.

Here we look at how an organization might account formally for their environmental and sustainability performance using that framework.

A management mantra has it that what gets measured gets managed, but that is not, of course, true. What's happened in the economy, for example, is ample proof of Einstein's observation that 'not everything that can be counted counts, and not everything that counts can be counted'. With the environment, so fervent are we about measuring in detail just how quickly and severely the natural world and its systems are degrading, and so languid are we about intervening, our species looks set to become the only one to have monitored minutely its own extinction!

Notwithstanding, there is a great flourishing of interest in environmental and, more lately, sustainability accounting, with the inevitable associated industry for designing appropriate metrics. David Aeron-Thomas, Forum for the Future's Head of Metrics cautions, though, that selecting the right metrics and using them in formal 'accounts' or in an informal self- or organizational assessment is 'both a science and a practical art'. A science because of the need to measure the right things in the right way and with just enough precision, and a practical art because of the need to work out what is worth measuring and how whatever data/information gathered will contribute to changing behaviour. Organizations like the RSPB and British Waterways use citizen observations about birds, bees and bugs to judge the health of the environment, for example, as well as data from specialist researchers.

There are two reasons for establishing environmental or sustainability accounts alongside or even integrated into traditional financial ones:

- Accountability – identifying where responsibility lies for direct or wider impacts of an organization.
- Knowledge – if organizations understand their impacts on the environment and on people they will be better able to manage them.

Both require measurement tools and techniques and although environmental ones are pretty tried and tested now, full sustainability accounting is flourishing more in theory than in practice.

For those wanting to delve deeply in a practical way, a good place to start would be with the work of two of the accounting professional bodies – the Association of Chartered Certified Accountants (ACCA) and the Chartered Institute of Public Finance and Accountancy (CIPFA). Both have been diligent in bringing the best forward for their members.[27] For the more theoretically inclined, some academics are asking 'what is it all for' questions and pushing the boundaries in methodology.[28] You could also look at a report from the Accounting for Sustainability (A4S) Group, convened by HRH the Prince of Wales *. From the same source is a (not uncomplicated) methodology for designing your own set of measures.[29] A few companies are at an early stage of using sustainability accounting as their principal method of reporting, with some electricity companies a little ahead. A good example of synergy between reporting on sustainability and performance is the Cooperative Bank *.

A different approach, from which someone new to all this might more easily derive a modest set of measures, is found via the work on ecological footprints or national 'well-being' accounts. Calculating your own 'footprint' or impact on the environment is now a popular way of identifying ways of reducing it. See examples by WWF, Global Action Plan and Defra.[30] All are *good enough* ways of working out personal or organizational emissions of CO_2, but none address the fact that on our own, it is almost impossible to reduce personal emissions to the recommended level for living a 'one planet' lifestyle. I can only rarely buy organic food that is grown locally for example. For most of us the choice is either local or organic. To do both needs the involvement of other people and organizations.

Also missing from the carbon footprinting approach is the people side of sustainability. Fortunately it is no longer heresy to say that the orthodox measure of whether a national economy is successful or not, gross national or domestic product, is a mortally wounded duck. It has broken the Einstein rule. Although never intended to be a measure of human or environmental well-being, that is just what GDP has been used to do for decades. Several initiatives are trying to put that right, and they are discussed in the reflection on economic growth in Chapter 3 (page 71).

Amongst all the different approaches and references you should be able to find a set of measures *good enough* for your own purposes whether you are starting from scratch or improving an existing suite of indicators. Using tools like the five capitals one to help you check you have covered all the relevant areas; with futures thinking to be sure you are including generations yet unborn. It is wise to talk to others, for their experience, but as you decide what to include, listen to those who will live the impacts of your actions – for better or for worse. That will keep your suite of indicators real.

Above all, don't let the cult of measurement become a substitute for action. There are shedloads of targets and indicators out there that either *prevent* or are a *substitute for* getting on with the right actions.

Think of Einstein and keep it simple.

 Belongs to the Climate Change family of understanding (see page 26 for explanation)

Box 8.1 Accounting for carbon

There is no escaping the need to understand carbon sufficiently if you are to be effective in implementing and talking about your plans for moving towards sustainability. So here I will try to cover *sufficient* basics about language, units of measurement and options for 'managing' carbon to enable you to navigate the complexity of both using and emitting less of it.

It has become common to talk about 'carbon' as a shorthand for everything. Even bodies like the Committee on Climate Change (CCC – the independent body that advises government on 'carbon – more accurately CO_2e – budgets' and monitors progress on sticking to them) and the Carbon Trust (which helps companies and organizations implement a low-carbon strategy) are not consistent in their use of language, and this is unnecessarily confusing. As Table 8.8 shows, carbon (C) is not the same as carbon dioxide (CO_2), which is, in turn, not the same as carbon dioxide equivalents (CO_2e).

Wherever possible stick to CO_2e, as this is the measure used by the CCC and countries reporting to the UN Framework Convention on Climate Change. And, although CO_2 is by a long chalk the largest gas in volume, methane and nitrous oxide are becoming more important. Scientists suggest both may not have been fully calculated up to now and are anyway on the increase, from thawing permafrost, for example.[31] When calculating your personal or organizational emissions, though, it will be mostly CO_2 that is counted even though the process is called carbon footprinting!

The reason for making such a fuss about language is that right now the biggest focus is on carbon dioxide (CO_2) *out*, while preventing carbon (C) from coming *in* to the economy in the first place, and then being ultra-efficient in what we do use is where we will make the quickest and deepest cuts. Because of the abundance, diversity and ubiquity of carbon in all life this is just another way of saying fossilized or otherwise sequestered carbon (peat bogs for example) should be left undisturbed. Knowing your C from your CO_2 will help you decide everything from personal and corporate strategies, to knowing when taxing or rationing carbon *in* would be more effective than penalizing *emissions* of CO_2 once produced, or indeed when both might be needed.

Table 8.8 What is carbon?

Carbon C	Carbon dioxide CO_2 or CO2	Carbon dioxide equivalent CO_2e or CO2e
One tonne of carbon = 3.74 tonnes of CO_2. May be solid, liquid and gaseous	I atom C combined with 2 atoms of oxygen. A gas. The most important human-generated greenhouse gas	The total emissions for all greenhouse gases (see below) expressed as equivalents of CO_2
Global warming potential The heat-trapping power relative to CO_2 over a time period (100 years usually). A methane molecule has 25 times the warming potential as a CO_2 molecule. CO_2 is more stable and longer lasting	Carbon dioxide Methane Nitrous oxide Hydrofluorocarbons Perfluorocarbons Sulphur hexafluoride	I 21 310 140–11,700 6500–9200 23,900

Note: Scientists talk of greenhouse gases as atmospheric concentrations expressed in parts per million (ppm). The concentrations of atmospheric CO_2 in pre-industrial times (c 1750) was 280ppm, rising by 2007 to 396ppm. If other greenhouse gases are included, the total warming effect is around 430ppm of CO_2e, and rising at about 2.2ppm per year. Staying under a ceiling of around 450ppm is what has to be achieved if we are to have a reasonable chance of limiting temperature rise to a 2° rise from 1750 levels, though some argue the ceiling should be lower.

Source: Table 1: 100 year warming potential for gases included in Kyoto Protocol, www.unfcc.int/ghg-data

Final point on language. There is no such thing as zero-carbon anything. It is scientifically impossible. Carbon is the fourth most abundant element in the universe and number two in our bodies. In the right place and in the right proportions it is good stuff. A zero-carbon home, therefore, is a fallacy. What is meant is a very, very, low-carbon one – both in a carbon *in* and CO_2 *out* sense. You may have to live with the mis-speaking of others, but being precise yourself minimizes confusion.

Figures 8.11 and 8.12 show where UK CO_2e emissions are coming from – by sector, and then by the contribution of each greenhouse gas to the total.

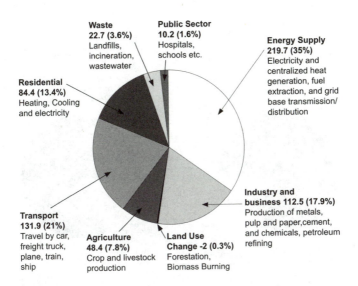

Source: UK emissions statistics via www.decc.gov.uk (16 April 2010 update)

Figure 8.11 UK 2008 greenhouse gas emissions by sector (in MtCO$_2$e)

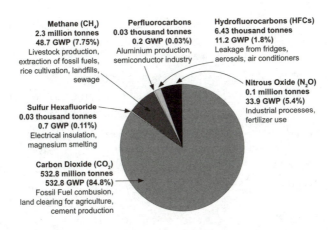

Source: UK Emissions Statistics 2010 via www.decc.gov.uk

Figure 8.12 UK 2008 greenhouse gas emissions by type, weighted for their global waming potential (GWP)

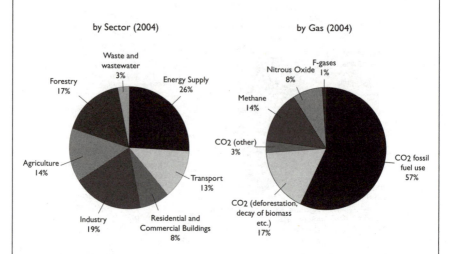

Note: Forestry includes deforestation

Source: IPCC Assessment Report 4 (2007), Summary of Policymakers: Figure SPM3

Figure 8.13 Global 2004 greenhouse gas emissions from human activity by sector and by gas

Figure 8.13 gives the same breakdown for global emissions, enabling you to see the differences and similarities.

Lots of people find it difficult to think in percentages. For example, the CCC says a 1.7 per cent year on year reduction of greenhouse gases from 2007 to 2020 will be needed to hit targets. Sounds straightforward, but is really hard to translate into meaningful actions for an organization or individual. Particularly as the first year's reduction might be as easy as the final year's is fantastically difficult, or even impossible if the necessary groundwork has not been laid in the first few years.

Table 8.9 shows the scale of the challenge between now and 2050 for UK sectors. For those who (as I do) find it easier to think about targets in tonnes rather than percentages, it gives the 'weight watchers' version with numbers rounded for clarity. It shows that we will need to find *at least* a 2 tonnes/person drop in CO_2e emissions each decade between now and 2050 to meet the *legally* binding targets. The challenge will be even more difficult if the predicted rise in UK population really happens.

Table 8.9 Targets for annual UK emissions of greenhouse gases between now and 2050

Year	Emissions ceilings as per CCC (in MtCO2e/year	Tonnes/person budget assuming:		Reduction from 2007 levels	Reduction from 1990 levels
		No population growth *	Projected growth occurs *		
2007 (actual)	680 **	11	11		
2020 (target)	540	9	8	20%	34%
2050 (target)	160	2.6	2	76%	80%

* Current UK population is 61.4 million. Projected (but not inevitable) rises suggest 65 million by 2020 and 77 million by 2050). See www.statistics.gov.uk and www.theccc.org.uk.
** this figure includes international aviation and shipping emissions.

Source: Adapted from CCC Adair Turner presentation 'Meeting carbon budgets: The need for step change', October 2009, overhead 7, www.theccc.org.uk/pdfs/report%20launchpresentation.pdf

These are very challenging targets indeed, whether expressed in percentages or in tonnes of CO_2e, and the UK Committee on Climate Change is in no doubt that progress is too slow and too unambitious. In October 2009 it pointed to three areas where new approaches by government are needed: electricity and carbon markets; residential energy efficiency; and support for electric cars.

How do ordinary people and organizations work out what is the best for them; how do you prioritize action so you are contributing enough to the collective targets? Forum for the Future has produced a very helpful brochure *Getting to Zero: Defining Corporate Carbon Neutrality*, aimed at business but applicable to all.[32] (Yes, that Zero again!) It uses a World Resources Institute model to set 'boundaries' within which to determine and prioritize action on reducing demand (carbon in) through efficiency, and on replacing high-carbon with low-carbon energy sources:

Scope 1 Emissions from sources owned or controlled by the organization.
Scope 2 Emissions from the generation of purchased electricity.
Scope 3 Indirect and other emissions.

The weakness of this framework is that Scope 3 tends to be neglected, even though it includes things like corporate air travel and procurement, which are hardly indirect as many organizations now have considerable influence over their suppliers and modes of staff transport. There is no excuse, therefore, to do anything but include them from the outset.

The brochure also promotes investing in CO_2-reducing activities elsewhere (forestry, renewable or efficiency technologies in poor countries) to offset reductions that are just too expensive where the company is based. The argument is that a tonne of CO_2 not emitted or soaked up is the same whether it costs £100 in the UK or £5 in India, and indeed more tonnes can be stopped from entering the atmosphere if the £100 is spent in India. In Figure 8.14 I've embellished the document's neat carbon management hierarchy process by adding the notion of befriending others where bigger effects could be had from collaborative rather than just individual organization action. For example, clubbing together with the local authority, hospital or university to install windmills or to make low-carbon procurement more viable for each organization and for suppliers. The new local authority auditing scheme – Comprehensive Area Assessment – demands local cooperation between public sector organizations (education, police, NHS, government, business, citizens) to get to a low-carbon economy, though the tax regime, unfortunately, doesn't – yet.

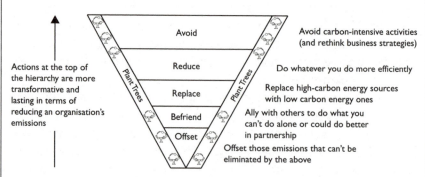

Figure 8.14 The carbon management hierarchy

Another important addition to this frequently used hierarchy is the inclusion of *simultaneous and continuous* investment in the environment's capacity to mop up after us as a constant and not just as an offset because we've failed to do it in other ways. By taking every opportunity to tear up the tarmac, grass over a roof, plant a tree and so on, we're adding to natural capital, and in return getting CO_2 out of the atmosphere. The Forum guide does makes clear offset is a last resort, but others view offsetting as rather like purchasing 'mediaeval indulgences' — buying the right to go on sinning, and so delaying the behaviour changes needed for a low-carbon economy to work!

The trick is to look for a triple whammy through simultaneously mobilizing a great deal less carbon in the first place, becoming *ultra*-efficient in that which is used, and increasing the biological capacity of the Earth to help us (more trees, more greenery) — regardless of whether you use offset to cover your emissions or not. Not one or the other, but all three together and at great scale and pace. Thinking of the *services* you want from energy (heat, power and light) helps illuminate how that could be provided in different, low-carbon ways. It also makes a case for thinking at the top of the hierarchy, as that is where the biggest gains and the greatest innovation are to be found. Enterprising organizations (e.g. student halls of residence, business units) are using front-of-pipe techniques to increase initial costs of energy with a 'levy' that creates a fund to invested in low-carbon technology or processes, or in otherwise incentivizing reduced demand for energy.

In summary, make the UK targets yours, and don't worry if you end up doing more than your 'share'. It will only be for the good and will make up for any double counting (of your effort by someone else or vice versa). Precision will not be possible and searching for it can easily become an excuse for not getting started. Use percentage reductions or tonnages in your strategies, whatever works best for you, though tonnes are real, and, like kilos lost at Weight Watchers, may motivate more than percentages. Talk to other organizations like yours or in the locality for collaborative ventures, look up the Carbon Trust (www.carbontrust.co.uk) for potential loans and support, learn lessons from others.

Conclusion
Practical wisdom

> Practical wisdom is a reasoned and true state of capacity
> to act with regard to the human good.
>
> _Aristotle[33]_

The intention of this book, and this section in particular, is to kit you out with _sufficient_ knowledge and skills to get out and be active in the pursuit of a more sustainable way of doing things with a confidence that your judgement will be wise _enough_ to ensure you are heading in the right direction. At least, I hope it will have helped you to think differently about how you do things right now.

To help us understand the magnitude of change before us, but in a way that sustains the mission possible thesis of this book, the next section considers a possible global sustainability To Do list. It fits with my compulsion for thinking in outcomes, and I like the idea of judging what I do today against its contribution to what good would look like tomorrow. And as good globally will depend on multiple goods happening locally, it helps to keep an eye on the larger goal as we busy ourselves near to where we are. It may be important to understand the causes of _un_sustainability well enough to steer clear of repeating wrong behaviours, but it is so much more uplifting – for the soul as well as our entrepreneurial minds – to be forward looking as we work out how to deviate around the perversities of life today.

Section Four

The Global Sustainability To Do List

The crisis is in implementation.
Kofi Annan, Johannesburg, 2002

Section Four

Introduction

Global challenges, local contributions

If this section had a slogan, it would pinch that of the supermarket Tesco: 'Every little helps'. Its purpose is to help you handle the argument that *un*sustainable development is globally so advanced that local contributions are pointless. Compared to the US or China, the UK's emissions are tiny, so why bother when the big countries don't? What difference will it make if I turn off the lights or you use a bicycle when those around us don't?

Both practically and morally, the answer to both those questions is: a lot. If unsustainable development is the outcome of zillions of (mostly) *unknowingly* wrong decisions and actions then the route to sustainability will be paved by a similar magnitude of *knowingly* right decisions and actions. Even a miraculous edict or wholesale policy change from top levels of leadership in an organization, country or even an international body, while greatly to be desired, will only become reality through a multiplicity of relatively small and mostly local acts of implementation. Many of these will have to be in positive deviance mode, because there won't be time to wait for top-down institutional reform before we get on with it. The challenge for the implementation brigade – the sustainability-literate positive deviants and those they motivate – is to maintain confidence over time that they are actually making a global contribution of value in what are bound to be turbulent times.

Tesco is well aware that a penny off this or that item in the weekly shopping trolley may not seem much, but actually adds up to a noticeable saving. In just the same way every contribution to a more sustainable way of doing things, however small, adds up. The talk of tipping points in relation to CO_2 emissions triggering runaway climate change, needs to be countered by the positive message of tipping points in the other direction – from multitudes of actions that bring emissions down. Moreover, opting out or preaching hopelessness sends the wrong message both ecologically and philosophically. If I don't, or you won't, then why should anyone else? A negative psychological loop is created. But if I do and you do, then together we can create a positive loop that is attractive to others. Being in a positive club not only does good, it feels good too.

The previous section considered many ways for you to develop your own capacity to provide sustainability-literate leadership, so you are able to decide and act in favour of sustainability, regardless of the perversities of the world around you.

This section should help you to tell a good story about what a sustainable world might look like and describe the grand lines that will get us there. Like the Five Capitals Tool, it should help you see and talk about the interconnections between different elements of sustainability, but most of all it should help you connect, for yourself and others, the way local efforts can contribute to global outcomes.

There is just one chapter – Chapter 9 – which starts with the list and a short explanation about how it came about. For those interested in the longer story behind the way the list is constructed, that comes at the end.

Returning to the metaphor of Chapter 1, the Global Sustainability To Do List could be seen as the fitness regime the patient ALOE+US needs to complete in order to return to full health – assuming, that is, we have learnt our lesson, taken our medicine and stopped gorging on an unreformed and resource- and soul-depleting human economic system.

Chapter 9

The global sustainability to do list

The list, summarized in Table 9.1, is compiled from an amalgamation and adaptation of two excellent models for thinking about the sustainability challenge on a global scale. The first, known as the IPAT equation, dates from the 1970s and is still in use today. The second, the Princeton Wedges, is from a more modern but nevertheless helpful way of identifying areas for action that, as an ensemble and interactively, would add up to sustainable development. From IPAT comes the grand lines that will take us from here to sustainability. The Princeton Wedges provide the principle that taking action on several fronts at once increases the chances of success. Originally designed around big energy solutions, the Princeton Wedges identified several 'candidate actions'. Pursuing several 'wedges' of them at once makes it more likely that some (either entirely or in part) will work out and thus add up to the desired target. There is absolutely no need to worry about overshoot here. So advanced are the symptoms of *un*sustainable development, it would only be a benefit. The bigger danger is undershoot through lack of imagination and effort. If you are unfamiliar with either model, you may wish to turn to page 250 first.

As you can see from Table 9.1 the five grand lines have targets for 2050, and apart from A, which is about reducing absolute consumption of energy and natural resources, and one relating to P (population numbers), all the candidate 'wedges' for action proposed are positive – doing more rather than less of something. This is a key point for positive deviants. Without pulling punches about the gravity of our current situation, or about the extent of the changes implied by a transition to a low-carbon economy, it is possible to provide a sustainability message that is essentially one of hope and positive action for growing a more satisfying and ecologically and socially just way of life.

Table 9.1 The Global Sustainability To Do List

N	**Grow nature's capacity to help**

Halt degradation and instead grow natural capital by 25% from now to 2050

+ Reduce tropical deforestation to zero, establish 300 million hectares of new tree plantations
+ Stop degradation and instead increase fraction of all terrestrial and marine biomes returned to original state (in urban as well as rural and wilderness areas)
+ Make it easier for water to get into aquifers and irrigation systems
+ Boost soil fertility – for food and to capture and store carbon
+ At least double the area of the Earth under sustainability conservation measures particularly for freshwater, marine and especially vulnerable and neglected land areas

P	**Reduce numbers of people**

Hit the lower UN world population prediction of 8 billion by 2050

+ Provide universal and easy access to appropriate contraceptive materials
- Bring fertility rates well under replacement levels in affluent countries, and at least halve current fertility rates in poorer countries
+ Improve reproductive health for women and men worldwide
+ Invest in women as those best able to determine their children's destiny
+ Value older people, make the most of their wisdom and experience

H	**Grow human and social capital**

Increase individual and communal sense of well-being by (say) 50% from today's levels by 2050

+ Provide universal health care and education
+ Provide knowledge and skills for successful personal relationships and social participation
+ Grow resilience of communities and neighbourhoods
+ Reform, develop and strengthen social institutions
+ Increase sense of security – of place and in international relations

A	**Reduce overall consumption of energy and raw materials**

Shrink human 'take' of (non-solar) energy and raw materials by 25% from today's levels by 2050 (i.e. leave it in the ground)

- Converge water used per person round a healthy optimum
- Converge calorie intake of affluent and poor around a healthy optimum
- Reduce absolute amount of energy needed for heat, power and light
- Reduce absolute amount of minerals and other materials taken from the ground
- Shrink land take for human infrastructure (built environment and agriculture)

T   **Grow efficiency/effectiveness of *any* energy and raw materials consumption**

Squeeze all waste and inefficiency out of energy (including solar) and materials use, by (say) 50% from today's levels by 2050
+ Increase efficiency of use for water that is used
+ Increase efficiency of use for all raw materials that are used
+ Ensure extreme efficiency in provision of all energy services – heat, power and light
+ Make all goods and services exchanged ultra-efficient in their use of carbon
+ Treat food production, like all land and marine resources, as part of an efficient ecological economy rather that as an industry

I'll be honest, I don't know if the percentages suggested are right, but they are good enough for the moment. Getting going on all factors in the equation will be the hard bit; more precise calibration can wait. What matters is that the direction of travel is established.

A necessarily brief commentary about each of the elements follows, with some references and websites to help you get at more information. See Lester Brown's book *Plan B 3.0: Mobilizing to Save Civilization*, for a range of candidate actions (Brown, 2008), but try to think of examples near to you.

N Grow nature's capacity to help

Halt degradation and instead grow natural capital by 25 per cent from now to 2050.

Commentary

Globally about 17 per cent CO_2e emissions come from deforestation and its consequences. As there are nearly two billion hectares of badly degraded land globally (every country has some) there is plenty of space for new trees in urban and rural areas. Planting 300 hectares is worth a reduction of 1 Gigatonne CO_2e according to Socolow and Pacala (authors of the Princeton Wedges).

The Millennium Ecosystem Assessment (MEA) found 15 out of 24 ecological systems degraded. Ending negative trends and restoring different local biomes[1] to healthy long-term quality and productivity can secure larger ecological systems services, like food, fertile soil. An urban area could be considered a biome too. So as well as wild spaces and coastlines, what you can make happen in your parish or town – urban parks and roof gardens, street trees – all contributes to CO_2e emissions reduction and growth in the main currency of a resilient ecological economy – a healthy environment (MEA, 2005).

Most of the rain that falls on drought hardened soil or on tarmac runs off, particularly if it falls in a heavy short storm. Instead of going into underground aquifers it disappears into rivers and storm drains. Ways of improving the chances of the water seeping down through the soil to reach the aquifers include green land cover, especially with deep-rooted plants (including trees), and replacing the tarmac with porous surfaces (Postel and Richter, 2003), www.environment-agency.gov.uk (search for SUDS).

Overgrazing, overploughing and overuse of fossil fuel fertilizers and other poor agricultural practices (like the removal of tree and hedge shelters) has made soil erosion, exhaustion and pollution epidemic in most countries and deadly for some of the poorest people. Restoring some good farming practice, like crop rotation, non-intensive rangeland, field boundary trees and hedges (themselves a source of food), and introducing new ones like high-efficiency irrigation and low- or no-tillage where seeds are drilled into uncultivated soil so previous crop residues can nourish and protect the soil from wind and rain. Improving the condition of the soil is a central objective of organic and permaculture methods of agriculture. These are techniques that reduce CO_2e emissions as well and are as relevant to countries in the US and Europe as they are in Africa and Asia. www.fao.org/organicag/en/; www.rainforestalliance.org/agriculture.

According to the International Union for Conservation of Nature (IUCN) 11.5 per cent of the world's land area is protected through reserves or 'parks'. United Nations Educational, Scientific and Cultural Organization (UNESCO) lists nearly 150 sites of 'outstanding natural value'. There are big gaps, however, and many 'paper parks' with little protection in practice. Under-represented are freshwater, marine and terrestrial habitats for some highly threatened species. Returning areas to the 'wild' gives the environment the chance to rebuild ecological resilience (especially for services such as climate regulation and resources such as fish). Indicators of successful protection include species diversity and improved local environmental quality. www.iucn.org.

P Reduce numbers of people   *or consumption ?.*

Hit the lower UN world population prediction of 8 billion by 2050.

Commentary

At present the world population of nearly seven billion is growing at around 80 million a year, on target for the high UN prediction of nearly ten billion by 2050. In poorer countries around 300 million women who want to use contraception have no access to it. In richer countries where access to contraceptive advice and methods is relatively easy and often free of charge, over a third of pregnancies (in and out of marriage) are unplanned. Improving services to meet expressed demand (no coercion needed) and making every conception a planned one, would enable us to hit the lower UN population prediction for 2050.

It is true that there is a strong link between consumption (affluence) and emission of greenhouse gases (see A below), but it takes a very special pair of blinkers to contest the fact that the more people there are, the harder it is for everyone to enjoy a fulfilled life. Everything is more difficult when there are more people – especially for women. (See Chapter 2 page 52.) A positive loop with wide benefits can be engaged – where having fewer children makes it easier for women (and families) to raise the children they do have safely to adulthood, improving the quality of everyone's life, and emancipating women *as well as* mitigating climate change. See UN State of the World Population: Facing a changing world: Women, population and climate, www.unfpa.org/swp/2009/en/pdf/EN_SOWP09.pdf for example. As the Optimum Population Trust (www.optimumpopulation.org) points out, $7 worth of contraceptives (preventing unwanted births) can deliver 1 tonne reduction in CO_2 between now and 2050, which, compared to the cost of investment in efficiency and renewable energy, represents excellent value for money – though all are needed of course.

If we were to continue emitting the level of greenhouse gases we do now, it is estimated the population would have to drop to around five billion by 2050 to keep warming to less than 2°C more than pre-industrial times. Such a reduction would not be possible without a dramatic rise in the death rate, which is precisely why a sensible approach to lowering the birth rate is needed.

Table 9.2 below shows the predicted difference between fertility rates (number of children per woman) now, and 2050. An average of one child less per woman is the global target. Although a drop is predicted amongst the poorest women, they have the most difficult challenges, while in more developed regions a rise in average fertility is predicted. This partially reflects the trend for more affluent couples to have three or four children. Justice suggests that, as with greenhouse gas emissions, richer couples could take responsibility for doing better than the lower fertility rate prediction for 2050. At the moment, the UK fertility rate is 1.8 on average, in the US 2.1 yet only 1.29 in Italy. An Ethiopian woman, by contrast, will on average, have more than 5.5 children – unless she is one of the 21 per cent lucky enough to have access to family planning advice and materials.

Table 9.2 Predicted fertility rates: Medium and low estimates of average number of children per woman by 2050, showing the difference between now (2005–10) and the predicted low 2045–50 rates*

Variant*	2005–2010 Actual	2045–2050 Predicted		Difference between column A and C (The fall in average number of children per woman needed to put world population numbers on track for lower UN predictions for 2050 and a steady reduction thereafter)
	Now A	Medium B	Low C	
World	2.56	2.02	1.54	1.02
More developed regions	1.64	1.78	1.31	0.33
Less developed regions**	2.73	2.05	1.56	1.17
Least developed countries	4.39	2.41	1.93	2.46

Notes: * UN Population Information Network (2008 revision) gives high, medium and low variants when calculating future growth of population, www.esa.un.org/unpp.
** Less developed regions, not including least developed countries.

Making the lower predictions for 2050 a reality would help all countries work through an ecological demographic transition – where populations stabilize at a lower level, and higher life expectancy is balanced by lower birth rates, as in Italy today. Getting contraceptive materials, especially the longer lasting ones, to women currently unable to get them, and raising the profile of the broader context for making a personal decision is the minimum that needs to be done in rich and poor countries alike. Add to that a sustained investment in improving reproductive health attitudes and practices for both men and women, investing heavily in emancipating women worldwide, and treating the elderly as a valuable resource rather than a burden, would make this particular 2050 target relatively easy to hit.

This may seem like a tough area for positive deviants to involve themselves with, but it should be the most straightforward. There is a lot of smog around family planning – raised by sexism, religion and, let's be frank, squeamishness about sex. It is possible to sidestep all that and advocate good population policies that in better-off countries help people consider the broader as well as the immediate considerations about having a child themselves, and an improvement in the way family planning services are promoted and delivered. The more the big carbon consumers can come in under the replacement rate of two children per woman the better. At the same time, strong and effective policies that get advice and materials to the women (and men) in poorer countries who want it but can't get it is something we can all advocate and contribute to practically. www.popoffset.com.

NB Promoting population policies and family planning is *not the same thing as advocating abortion*. Abortion is the result of failed contraception, and I know of no research that shows women choose abortion as their preferred method of fertility control. So, whether you are in favour of a woman's right to decide about terminating an unwanted pregnancy or not, it has nothing to do with rest of the argument here.

H Grow human and social capital

Increase individual and communal sense of well-being by (say) 50 per cent from today's levels by 2050.

Commentary

A successful move onto a sustainability trajectory will not happen if people do not have a good enough education, and sufficient health (physical and psychological) to learn and apply knowledge. Moreover, unless people see that sustainability is as much about improving their lot as it is about protecting the environment, there is a danger they will become disillusioned and resentful of efforts to create an economy as low on carbon as it needs to be.

This particular grand line assumes an enormous amount of growth in both human and social capital can be achieved with very little mobilization of environmental capital. Delinking growth in people's wellbeing and life satisfaction from high utilization of natural resources and greenhouse gas emitting materials will be a key challenge for positive deviants.

At the moment, health care is far from universal, even in the richest of countries, and it is more about care of the sick than about maintaining good health. The outcome of universal health care should – at least – *prevent* the easy to treat diseases affecting infant, child or adult mortality rates, including malnutrition (caused by either under- or overeating) and HIV/AIDS. www.who.int.

Amarta Sen points out that 'illiteracy and innumeracy are greater threats to humanity than terrorism,'[2] especially true in a world with a booming number of young people finding hunger a major impediment to learning. Globally, one fifth of adults are currently unable to read or write (around one in ten in the UK) but worse in very poor countries where girls especially lose out. The UN says education is the essential 'fertilizer' for any sort of development. www.unesco.org (see Education for All Monitoring Report).

Consequently, understanding and having sufficient health and education to be able to fulfil one's own potential in a socially and environmentally responsible way does form a sensible baseline for growing 'human capital'. Progress everywhere is needed, especially in the light of evidence that, by and large, people in richer countries are not all that happy. So care of mental as well as physical health and a broader idea of what constitutes a satisfactory life is part of being a full human being. It is also part of forging satisfactory relationships – be they intimate, within the family or neighbourhood, at school or work, at social events, or participating in public life generally. As well as the good things modern culture and technology brings, research has identified three messages that are affecting children: the view that to be happy you have to be wealthy and beautiful; a conflictual and often violent model of human relationships; physical inactivity and eating, drinking and smoking to excess (Layard and Dunn, 2009). Confidence in one's own identity is a good thing, but sterile without two-way responsibilities met and enjoyed in the company of others (see *ubunto* in Chapter 8). Music and all creative arts are immensely important to personal growth and social interactions, even in conflict zones (see Daniel Barenboim ✱).

The quality and growth of human capital is, arguably but perhaps instinctively, a matter for localities to assure, not in competition with neighbouring communities and institutions, but in partnerships, reflecting an understanding of our interconnectedness one with another and the environment we all share and the need for justice that transcends generations and geographical boundaries. Nowadays, too few political or institutional structures support or reward this way of living, but people like former UN Ambassador Sir Jeremy Greenstock are unequivocal that global security and ecological stability depends on multitudinous resilient localities (see also, www.undp.org and Sen, 2000).[3]

None of which is to underestimate the necessity to get national and international institutions into good shape. Devolution of responsibility and action quickly dissolves into anarchy or local baronetcies without a larger framework of confidence in systems of democracy, justice and freedom of information. Cultural and creative activities are as important at national and international level as they are at local level and, like the environment, could form a baseline of shared values around which new or reformed institutions could be built. For a very long time music, art, literature, poetry and crafts have provided a language that crosses international and cultural boundaries, but like the universal need for a life supporting environment are not used as strategically as they might be in building good relationships between communities and countries. For example, until Islam took a violent interest in the West, we were not much interested in its culture. Wonderful Persian poetry went untranslated and the debt of William Morris to Islamic textile design forgotten. Distilling, fountain pens, windmills and cheques are other unacknowledged Islamic innovations. If we had been more interested sooner, things might have been different.

Through raising understanding of the role of growing human and social capital to achieving sustainability, positive deviants can advocate, influence and push investment in that direction. Around the world, social enterprises, using a range of different business models, are springing up as people sidestep business as usual to activities that contribute directly to sustainability (Elkington and Hartigan, 2008) while some existing firms, like BT (www.btinsights.co.uk), are becoming adept at gaining maximum social as well as environmental outcomes from straightforward business adaptations.

A   Reduce overall total consumption of energy and raw materials

Shrink human 'take' of (non-solar) energy and raw materials by 25 per cent from today's levels by 2050 (i.e. leave it in the ground).

Commentary

This grand line is about the absolute reduction we need to make in the way the human economy uses energy and raw materials. Efficiency in the context of a rising, or even a level, 'take' of environmental resources will not be sufficient. There has to be an absolute reduction, on top of a major increase in the efficiency of what we do use (see T below) if we are to get anywhere near the sort of levels that are sustainable into the long term. Not only because of a shortage of resources, but because of the need to design and move into low-carbon, low-resource intensive lifestyles. Attempts to delay absolute reduction through sticking with efficiency-only strategies will cost dearly in future. Our addiction to profligacy will have to be cured.

For example, the recommended basic water requirement is 50 litres per person per day – but 30 should be sufficient, 5 for food and drink and 25 for hygiene. The UN say the minimum is 20 litres per person per day, but in places the average use is less than 10 litres/day – 8 in Mali, 4.5 in Ghana, for example. In the US the average consumption of water per person is 500 litres/day, UK residents use 200 litres/day, both countries practise the financial and environmental lunacy of buying bottled water while paying for drinking-quality water on (all) taps at home.

Replenishing aquifers and other water stores for household, industrial and agricultural use in case of prolonged drought is an important climate change adaption strategy for many regions already. Already, composting toilets (some approved by the US Environmental Protection Agency) are gaining popularity for water conservation reasons. Mongolia has installed them in a new block of flats housing 7000 people. As Sunita Nurain of India's Centre for Science and the Environment points out, water-based systems for treating human waste don't make sense in countries like hers. They are wasteful of water, damaging to rivers and human health and the cost of infrastructure to treat the sewage is cash and energy expensive. (There are many relevant references and websites on water. See also Pearce, 2007.)

The recommended calorific intake for a man is about 2500, and a woman 2000 (more if heavy labour is involved). Yet so great is the malnutrition in the world that WHO says 1.6 billion adults are significantly overweight (one third of them obese) while around one billion are hungry. Converging rich and poor around the recommended calorie intake and eating lower down the food chain (less meat, more plants) will contribute to human and environmental health. Moving to an average of 25kg of meat per person/per year (roughly half a kilogramme per week) would drop global consumption from today's 267 million tonnes/per year to 175mt/yr and reverse a trend heading for 465mt/yr by 2030 (a cut of 75 per cent for the US, c. 30 per cent in Japan and c. 20 per cent in the EU). While cows do convert roughage to energy more efficiently than biofuel production, lower quantities of red meat in the diet will also take some of the pressure off land, and reduce greenhouse gas emissions (methane and CO_2).[4] It is not necessary to become a vegetarian or a vegan, except for personal preference. Human beings evolved as omnivores and a resilient agricultural system will depend on *enough* animals for fertilizers, land management, wool and leather as well as nutrition. For an analysis of the calorie/land equation under different agricultural regimes in the UK, see Simon Fairlie's 'Can Britain Feed Itself?' in *The Land* 4, Winter 2007–08. A pdf version is available from www.transitionculture.org.

'Current trends in energy supply and consumption are patently unsustainable – environmentally, economically and socially – they can and must be altered', said Nobuo Tanaka, chief executive of the International Energy Authority (IEA) at the end of 2008. Few now argue that the more oil and coal – and gas – we can leave in the ground soonest, the easier it will be to avoid dangerous global warming. The most active naysayers for that scenario are unsurprisingly the major extractive and refining industries (see www.iea.org and Leggett, 2005; Monbiot, 2007).

Non-agricultural emissions of greenhouse gases make up 65 per cent of the total, so at least halving the current annual rates of fossil fuel use in power generation (24 per cent of total emissions) will, combined with similar scale efficiency gains in what we do use, be where a core contribution to avoiding dangerous global warming will be made. Pacala and Socolow say things like reducing vehicle use from 10,000 to 5000 miles per year (at 30 miles per gallon (mpg)) would remove 1 gigatons of carbon per year (GtC/yr) by 2054. A further 1GtC/yr reduction is available by replacing coal power with two million 1MW-peak windmills. This would mean building at 50 times the current rate. Challenging, but technologically speaking, not impossible. As yet unproven technologies like those to capture and store CO_2 emissions from burning fossil fuels have been reviewed by the Royal Society, and published with warnings that using more big kit to put right the wrongs of other big kit, doesn't make too much sense. More sure and quicker reductions in energy demand could come from distributed, smaller, even home-based, systems connected by an intelligent grid that can smooth out demand and assure resilience should a locality get into difficulties (see www.royalsociety.org and Mackay, 2009).

As for minerals other than coal and oil, such as uranium and the rare elements that, literally, keep our information and communication technologies functioning, see Table 1.1 (page 21). Despite modern society's dependence on many of these minerals, very soon there will be less available anyway, not least because China already dominates the extraction and processing of 95 per cent of the world's supply.

In relation to land under forestry (30 per cent globally) and woodland/grassland (26 per cent) or agriculture (11 per cent), the percentage of all land covered in brick, concrete and tarmac comes in at under 0.5 per cent. However, according to the UN Food and Agriculture Organization (FAO), land used for human settlements and infrastructure such as roads is growing at a rate of 20,000 square kilometres/year at the expense of mostly agricultural land, but also forestry and woodland/grassland.[5] In the spirit of every bit counting when it comes to putting nature back into the ecological driving seat, chiselling away at precious agricultural and wild land is as counter-intuitive as it is daft and unnecessary. Most cities and towns, and many villages, in rich and poor counties, are wasteful in the way they use land. Even in densely populated areas much land can be liberated from concrete and tarmac, with many collateral benefits that make cities 'liveable'. London for example, has 3000 hectares of 'previously developed land'. Trees capture rain and protect against flood risk, for example, and US cities find a mature tree canopy can reduce summer air temperatures by around 3°C. If evergreen, even in severe winters, trees can reduce the wind speed and therefore the chill, so lowering heating bills. www.forestry.gov.uk (search The Read Report); www.fao.org.

Just by differentiating between where *less* of any resource can be used and the efficiency measures that should be applied to those resources that are brought into use will help open minds to more effective ways of achieving both.

T   Grow efficiency/effectiveness of *any* energy and material consumption

Squeeze all waste and inefficiency out of energy (including solar) and material uses, by (say) 50 per cent from today's levels by 2050

Commentary

You will remember from Chapter 8 (page 218) the two life cycles Michael Braungart and Bill McDonough advised for ensuring maximum efficiency and minimum pollution from human activities – one integrated in a non-damaging (even contributing) way to the nutrient and chemical cycles of the natural world, the other a technological one in which the non-biodegradable resources live in a perpetual reuse and recycle relationship. This is a very good way of thinking how we can make the best use of the resources we do use. I've just suggested an overall 25 per cent reduction in resources mobilized in the first place, and here propose a further 50 per cent improvement in those we do use – from today's level. Tough, but achievable, if you recall the waste diagram on page 25.

For example, if US and European citizens had to carry the water they used from a central point – even ten metres away – would they use so much? A toilet flushed in London uses 50 litres of water. Calculating the 'embedded' water in a product or service can be as sobering as the same calculation for embedded energy (embedded means the amount of energy or water used in the whole life cycle of something). For instance, a cotton T-shirt takes 27,000 litres, one kilowatt of coal power energy uses 1.6 litres, nuclear energy, 2.3 litres/kW. The opportunities for industry and households to squeeze waste out of the whole water capture and use cycle is enormous. For example, water in large dams and reservoirs evaporates more quickly, usually has to travel a very long way and needs treatment before use. Two thirds of UK water comes from rain captured and brought to our doors in this way, the rest from ground sources – aquifers, wells and springs. Huge efficiency gains could be had from more local capture and differentiated use, especially for drought susceptible areas like the South East: roof capture for toilets and washing machines, water butts and washing up water for gardens, for example. Globally, 70 per cent of water is used for irrigation, with variable efficiency. Widespread introduction of drip irrigation techniques using captured rainwater would help the gravely water-stressed regions of the world where currently over a billion lack access to clean water and well over two billion lack safe sanitation.

Whether it is the aggregate for constructing roads or the silver that is found in almost every gadget you own, we are profligate. Using a bottle many times over is more energy efficient than recycling aluminium cans. To create a proper closed circuit for use and reuse of rare metal we may have to change the way we 'own' things like mobile phones and computers. In future we may 'rent' them, making a substantial deposit to ensure the manufacturer gets them back.

No one really wants to buy energy. What we do want are the *services* provided – heat, power and light. The minute you start to think of the most efficient way to get those services near to where you live or work, a whole new perspective on generation and distribution is opened up. The *least* efficient is large centralized generation with long distribution lines. The most efficient – and the most resilient should things go wrong here or there – is very local generation (using the best options for that particular geographical location) and a hugely intelligent grid that allows flows of electricity in and out of your building. Already 'smart' gadgets to go into white goods like fridges are being tested. They can switch your fridge on and off, balancing its needs with that of the grid to smooth out peaks of demand (like mass switching on of kettles at half-time in the Football Association Cup Final). Energy expert Amory Lovins underlines the 90 per cent wastage built into the current system, a great deal of which is the responsibility of the end-user of the heat, power and light. Another 1GtC/yr wedge from Pacola and Sacolow comes from reducing the carbon emissions from all buildings by a quarter by 2054. Cutting back on what comes into the building, and becoming ultra-efficient in what is used is not a practical problem with the technologies and process we have now, it is just that we don't use them. Car makers too know how to produce ultra-efficient vehicles, it is just that they don't. Perversely, policy and infrastructure are geared to consuming more energy, rather than securing *enough* heat, power and light in the most carbon effective way (see www.rmi.org, the website of Amory Lovins' Rocky Mountain Institute).

It is not easy to calculate how much embedded water and energy there is in the goods and services that are exchanged in the high street, online, or through providers of services, like information and communication technologies (ICT), the NHS, universities, local authorities or banking. But it is likely that all of them could achieve large efficiency savings. Some supermarkets and service providers like BT and Eurostar have taken on the challenge, but as the section on corporate responsibility in Chapter 5 points out, progress is too slow for comfort. The physics of being ultra-efficient in energy and water use are not the problem. The fact it is still cheaper to be wasteful, is. Here consumer power could make the difference, as the growth in socially responsible investment, fair-traded and organic goods suggests it might. Key to efficiency will be to learn from poorer communities about thrift, craftsmanship and making things to last.

In the UK, of the food we purchase around 40 per cent is thrown away. Even more is wasted through the now vast food processing industry. Globally, the FAO estimates one third of food grown goes into animals, one fifth into fuel tanks. Immoral in a world where so many starve. It is better and cheaper to cook your own food, not least because the fewer the number of processes between field and mouth, the less the nutritional loss and chances of contamination – though in countries like the UK many people have never learnt to cook, or say they are too busy.

On the other hand sharing the cooking load around family members and friends has increased, and growing your own has become popular, with London (80 per cent dependent on food imports) hiring its own food champion, www.lda.gov.uk (search Chair of London Food), and Michelle Obama starting a White House allotment.

Buying native food from other countries, like runner beans from Kenya, is contested as a way to feed rich cities like London, and whatever the energy budget it is certainly not ideal. Creating dependences on one or two 'cash crops' in poor countries is probably unethical. What happens if the crop fails, or we stop buying? Long distance trading relationships need to be efficient in not only energy and other resources, but also socially responsible. That means not only fair trade but also trade that is regenerative and sustaining of locally resilient communities at both ends. If a Ghanaian community is dependent for its livelihood on selling pineapples to the UK, it is not resilient. As with all land and marine resources, the production of food for human consumption should be a matter for conservation and intensifying quality – the foundations of an ecologically resilient economy. Not, as it seems to be at present, an extractive industry.

If you haven't jumped ahead already to learn more about the IPAT equation and the Princeton Wedges that inspired this chapter, here is more about them. In their own right they are helpful models for working out what to do next.

Two models for thinking about sustainability on a global scale

These two models for thinking holistically about *un*sustainability (IPAT) and about how to tackle it (Princeton Wedges) I've found really helpful, both in explaining the challenge to others, and in maintaining some clarity about the interconnectedness of it all in my own mind. Neglecting that interconnectedness in resolving particular problems is, of course one reason we've got into such a mess. Only problem solving across the grand lines and linking local action to global as well as local benefits will get us out of it. Here is some background to both IPAT and the Princeton Wedges.

IPAT – The 'all important equation'

In 1971, in time for the first Earth Summit, Paul Ehrlich and John Holdren published a paper in *Science* to explain the relationship between environmental impact and human activity (the subject of the conference).[6] The equation they used was picked up and elaborated into the I=PxAxT equation by Barry Commoner who said 'Pollution emitted is equal to the product of three factors – population times the amount of a given economic good per capita times output per unit of the economic good produced.'[7]

I   is **Impact** on the environment

=

P   is **Population** (number of people)

x

A   is **Affluence**, or consumption per capita (of energy and materials but as manifest in the gross national product calculations of goods and services produced by the human economy)

x

T   is the **Technology (or Techniques)** of that consumption that determine how efficiently it uses those resources.

Although presented as a matter of multiplication, with the state of the natural world determined by the total number of people multiplied by both the total amount of raw materials and energy they consume and the manner (efficiency) of that consumption, a crude relationship between the factors does not necessarily hold good. For example, a doubling of a population does not necessarily mean a doubling of resource consumption. But for people like me, this equation provided an intellectual lifeline for explaining the relationship between the different factors contributing to *un*sustainable development.

Paul Ekins and Michael Jacobs were amongst those who tried to extend understanding of the relationship by attempting to 'solve' the equation while recognizing the constraints involved. Using available evidence they set the value of I by concluding that our impact on the environment needed to halve by 2050. Filling in the other known information for P and A, they were able to analyse what the value of T needed to be if environmental sustainability (50 per cent reduction in impact) was to be achieved.

I   50 per cent reduction from current (c. 1997) impact by 2050 (various sources)

=

P   Population set to rise by 9–11 billion by 2050 (United Nations)

x

A   Growth of consumption (GDP) of about 3 per cent per year

x

T   the value of which has to represent
50 per cent (more efficient use of resources) if no growth in P or A
66 per cent if growth in P but no growth in A
81 per cent if growth in P and A in South
89 per cent if growth in P and A takes place in the North
91 per cent if growth in P and A takes place in both North and South

(Ekins and Jacobs, 1995; Ekins, 2000)

The value for T, as with the value of other components of the equation thus moves under different assumptions about each of them. A lower population, consuming fewer resources (lower GDP as it is currently calculated), might mean we could get away with lower efficiency rates, for example.

For me, what is missing from the IPAT equation is the inclusion of people in any way other than their number. And the potential variability of I. Nature, as represented by I, can have its capacity to clean up after us augmented. Trees and other greenery can be planted as well as destroyed. Furthermore, in both these areas – that of natural and human/social capital – a lot of growth could be enjoyed without using a lot of resources. Including these two refinements, the IPAT equation becomes NPHAT – not at all elegant, but definitely offering a more positive and realistic agenda for future action than IPAT could do on its own.

So, maybe overboldly, I have amended this revered method for conceptualizing the relationships between the environment and human activity. First by making much clearer that the natural world can be recruited as a partner in mopping up our mess, and secondly by incorporating people as a positively contributing factor, cashing in, literally, on our innately collaborative and creative selves to work with the environment and for each other. As argued elsewhere in this book, that is the sort of economic transformation that has to take place.

The new formulation is therefore as follows, with the reminder that the equation is not technically solvable, but designed to help think of the whole and the magnitude of the challenge, rather than its mathematical precision. For me, these are the five grand lines we need to think along from where we are now to where we want to be 40 years from now.

Natural capital: Halt degradation and instead grow natural capital by 25 per cent (from now) by 2050

=

Population: Hit the *lower* world population prediction of 8 billion by 2050

x

Human/social capital: Increase individual and communal sense of well-being by (say) 50 per cent from today's levels by 2050

x

Affluence: Shrink human take of (non-solar) energy and raw materials by 25 per cent from current levels by 2050 (i.e. leave it in the ground)

x

Technology/techniques of consumption: Squeeze all waste and inefficiency out of energy (including solar) and material use by (say) 50 per cent from today's levels by 2050

The Princeton Wedges

The Princeton Wedges are so called because they were developed by two academics from the Carbon Mitigation Institute at Princeton University: Stephen Pacala and Robert Socolow.[8] Cited in the Stern Report (2006) and forever after, the authors are primarily concerned with climate energy and activities that would first stabilize greenhouse gas emissions within 50 years and then set them on track to reduce by half between then and the end of the century. As Figure 9.1 below shows, there is a triangle formed by the deviation of the stabilization-to-reduction path from the business as usual (BAU) path. Into this triangle, Pacala and Socolow introduced seven wedges, each representing a '50 year mitigation strategy' for reducing annual greenhouse gas emissions by one gigatonne, so bringing the BAU line down to meet the stabilization-to-reduction trajectory. They propose a number of 'candidate' actions (15) that, in any combination of seven, would produce the same outcome. For example, strategies to replace 1400GW 50 per cent efficient coal plants with gas plants, or cutting carbon emissions by a quarter in buildings and appliances, or increasing fuel economy for two billion cars from 30 to 60mpg each have the potential to remove 1GtC/yr from the emissions inventory by 2054. Many strategies cannot plausibly grow big enough to provide a whole 'wedge', say Pacala and Socolow. But by considering candidate actions together as whole or partial contributions to one or more wedges, trade-offs and synergies

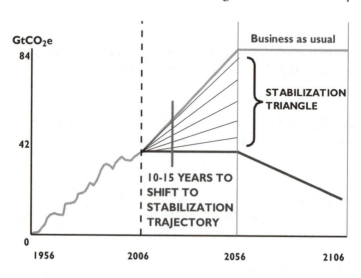

Source: adapted from Socolow and Pacola, 2004

Figure 9.1 The Princeton Wedges

can be identified. Putting too few eggs in the basket too soon might also mean missing critical CO_2 emission reduction targets should some eggs fail to hatch after it was too late to incubate different options.

In my variation, I've suggested five 'wedges' for each of the five grand lines (NPHAT) of the sustainability to do list. Each wedge could have several 'candidate actions'. The same principles would apply as for an energy only model – the more wedges and candidate actions tackled the better to increase chances that some will, wholly or in part, come good within the timescale.

Conclusion

Design your own

The purpose of this chapter is to offer a framework to help sustainability-literate leaders make the interconnections between the grand lines of our global sustainability to do list, and our own efforts back home. There should be enough in it to provide a useful conceptual framework to keep day to day decisions on track for the larger goals of sustainable development. As before, readers are encouraged to adapt NPHAT and the models behind it to their own needs. No model should come in the way of practical wisdom and our ability to do the right thing.

So, like other tools in this book, you can use the basic NPHAT equation to customize the 'wedges' yourself. Best of all, whether you are learning about sustainability or implementing actions, you can involve others to design wedges of actions that best fit local circumstances. Self-designing a suite of actions is motivating, and one of the best ways to turn words into reality. Pacala and Socolow came to the same conclusion and have developed a teaching tool where learners are asked to debate the merits of different contributions and design their own wedges. See The Teachers Guide to the Stabilisation Wedge Game on Princeton University's Carbon Mitigation Institute, www.cmi.princeton.edu. It is concentrated on energy and water, but can be easily adapted to take in the broader NPHAT sustainability factors, without which, it could be argued, the necessary reduction to dangerous levels of greenhouse gases will be unachievable.

Prologue

The Future Starts Now

Do the right thing. This will gratify some, and astonish the rest

Mark Twain

The future starts now

Prologues normally come at the beginning not the end of a book. This one, however, is designed to come at the start of your career as a sustainability-literate leader who is wise to, and increasingly confident in, the arts of positive deviance. Not as an epilogue to what has come before, but as a prologue to the rest of your life.

By now, I hope, you will understand *sufficiently* your own role in these spectacularly challenging times, and will be ready to heed the message that it is leadership that changes the game. Nothing is preordained. Good leadership can decrease the severity of negative developments and increase the likelihood of positive ones. You will be brave in letting governments and organizations know what you expect from them, and no less ambitious for yourself and your neighbours. Your powers of persuasion, imagination and example will mobilize ever more recruits to the cause of sustainability.

What *you* do from now on could not matter more.

The other reason for making now – the moment you arrive at the end of this book – the point where the future really starts, is because we have been here before. Coincident with the first Earth Summit in 1972, a team from the Massachusetts Institute of Technology (MIT) published a book, *Limits to Growth* (LtG) (Meadows et al, 1972). Using newly developed 'systems dynamic' computer modelling they, for the first time, linked the world economy with the environment and ran a series of scenarios, including a business-as-usual one, called the 'standard run'. This scenario predicted 'overshoot and collapse' of populations and economic systems sometime in the *21st century* unless there were early changes in behaviour, policy and technology. Immediately, the authors were subject to sustained false claims and criticisms, as Rachel Carson was ten years earlier when she published *Silent Spring*. The biggest lie, still repeated, is that LtG predicted collapse during the *20th century* and as this didn't come to pass the whole thesis was thus discredited.

In 2008, academic Graham Turner reran the LtG scenarios, adding 30 years of *real* historical data from 1970 to 2000. He found a close fit between reality over that period and the LtG business-as-usual scenario, proving their predictions are indeed coming to pass – *in the 21st century*. On the other hand, reality did not fit with the mitigating scenarios based on different policies for stabilizing growth, or relying on technological change. Turner proved 30 years on, and several international conferences later, that policy has so far not made any significant dent in the worst-case scenario or any of its environmental or economic variables.[1]

So, here we are again, nearly 40 years later, after yet another big and unsatisfactory conference (on climate change, in Copenhagen) and with a redoubling of the efforts of the deniers, naysayers and those who work cynically to subvert any attempt to change the business-as-usual scenario – just as they did in 1972 and at every twist and turn since. Early in 2010, *Nature* magazine warned climate scientists that attacks on them are only superficially about the science, and that they 'must acknowledge they are in a street fight'.[2] So, what will be different this time?

Quite a lot, I would say. The perversity of the way we run our affairs and the corruption or carelessness of too many people in leadership roles may not melt away as quickly as you and I might wish, but never before has the failure of current leadership models and priorities been so visible. Their negative effects on people and the environment, and their dependence on bad governance practice, have exposed the nakedness of the business-as-usual Emperor. That *Nature* editorial would not have been written even five years ago.

Consequently, as we square up to a fiendishly difficult couple of decades that will determine whether the 21st century is a human triumph or a tragedy, there is a search on for a new logic in which to make sense of what to do next. For me, and I hope by now for you, the only logic that seems to fit the bill is sustainability, where growing environmental and human and social capital in pursuit of a good life well lived becomes the purpose of the 'toil and bustle' of our lives. In that logic there is what Susan Neiman calls a philosophical basis for understanding the difference between the actual and the possible, and a framework for getting there (Neiman, 2009, p92).

A cautionary word. We will have to mobilize all our leadership skills to defend this new logic. 'It's unrealistic' will be the most common objection you will hear. But don't fall for it. Calls for reality are calls to lower your expectations. The counter question has to be: 'Where will your reality take us, what logic is it pursuing?' Arguing for sustainability means that, if we want the ideal, we will have to strain very hard for it. Aim high and we might get most of it, if not all. And even if we do fall short, that is likely to be *good enough*. Aim low and we are bound to fail. Being asked to accept the *realpolitik* means bowing to someone else's reality.

Part of championing sustainability will mean differentiating it from an ideology. That is a bounded collection of ideas, like Thatcherism or socialism, which, if applied to a given situation, is expected to come up with a recognizable solution or policy. As we are surrounded by the failure of the ideological approach to governing and to solving the very 'wicked' (complexly interrelated) problems we face, why develop another one? Gillian Tett remarked that it is the finance world's lack of interest in wider social matters that goes to the very heart of what went wrong (Tett, 2009). No, sustainability is not a hard edged 'ism'. Nor, though it is a new way of thinking about the world around us and our place in it in a spiritual as well as a practical sense, is it a religion. Sustainability is more like a moral obligation, something that can take each of us in a different way even though we may be joined by a commitment to a similar end. Because we are all starting from a different place, there are many paths to sustainability. Anyone can join in without taking an oath or paying a membership fee.

Susan Neiman also argues that morality is not God-given, and that is not even discernable in the rest of nature. It is human made. If the world is not what it should be, it is up to us to open our eyes and close the gap between what is, and what ought to be. If we want moral clarity, she says, we have to put it there. We have to do the living in truth. We have to do the right thing. No one can do it for us. Our ideas and words must be powerful, of course, but in the end it will be our actions that are convincing.

For me, that sounds like a *good enough* creed for sustainability-bound positive deviants!

The purpose of this book is to help you feel the same. I've tried to expose you to a deeper and broader way of thinking about sustainability, as well as to the excitement around the new ideas for making it happen, in a way that is interesting and sometimes provocative. I hope I leave you stirred and confident enough to set out on your own sustainability leadership journey, starting on Monday.

Even though our various paths mean we may never actually meet, I nevertheless look forward to working with you from now on.

Sara Parkin
Isle of Islay,
March 2010

I don't mind if my future is long or short, as long as I'm doing the right thing. And as long as I behave for other people

The late Henry Allingham, First World War veteran, when aged 112
(Observer Magazine, 9 November 2008, p13)

Appendix
Positive deviants

DANIEL BARENBOIM has spent a lifetime in a passionate relationship with music, and has played with and conducted great orchestras
around the world. Barenboim's other passion, the situation in the
Middle East, however, causes him daily pain: 'I can't stand injustice.
Every day it brings suffering; both to Palestinians and Israelis.' In 1999
Barenboim set up the West-Eastern Divan Orchestra, with young musicians from Israel, West Bank, Syria, Lebanon, Egypt, Jordan, Turkey
and more recently Iran. The orchestra now plays concerts around the
world, including famously and only after intense diplomatic negotiations, Ramallah in 2005. He also challenged Israeli audiences when he
performed Wagner in Jerusalem in 2001. 'Doing the impossible has
always attracted me more than doing the difficult. When you attempt
the impossible, failure is what is expected, so whatever you do to avoid
that is already a positive result.' He believes in music as a force for
harmony and change: 'There is a lot one learns from music... You have
to express yourself but, simultaneously, you have to listen to what the
others are playing. Just think what a lesson that is for life: how our life
would be and how our politicians would be if they could think like this.
That is why every child should have a musical education.'

On a different continent, another to see the potential of music to
heal and tackle crime and poverty is the Venezuelan Jose Antonio Abreu
who established *El Sistema*, a network of music education and child and
youth orchestras for the poor. Participation in music, he has proved,
helps 'the fight of a poor and abandoned child against everything that
opposes his full realization as a human being'.

www.danielbarenboim.com; Anthony Holden (2009) 'The whole world
in his hands', *The Telegraph*, 3 August; Paul Kendall (2009) 'Playing for
peace', *The Telegraph*, 9 August; Ivan Hewitt (2008) 'El Sistems: Music
of hope from the barrios', *The Telegraph*, 30 May.

The BAREFOOT COLLEGE started by training poor, usually rural, illiterate or semi-literate men and women to be 'barefoot engineers' who could, for example, install solar energy equipment in remote areas. The idea of *good enough* knowledge and *sufficient* skills to get on and do what is needed, is not new, but Bunker Roy, who set up the Barefoot College in Rajasthan, India has taken the 'barefoot' concept to scale in different areas delivering social and environmental benefits – water collection, night schools, health centres, housing.

www.barefootcollege.org

JOHN BIRD, himself a one-time social deviant in the negative sense, is now a leading activist and social entrepreneur on behalf of the poor, homeless and otherwise socially excluded. With the backing of Body Shop founders Anita and Gordon Roddick, in1991 he founded the *Big Issue*, to be sold by homeless people as an alternative to begging. Now sold all over the UK and in different versions in many other countries, the *Big Issue* is typical of John Bird's approach – instead of handouts, help people to help themselves: back to self-esteem and dignity, back to control over their own lives. Which is why he objects to soup kitchens, saying: 'we wouldn't feed our dogs on the street, so why feed people there?' His many schemes, events and other services for his 'vendors' he runs through the *Big Issue Foundation* set up in 1995. In 2006 he launched the *Wedge Card*, a loyalty card for independent traders in London.

www.bigissue.com; www.wedgecard.co.uk

DAVID CADDICK was the presiding judge at the trial of the six Greenpeace activists accused by owner E.ON for causing criminal damage to the UK Kingsnorth coal fired power station in September 2008. Activists climbed a smoke stack to protest against government plans to build a new station on the site. Summing up, Judge Caddick said the case centred on whether or not the protesters had a lawful excuse for their actions. For this defence to be used, he explained to the jury, it must be proved the action was due to an immediate need to protect property belonging to another. The defence argued this was the case, bringing evidence that the daily 20,000 tonnes of CO_2 emitted by the existing plant caused damage to the climate, to species and to the parts of Kent vulnerable to sea-level rise. Moreover, it was not reasonable to argue against similar plants proliferating in China, yet let them proliferate in the UK. The jury agreed, setting a legal precedent with potentially significant consequences. In December 2008 *The New York Times* included the Kingsnorth defence in its list of influential ideas that will change our lives.

www.greenpeace.org; Fiona Harvey, 'Greenpeace six cleared of damaging power plant', *The Daily Telegraph*, 11 September 2008.

JAMES CAMERON is an international lawyer who specialized in climate change for many years. His expertise in developing policy responses is recognized globally. Cameron negotiated the UN Framework Climate Change Convention and the Kyoto Protocol, provides legal advice to the Alliance of Small Island States, and advises or is on the board of a wide range of not-for-profit, campaigning and private organizations – all concerned with tackling climate change. Frustrated at the slow pace of real action to prevent CO_2 entering the atmosphere from human sources, Cameron set up a new company, Climate Change Capital, to demonstrate that a low-carbon economy can offer attractive returns to investors through funds that invest in companies, projects and technologies that provide products and services that facilitate climate change mitigation or adaptation. The company's philosophy and values are enshrined in its strapline: Creating Wealth Worth Having.

www.climatechangecapital.com

The CARROT MOB organizes 'gangs' of consumers to make purchases that give financial reward to a local shop or bar that agrees to make socially beneficial changes to the way it does business. The focus is on providers of weekly staples and everyday activities in neighbourhoods rather than on specialist outlets. Local stores are invited to 'bid' the percentage of the takings they will spend on environmental upgrades and the Carrot Mob arranges the mob of consumers. Better a positive incentive than the stick of a boycott, the organization claims. Word about 'mobs' is spread through MySpace, Facebook, blogging, Twitter, Digg and YouTube. The idea was started in the San Francisco neighbourhood of founder Brent Schulkin and has been emulated elsewhere in the US, and other countries, including the UK.

www.carrotmob.org and www.carrotmobUK.org

THE CO-OPERATIVE BANK rather gleefully describes itself as 'good with money'. The difference – the innovation – that keeps the Co-operative Bank good with money is not, paradoxically, being a cooperative as such, but the fact that it has operated an ethical policy for 15 years. The policy is set by a poll of its own customers and governs where the bank and its financial and insurance operations lend and invest. Since 1992, the Bank has turned away £1 billion worth of corporate loans in conflict with its customers' concerns, yet grown its commercial lending over the same period by 13 per cent per year to £4.2 billion. A refresh of the bank's ethical policy at the end of 2008 adds high global warming potential fuels, cluster bombs, or activities that involve exploitation of great apes to its no-go areas. In these muddy financial times, The Co-operative Bank is 'a clear demonstration that ethics can deliver a sustainable business model'.

www.cfs.co.uk

DIVINE CHOCOLATE became the first farmer-owned Fairtrade chocolate bar aimed at the mass market when it was launched in 1998. A cooperative of cocoa growers in Ghana called Kuapa Kokoo decided to start making their own chocolate in 1993, and then to go on and make and sell their own chocolate bars via the Day Chocolate Company. Kuapa Kokoo remains a cooperative, holding an ownership stake in The Day Chocolate Company, where two Kuapa Kokoo members are board directors. Co-founders of The Day Chocolate Company, The Body Shop, donated its shares to the Kuapa Kokoo in 2006. Divine entered the US market in 2007. It is delicious.

www.divinechocolate.com

THE ECOLOGY BUILDING SOCIETY was founded by Yorkshire solicitor David Pedley in 1981. Struggling to find a mortgage for an old property he wanted to renovate, he decided to start his own building society. Currently the society has 10,000 open accounts and assets of over £60 million. Savers (and borrowers) are thought of as members and 'share' in the objectives of the society, which includes a special deposit fund for charities. The society has unique lending criteria, including an assessment of the environmental impact of the project, and will lend on non-conventional things like earth shelters and breathing walls. It also lends on properties that have been turned down by other lenders, offering flexible arrangements that, for example, release 'up front' funds based on the unimproved value of the property, with further releases as the work progresses and the value rises.

www.ecology.co.uk

W L GORE and Associates is a private company, founded in 1958, which specializes in applications of polytetrafluoroethylene (PTFE – to be found in Gore-Tex® outdoor clothing, Teflon and heart valves for example. See www.masds.chem.ox.ac.uk for information about PTFE). However, W L Gore is cited here for the way it organizes itself, something that regularly earns it top scores in 'best company to work for' listings. Technically, the Gore management model might be classed as 'organized chaos' with a flat corporate hierarchy and associates instead of employees. CEO Terri Kelly says that the firm's corporate culture doesn't mean there is no discipline, but 'you have to *almost* give up power'. Business units are split if they get too big and teams self-organize. Decisions are reached by agreement, leaders emerge through a democratic process (even the CEO), and peer appraisal decides salary levels and career advancement. Essentially, W L Gore is an advanced engineering company, focusing on the needs of customers, and on the lookout for new markets. It has a third and equal objective – 'to enable our associates to grow and develop, expanding their horizons' – because it finds that the best way to achieve the first two. Associates sign up to core values designed by founder Bill Gore: fairness, freedom, commitment, waterline (meaning don't do anything that might harm the company without consulting other associates). It's the nearest I've seen ecological principles manifest in an organizational structure.

www.gore.com; Stefan Stern and Peter Marsh, 'The chaos theory of leadership', *Financial Times*, 2 December 2008.

VACLAV HAVEL was the last President of Czechoslovakia, and then the first President of the Czech Republic, serving until 2003. It was as a playwright, poet and dissident that Havel first reached international attention, when, after the 1968 Prague Spring, when Russia crushed Czech reformist leader Alexander Dubek's plans to install more freedom, Havel's works were banned in his own country. He chose to stay in Czechoslovakia but to 'live in truth' – that is, behave as if his freedoms had not been snatched away. Consequently, he was frequently in prison and continually harassed. In 1977 he published the dissidents' manifesto, *Charter 77*, and after the collapse of communism in 1989, went on with Civic Forum to win 80 per cent of the vote and become president. He kept the fissiparous factions on track for the main objective and reminded everyone once they were in power what power was for. In his *Summer Meditation: A meditation on politics, morality and civility in a time of transition*, Havel concludes that a state should be 'an intellectual and spiritual state – a state based on ideas not ideologies … as something [its people] see as their own project and their own home, as something they need not fear, as something they can – without shame – love, because they have built it for themselves'. Dubbed the 'philosopher-king', Havel's is an exemplar of how to behave with public probity when out of, and in, power.

www.vaclavhavel.cz is his personal official website (in English)

WANGARI MAATHAI won the 2004 Nobel Peace Prize for her contribution to sustainable development, democracy and peace. She founded the deliciously subversive but anodynely titled Green Belt Movement of Kenya in 1977, under the auspices of the National Council of Women of Kenya. On the face of it a tree-planting exercise promoting the benefits of plantations to villages of shade, soil improvement and so on, the Green Belt Movement simultaneously and often covertly built the capacity of women, passing on information about nutrition, family planning, education, environmental protection. Over 30 million trees have been planted in Kenya, and the UN picked up on the Green Belt's development model for other countries. Wangari challenged President Daniel arap Moi's regime to move to multi-party elections and end corruption and tribal politics, which earned her much harassment and several periods in prison. Like Havel, her international network of supporters ensured she could not 'disappear'. Eventually, in 2002, she was elected to parliament. Her citation for the Nobel Peace Prize said she 'stood up courageously against the former oppressive regime in Kenya. Her unique forms of actions have contributed to drawing attention to political oppressions – nationally and internationally. She has served as inspiration for many in the fight for democratic rights and has especially encouraged women to better their situation.'

www.greenbeltmovement.org

NELSON MANDELA served as the first democratically elected President of South Africa from 1994 to1999 after a total of 27 years in prison for crimes committed as an anti-apartheid campaigner and leader of the armed wing of the African National Congress. His enforced reflection during his years in prison could have made him crazy and bitter, but didn't. Instead Mandela concentrated on strategies to end apartheid peaceably, the most important of which was the doctrine of truth, reconciliation and non-violent negotiation. During his time in prison, Mandela studied law by correspondence course, and formed a clandestine 'university' in which fellow inmates taught each other all they knew. ANC members outside prison were asked to do the same and to encourage young people into education, all in readiness to participate in the new South Africa. All the time, Mandela was single-mindedly preparing for the moment when Africans could share power, and with his colleagues thinking through the negotiations with the white leaders and the route to peaceful elections. An extraordinarily positive and hopeful agenda with no guarantees it would ever be implemented, Mandela's stature and authority grew, and by the time he was released, his quiet reasonableness was a major factor in the smooth transition to democracy. Mandela also established The Elders, a group of people, working largely behind the scenes, who 'have the trust of the world and can speak freely, be fiercely independent and respond fast and flexibly in conflict situations'.

www.nelsonmandela.org for Mandela's foundation and his own writings, www.theelders.org for The Elders

PRESIDENT FESTUS MOGAE of Botswana received the 2008 Ibrahim Award for good governance, a refreshing, positive story from a continent that has suffered more than its fair share of bad leadership. Mogae took his country from civil war to multi-party democracy, tackled corruption (particularly around the diamond industry) and diversified the economy. With HIV/AIDS at epidemic levels (30 per cent of the population infected) he put in one of Africa's most progressive programmes and is now working on a continent-wide campaign. His guiding principle and code of conduct, he told the people of Botswana in his final address as president, was 'prudent, transparent and honest use of national resources for your benefit'. By the time he stepped down after two terms in 2008 (in itself commendable) Mogae had established strong and independent institutions to maintain the rule of law and respect for human rights, and improved the country's infrastructure, including health and education. During his presidency Botswana achieved gender parity in tertiary education. It may seem odd to cite as a positive deviant someone who was simply committed to good governance. But the story of Mogae, and Botswana under his presidency, is a story of how it is sometimes necessary to tackle a lot of big challenges at the same time, as each can reinforce the other. Doing lots of right things, whatever the difficulty. Mo Ibrahim and his foundation deserve special mention too for establishing the Africa prize.

www.moibrahimfoundation.org

BARACK OBAMA is 44th President of the United States of America. It may be early days, but I suspect we may have a positive deviant in the White House. Even Obama's campaign broke free of the negative grind of political fund-raising, through clever use of modern technology and careful re-engagement of citizens in the political process – especially those most alienated by it – young people, women, non-whites. And, like President Mogae, there is evidence Obama knows his success will depend on tackling many big challenges simultaneously, and that he is thinking strategically both for that, and for himself personally. He appears committed to 'living in truth' (as a basis for trust) and has made it clear he understands the powers (and the vulnerabilities) of the US, and therefore its responsibilities. Let's hope he can – come good, that is.

www.whitehouse.gov

ONLY CONNECT is a creative arts company and resettlement charity that works with prisoners and ex-offenders. Using drama, offenders are helped to restore their lives practically and emotionally. Different from the other sorts of good work that go on in this area, Only Connect not only makes the effort to help the offender reach deep into themselves, buts also sticks with them as long as they need. The organization's purpose is to avoid recidivism and it uses customized evaluation methods to assess progress. 'Only Connect is remarkable. Those [prisoners] engaged with their projects receive an extraordinarily high quality of both professional and personal support. Only Connect assists offenders' effective rehabilitation in ways that many organizations are unable to achieve', says Jacquie Harvey, Head of Learning and Skills, HMP Holloway.

www.onlyconnectuk.org

THE PRINCE OF WALES has carved out a singular career as King-in-Waiting, fulfilling duties expected of the role, but also going further to champion a wide range of initiatives and causes. He uses his convening powers to bring together people, money and ideas around areas that interest him or that he thinks matter – often the same thing. His positive deviant status comes from his judicious, often brave, use of his position to bounce urgent issues out of the shadows and into wider public attention. A few examples of where HRH has acted like an early warning system include spirituality and multi-faith engagement, food in schools, climate change, sustainability accounting, business leaders' responsibility to the environment, integrating conventional and complementary health. Unfazed by the sometimes hostile response of the press, The Prince of Wales usually comes in behind his call to action with a pre-planned initiative designed to keep up the pressure for change. He doesn't have to do all this, but he does.

www.princeofwales.gov.uk

The RushCard is the brainchild of **RUSSELL SIMMONS**, a US 'street entrepreneur' and 'godfather of hip hop', who is revered by urban youth. Essentially a prepaid Visa card, the RushCard is targeted at the estimated 48 million Americans, but particularly the young, who either have a bad credit history, or no credit history at all. It is the only credit card not to charge for its services, and enables individuals to enjoy the freedom of a credit card (obtaining money from ATMs, in stores or online) while staying in control of their spending. After five years of operation, RushCard is celebrating the management of over $2 billion worth of deposits. Cardholders can save with RushCard, track their spending, receive text alerts (on balances), and even transmit their payment history to consumer credit checking agencies in order to (re)build positive money management profiles.

www.rushcard.com

SANDBAG is an organization founded by seasoned climate campaigner Bryony Worthington in September 2008. Bryony became frustrated with the small effect the various trading schemes were having on actually reducing the tonnes of CO_2 emitted, so she set up Sandbag. Members are able to buy 'permits to pollute', each worth 1 tonne of CO_2, but instead of using or trading them through the EU Emission Trading Scheme, for example, Sandbag 'retires' them for you instead. So for each 'permit' retired, 1 tonne of CO_2 is not emitted and the overall 'cap' on available permits is brought down. At £25 a tonne this makes a novel gift, but potentially a significant example of civilian activism if enough people and organizations get involved.

www.Sandbag.org.uk.

The SEIKATSU CLUB CONSUMERS' COOPERATIVE UNION (SC) started life as a Japanese housewives' social movement in1965. Members are committed to 'alternative economic activity against industrial society's prioritization of efficiency'. Seikatsu means life and the club is seeking 'a fair world and a higher quality, more sustainable way of life, through people's actual daily life activities'. With around 22 million members, organized in local groups (99 per cent of them women) and a turnover of $640 million (2006) the SC works with dedicated suppliers for chemical-free food and other household goods that meet their standards. The Seikatsu Club is also a social movement reaching far beyond its household consumables activities. From the start, the women became active in local politics, through a Seikatsusha (inhabitants) Network that now has 140 elected representatives working to protect the environment and improve the welfare system. Highly democratic and devolved, the SC is also active in Japan on home and institutional care for the aged, and internationally through campaigning on issues (pesticide-free bananas) or injustice and worse to local communities by the huge multinational corporations.

www.seikatsuclub.coop/english

MUHAMMAD YUNUS is a serial social entrepreneur. Best known for the Grameen Bank (meaning village bank) he established in Bangladesh, in 1983 he launched the micro-credit movement by lending to poor people for income-earning activity. He thus liberated many people from the grip of extortionate moneylenders and rapacious middlemen and gave hope to what he calls the bottom 50 per cent. Yunus banks, literally, on the capacity of people to help themselves, saying trust and positive incentives (including saving) are more effective than legal documents. About 95 per cent of the customers are women, no collateral is required, but far from being subprime, about 98 per cent of the loans are paid off. Grameen Bank has about 7.5 million borrowers, with an average loan of $150. The bank is 96 per cent owned by its borrowers, and 9 of its 12 directors are women. Yunus is campaigning to remove the legal barriers to ethical micro-finance programmes and social enterprise becoming more mainstream. He's proposed an equivalent of the Hippocratic Oath (and some laws) to sort out the speculators from the social financiers.

www.grameen-info.org; Muhummad Yunus, 'How legal steps can help to pave the way to ending poverty', *Human Rights Magazine*, Winter 2008, vol 35, no 1 (published by the American Bar Association)

ZOPA (Zone of Possible Agreement) has been called the eBay of capitalism. It is an on-line service that enables people (members who pay a small fee) to borrow from and lend to each other directly without a bank in sight (person to person (P2P)). Over the 2008/09 financial year ZOPA lenders enjoyed a 9 per cent return on average. In the UK there are 260,000 members with over £37 million in loans arranged since its start up in 2005. The matchmaking service provided by ZOPA includes checking the credit-worthiness of borrowers, and for the lenders, classifying into five different risk 'markets' – A, B, C, D and Young for those too young to have history of repaying debts. Lenders pick a market, and set a time limit and an interest rate. To manage risk your money is spread across a number of borrowers. So far the bad debt rate is 0.3 per cent. There is no category for sustainability right now, but there could be.

http://uk.zopa.com

Notes

Introduction

1 *The Guardian* (2009) 'Climate change summit hijacked by world's biggest polluters, critics claim', 25 May
2 Playfair, J. (1805) 'Biographical account of the late Dr James Hutton FRSEdin', *Transactions of the Royal Society of Edinburgh*, vol 5, pp18–19.
3 For a very understandable description of the scientific foundations for the 'social brain' see Appendix B in Daniel Goleman (2006).
4 Grayling, A. C. (2008) 'Mindfields', *New Scientist*, 3 May.

Chapter 1 The Symptoms

1 Daly, H. E. (2005) 'Economics in a full world', *Scientific American*, vol 293, issue 3.
2 Vitosek, P. M., Erlich, P. R., Erlich, A. H. and Matson, P. A. (1986) 'Human appropriation of the products of photosynthesis', *Bioscience*, vol 36, no 6, pp368–373. See also Vitosek, P. M., Mooney, H. A., Lubchenco, J. and Melillo, J. M. (1997) 'Human domination of earth's ecosystems', *Science*, vol 277, 25 July.
3 WWF (2008) Living Planet Report.
4 'UK troops face Congo ordeal', *The Observer*, 2 November 2008.
5 UN Environment Programme, 'From conflict to peacebuilding: The role of natural resources and the environment', February 2009, UNEP, Nairobi.
6 www.worldcoal.org (accessed 6 March 2010). The estimate has dropped from 130 years in less than two years.
7 Could be as soon as 2020 according to the UK Energy Research Council. Sorrell, S. and Spiers, J. (2009) *Global Oil Depletion: An Assessment of the Evidence for Near-term Physical Constraints on Global Oil Supply*, UKERC unpublished report. www.ukerc.ac.uk.
8 International Energy Authority, www.iea.org. See also Global Witness (2009) *Heads in the Sand*, www.globalwitness.org, and Leggett (2005).
9 Toni Johnson, 'The return of resource nationalism' in Council on Foreign Relations, 13 August 2007. www.cfr.org/publications.
10 www.domino.lancs.ac.uk.
11 Worldwatch Institute (2006) *Vital Signs 2006–2007*, Worldwatch, Washington DC, www.who.int/heli.

12   McMichael, A. J. (2009) 'Human population health: Sentinel criterion of environmental sustainability', *Current Opinions in Environmental Sustainability*, vol 1, pp101–106.

13   Figure 1.4 is adapted from one in a 2000 Report of BIFFA, a UK waste company. See also Cradle to Cradle, modern life cycle analysis in Tools for change in Chapter 8.

14   www.wupperinst.org. A German research institute that has worked extensively on the concept of the ecological rucksack.

15   See report *Ocean Acidification: The facts,* at www.naturalengland.org.uk.

16   This list taken from a *Climate Science Statement* published by the Royal Society on 24 November 2009, www.royalsociety.org. See also www.aaas.org; Anderson, K. and Bows, A. (2008) 'Reframing the climate change challenge in light of post-2000 emission trends', *Phil. Trans. R. Soc. A* doi:10.1098/rsta.2008.0138 and 'Climate change and human influence', www.metoffice.gov.uk.

17   John Beddington, Government Chief Scientific Advisor, in a speech to UK Sustainable Development Conference, 19 March 2009. The term 'perfect storm' is also used by Dr James Hanson of NASA.

18   Robins, N., Clover, R. and Singh, C. 'A climate for recovery: The colour of stimulous goes green', HSBC Global Research, www.research.hsbc.com.

19   *Public Attitudes to Climate Change 2008: Concerned but still unconvinced*, Ipsos MORI, May 2008 and Climate Change Omnibus: Great Britain, Ipsos MORI, 24 February 2010.

20   Ekins, P. (2008) 'The government's fallacious use of carbon pricing means that it can disguise its aviation expansion as alleviating climate change', *The Guardian*, 13 February 2008.

21   Prins, G. and Raynor, S. (2007) 'Time to ditch Kyoto', *Nature*, vol 449, pp973–975, 25 October.

22   www.greenfiscalcommisssion.org.uk.

23   Omana, A., Orr, D., Ostrom, E., Young, O., Hawken, P., Barnes, P., Costanza, R. (2008) 'Creating an Earth Atmospheric Trust: A system to control climate change and reduce poverty', *Grist*, 2nd January 2008, www.grist.org.

24   www.teqs.net.

25   www.sandbag.org.uk.

26   'A changing climate of opinion', *The Economist*, 4 September 2009.

27   'Geoengineering the climate: Science, governance and uncertainty', *The Royal Society*, September 2009, www.royalsociety.org.

28   www.climatecongress.ku.dk.

29   Holdren, J. P. (2008) 'Convincing the climate-change skeptics', *The Boston Globe*, 4 August.

30   Paul Brown (2003) 'Debunker of a global warming found guilty of scientific dishonesty', *Guardian*, 9 January.

31   www.ejsd.org; The Scientific Alliance via the Cambridge Network, www.cambridgenetwork.co.uk/directory or directly at www.scientific-alliance.org.

32   Try www.lobbywatch.org or The Centre for Media and Democracy at www.sourcewatch.org. See too articles by *The Guardian* correspondent George Monbiot, www.monbiot.com (search climate change deniers).

33   www.heartland.org for the naysayers climate change conference in New York, 8–10 March 2009.

34   www.davidmiliband.defra.gov.uk/blogs/ministerial (now discontinued) and www.channel4.com/science/microsites/G/great_global_warming_swindle/; Tom Burke,

Ten Pinches of Salt: A Reply to Bjørn Lomborg, August 2001, www.greenalliance.org; and 'This is neither skepticism nor science – just nonsense', in *The Guardian,* 23 October 2004. The Royal Society: www.royalsociety.org.

35　In 1990, when the population of the world was 4.5 billion, the number living under a $1 a day was 1.8 billion or 42 per cent. The proportion today may be 21 per cent of a world population of 6.5 billion, but the absolute number 1.4 billion represents poor progress for 20 years of effort.

36　Millennium Development Goals, www.un.org/millenniumgoals.

37　Ban Ki–Moon (2010) 'Keeping the promise: A forward-looking review to promote an agreed action agenda to achieve the MDGs by 2015', *Report of the Secretary General to the UN General Assembly,* 16 March 2010.

38　António Guterres (2008) *Statement to the UNHCR Executive Committee,* 6 October 2008, Geneva

39　David Hirsch, Joseph Rowntree Foundation (2004). According to the US Census Bureau, one in eight Americans is living in poverty.

40　Paul Krugman, speaking in October 2007 at the Commonwealth Club of California.

41　UNDP Report (2001) *Deepening Democracy in a Fragmented World,* New York, UN Development Programme, p19.

42　Liddle, R. (2008) *Social Pessimism: The New Social Reality of Europe,* Policy Network Essay, October, www.policy-network.net.

Chapter 2 Anatomy and Physiology

1　Riddle, John M. (1992) Contraception and Abortion from the Ancient World to the Renaissance, Harvard University Press, Cambridge, Mass.

2　Adair Turner chaired a commission to review UK pensions. It published several reports, see www.pensionscommission.org.uk.

3　See, for example, Satterthwaite, D. (2009) 'The implications of population growth and urbanization for climate change', *Environment and Urbanisation,* vol 21, October, pp545–567, available at www.sagepublications.com. Also Fred Pearce, 'The overpopulation myth' *Prospect,* 11 March 2010.

4　See www.un.org/popin/data for the historic and predicted trends.

5　Jasanoff, S. (2007) 'Technologies of humility: Citizen participation in governing science', *Nature,* vol 450, pp33–34, 1 November.

6　See Palmer, M. and Finlay, V. (2003) *Faith in Conservation,* The World Bank, Washington DC; WWF International and Alliance of Religions and Conservation (2003) *Beyond Belief,* WWF, Gland. Also, Palmer, M. (2008) 'Sites of significance', *Resurgence,* no 250, Sept/Oct 2008.

7　In an interview published in *Green Futures,* 25 April 2008, Forum for the Future.

8　Luis Garicano is Professor of Strategy and Economics at the University of Chicago Graduate Business School and Director of Research at the London School of Economics Managerial Department, where this exchange took place. Reported by Simon Jenkins, 'It's not only the Queen. We're all screaming for an answer', *The Guardian,* 12 November 2008.

9　Taken from Denis Healey (1989) *The Time of My Life,* Michael Joseph, London pp550, 551. Healey was Chancellor of the Exchequer from 1974 to 1979.

10   Luca Pacioli (1495) *Summa de arethmetica, geometria, roportioni et proportionalita*. St Andrews University collates texts, articles and facts about Pacioli, who was an extraordinary man. He roomed with Leonardo da Vinci and is credited with teaching Leonardo about the 'golden rule' for proportionality in paintings. He also wrote a treatise on maths and magic!
11   See for example Herman, A. (2003) or Buchan, J. (2003) for an overview of the radical thinkers (the positive deviants) of the Enlightenment period.

Chapter 3 The Treatment

1   MacKenzie, D. (2008) 'Rich countries carry out 21st century land grab', *New Scientist*, 4 December, and Vidal, J. (2010) 'How food and water are driving a 21st century African land grab', *The Observer*, 7 March.
2   Over 1000 goods and services have been compared to establish an equivalence of different currencies. See the latest update of PPP by the International Comparison Programme at www.worldbank.org (these are 2005 figures, the latest available end of March 2010).
3   For more see Josh Ryan-Collins, 'Let's not put all our pounds in the one basket', 4 February 2009, www.neftriplcrunch.wordpress.com (accessed 7 February 2009), Ryan-Collins, J., Stephens, L and Coote, A. (2008) *The New Wealth of Time*, New Economics Foundation, 2 November, and www.letslink.org, and www.timebanking.org.
4   In UK Fair traded goods have risen from £17m to £713m in the decade to 2008, www.fairtrade.org.uk. Bachelor, L. (2010) 'Ethical funds feel investment surge', *The Observer*, 21 March.
5   Handy (1997, p155); Prospect, September 2009, p36.
6   There is in fact a tiny loss, so infinitesimal that it is a consideration only in timescales calculated in millions of years.
7   Turner, A. (2008) 'Dethroning growth', in Sims, A. and Smith, J. (eds)
8   Daly, H. E. (2010) 'A steady state economy: A failed growth economy and a steady state economy are not the same thing, they are very different alternatives we face', paper for UK Sustainable Development Commission, 24 April, p3.
9   Daly and Cobb (1990), Jackson (2009) and Victor (2008). See also Daly, H. E. (2005) 'The Illth of nations and the fecklessness of policy: An ecological economist's perspective', in the wonderfully titled *Post-autistic Economics Review*, issue 30, 21 March, www.paecon.net.
10   Quoted in *Responses to the Global Crisis: Charting a Progressive Path*, handbook of ideas produced for progressive governance conference, Chile, March 2009, www.policy-network.net.
11   Leading economists like Freidrick von Hayek and Milton Freidman saw themselves as 'freedom fighters' using guerilla warfare to get their ideas into power. UK economist Samuel Brittan described them as 'post-Keynsian counterrevolutionaries' engaged in a world war that would affect billions of people (Brittan, 1996). Their apogee of influence started when disciples Ronald Reagan and Margaret Thatcher came to power.
12   Macalister, T. (2008) 'Rebuild global economy through green investment', *The Guardian*, 22 October.
13   Turner, A. (2009) 'How to tame global finance', *Prospect*, September.
14   See for example Huber, J. (1999) 'Plain money: A proposal for supplying the nations with the necessary means in a modern monetary system', October, Institut fur Soziologie,

Martin-Luther-Universitat Halle Wittenberg. Huber and Robertson (2000) explain how this can be done with little disruption (a little big bang) and great simplification to the way the money supply is assessed and managed. See also the work of James Robertson, for example at www.jamesrobertson.com.

15   See James Robertson at www.jamesrobertson.com on monetary reform.

16   See also a range of examples in the UK and elsewhere via www.transitiontowns.org, or for cities, www.c40cities.org

17   This is not an ideological pitch for public ownership of banks. A more appropriate model would be a trust, like the National Trust. It may well be that a similar question will arise over water and energy companies, should business failure or strategic concern over shared resources occur. See, for example, Press Release R5 (3 February 2010) from Ofgem, UK's gas and electricity generator.

18   Adair Turner, Turner Review Press Conference, speaking notes, 18 March 2009, www.fsa.gov.uk.

19   Quoted in Hazel Henderson, *More advice for summiteers on reforming the global casino*, presentation to the Emergency Congress, 23–25 February 2009 in London, www.rightsandhumanity.org.

20   Jackson, T. (2008) 'The challenge of sustainable lifestyles', in *Worldwatch State of the World 2008: Innovation for a Sustainable Economy*, W. W. Norton, New York

21   Just a few examples to add to the others like Daly and Cobb (1990) and New Economics Foundation: Costanza, R., Hart, M., Posner, S. and Talberth, J. (2007) *Beyond GDP: The Need for New Measures of Progress*, Boston University, The Pardee Papers No 4, January 2009; Environment Commission (2007) *Summary notes from the Beyond GDP conference: Measuring progress, true wealth, and the well-being of nations*, European Commission, Brussels; Calvert Group (corporate author), Henderson, H., Lickerman, J. and Flynn, P. (2000) *Calvert–Henderson Quality of Life Indicators: A New Tool for Assessing National Trends*, Calvert Group, Bethesda, MD, www.calvert-henderson.com.

22   See Daly and Cobb (1990) for an American version, and for the UK see Jackson, T., Laing, F., MacGillivray, A., Marks, N., Ralls, J. and Stymne, S. (1997) *An Index of Sustainable Economic Welfare for the UK 1950–1996*, University of Surrey Centre for Sustainable Strategy, Guildford; and Jackson, T. and Marks, N. (2002) 'Measuring progress', new economics foundation and Friends of the Earth, London.

23   www.happyplanetindex.org.

24   www.stiglitz-sen-fitoussi.fr.

25   Robert Kennedy, address at the University of Kansas, Lawrence, Kansas, 18 March 1968.

26   In fairness, the FSA Chair, Adair Turner, is doing some pretty radical thinking. See, for example 'What do banks do? What should they do and what public policies are needed to ensure best results for the real economy', speech to the Cass Business School, 17 March 2010, available via www.fsa.gov.uk.

27   Elliot, F. (1999) 'President Lula of Brazil blames crisis on white and blue-eyed', *The Times*, 27 March.

Chapter 4 The Best and Worst of It: Leadership Today

1   Corbyn, Z. (2008) 'Did poor teaching lead to crash?', *Times Higher Education*, 25 September.

2   'The three habits of highly irritating management gurus', *The Economist*, 24 October 2009.

3   AACSB, *Management Education at Risk*, August 2002, www.aacsb.edu/publications, and Net Impact, *New Leaders, New Perspectives*, March 2009, www.netimpact.org.

4   British Library Research Service advanced search on its Integrated Catalogue on 2 April 2009, by Rupert Lee – to whom many thanks. Likewise thanks to the anonymous researcher at the Library of Congress for her/his comprehensive reply to my inquiry (received 6 April 2009).

5   Even the rock stars of management theory are not immune from bewitchment by some of the big villains. For example, described by *The Economist Magazine* as the 'world's reigning strategy guru', Gary Hamel extolled the leadership virtues of Enron's subsequently criminally disgraced CEO Kenneth Lay in a (non-ironically titled) 1997 article in *Fortune Magazine*: 'Turning your business upside down'.

6   Boehm, C. (1999) *Hierarchy in the Forests: The Evolution of Egalitarian Behaviour*, Harvard University Press, Cambridge, MA, p10.

7   Goffee, R. and Jones, G. (2001) 'Followership: It's personal too', *Harvard Business Review*, December.

8   Vidal, J. (2008) 'Not guilty: The Greenpeace activists who used climate change as a legal defence', *The Guardian*, 11 September.

9   After the Second World War, the Nuremburg Trials established a defence that the accused were following orders to be not legitimate.

10   Sun Tzu (544–496BC), a contemporary of Confucius who wrote *The Art of War*, a treatise on strategy and tactics that has influenced military and other leaders ever since.

11   Field Marshall Montgomery (1958) *Memoirs*, Collins, London; see Chapter 6: 'My doctrine of command'.

12   The John Adair Action Centred Leadership model – 'grip task, grip self, grip team' – is used by The Leadership Trust with Forum Leadership for Sustainable Development Masters students.

13   *Connect, collaborate, innovate*, Policy Briefing CCI/09, June 2007, NESTA, London.

14   National College of School Leadership, *Leadership Development Framework*, www.ncsl.org.uk.

15   *Financial Times*, 20 March 1998.

16   Mintzberg, H. (1987) 'The strategy concept 1: Five Ps for strategy', *California Management Review*, vol 30, no 1, pp11–24.

17   It is worth recalling Albert Einstein's remark: 'if a cluttered desk signs a cluttered mind, of what, then, is an empty desk a sign?'

18   Chapman, J. (2003) 'Public value: The missing ingredient in reform', in Bentley, T. and Wilsdon, J. (eds) *The Adaptive State: Strategies for Personalising the Public Realm*, Demos, London, p128.

19   Bennington, J. and Hartley, J. (2009) *Whole Systems Go!: Improving Leadership Across the Whole Public Service System*, National School of Government, August.

20   Ratzinger, J. (2004) *Letter to the Bishops of the Catholic Church on the Collaboration of Men and Women in the Church and in the World*, 31 July, Vatican.

21   Sealy, R., Vinnicombe, S. and Doldor. E. (2009) *The Female FTSE Board Report 2009*, Cranfield School of Management, www.som.cranfield.ac.uk.

22   Hausmann, R., Tyson, L. D. and Zahidi, S. (2009) *The Global Gender Gap Report 2009*, World Economic Forum, Geneva, Switzerland, www.weforum.org.

23 Equality and Human Rights Commission (2008) *Sex and Power 2008*, September, www.equalityhumanrights.com.

24 'The great pay divide', *Financial Times Magazine*, 26/27 September 2009.

25 Higher Education Statistics Agency (2007) *Destinations of leavers from HEIs*, October, HESA, www.hesa.ac.uk.

26 But see a comprehensive listing at www.guide2womenleaders.com for women in power in different cultures down the ages.

27 Chartered Institute of Personnel Development (2004) *Women in the Boardroom: A Bird's Eye View*, www.cipd.org.uk.

28 Adapted from Eagly, A. and Carli, L. (2007) 'Women and the labyrinth of leadership', *Harvard Business Review*, September.

29 'The double bind dilemma for women in leadership: Damned if you do, doomed if you don't', *Catalyst*, 17 July 2007, www.catalystwomen.org.

30 www.walmartclassaction.com for details of slow moving court procedures.

31 Halls, S. (2009) 'FT Top 50 women in world business', *Financial Times*, 25 September.

32 Quoted in 'Why women in business became the solution, not the problem', *The Guardian*, 5 February 2008.

33 'In ranks of millionaires, sisters are doing it for themselves', *The Scotsman*, 12 June 2007.

34 Joy, l., Carter, N., Wagner, H. and Narayanan, S. (2007) 'The bottom line: Corporate performance and women's representation on boards', *Catalyst*, October, www.catalyst.org/publications.

35 www.ifpri.org.

36 Sweetman, K. (2009) 'How women have changed Norway's boardrooms', from blogs.hbr.org, 27 July.

37 Coates, J. M. and Herbert, J. (2008) 'Endogenous steroids and financial risk taking on a London trading floor', in *Proceedings of the US National Academy of Science*, 22 April, vol 105, no 16, pp6167–6172. John Coates made the comment about tennis players when interviewed about this and other research on BBC Radio 4 lunchtime news on 13 January 2008.

Chapter 5 Business School Betrayal

1 Caulkin, S. (2008) 'When it came to the crunch, MBAs didn't help', *The Observer*, 25 October.

2 Walker, P. (2009) 'To what extent are business schools' MBA courses responsible for the global financial crash?', *The Observer*, 8 March.

3 Though even earlier examples exist, such as the Fenwick Weavers Society, which flourished in 1761.

4 Veracity Index 2009, www.ipsos-mori.com (accessed October 2009).

5 www.globalreporting.org.

6 *The Economist*, 'Just good business: A special report on corporate social responsibility', 19 January 2008.

7 See also Crook, C. (2005) 'The good company: A survey of corporate social responsibility', *The Economist*, 22 January.

8 Porter, M. and Kramer, M. (2006) 'Strategy and society: The link between competitive advantage and corporate social responsibility', *Harvard Business Review*, December.

9   Pearce, B. (2003) *Sustainabiltity and Business Competitiveness*, DTI and Forum for the Future, December.

10   Uren, S. (2007) 'Leaders of the pack', *Green Futures*, July.

11   Draper, S., Staafgård, L. and Uren, S. (May 2008) *Leader Business 2.0: Hallmarks of Sustainable Performance*, Forum for the Future, London.

12   www.wbcsd.org.

13   Grant Thornton LLP, 'Corporate Responsibility: Burden or Opportunity?', Survey of US Business Leaders, September 2007.

14   Corporate Leaders Group on Climate Change, 2006, *Letter to the Prime Minister*, 6 June 2006; on www.cpi.cam.ac.uk.

15   Bonini, S., Mendonca, L. and Oppenheim, J. (2006) 'When social issues become strategic: Executives ignore sociopolitial issues at their own peril', in *McKinsey Quarterly*, no 2, May 2006.

16   Oppenheim, J., Bonini, S., Bielak, D., Kehm, T. and Lacy, P. 'Shaping the new rules of competition: UN global compact participant Mirror' *McKinsey Quarterly*, July 2007

17   McLellan, A. (2007) 'CSR: The new climate', *The Independent*, 18 October.

18   Elkington and Hartigan (2008) p17.

19   Muhammad Yunus, *Nobel Lecture*, 10 December 2006.

20   Linklaters, with the Schwab Foundation for Social Entrepreneurship, *Fostering Social Entrepreneurship: Legal, Regulatory and Tax Barriers,* January 2006, www.linklaters.com/community/Schwabsummary.pdf.

21   *The New York Times Magazine*, 12 September 1970.

22   Henderson, D. (2001) *Misguided Virtue: False Notions of Corporate Social Responsibility,* Institute of Economic Affairs, London.

23   Cited in Nelson, J. (2006) 'A responsibility for governments: How far should companies go?', in Jordan, A. and Lunt, A. (eds) *Whose Responsibility: The Role of Business in Delivering Social and Environmental Change*, Smith Institute, London.

24   Kearney, A. T. (2009) 'Green winners: The performance of sustainability-focused companies during the financial crisis', www.atkearney.com (accessed 30 March 2010).

25   *Acting Now for a Positive 2018, Preparing for Radical Change: The Next Decade of Business and Sustainability*, Forum for the Future, December 2008.

26   Gloeckler, G. (2008) 'Here come the millennials', *Business Week*, 24 November.

27   www.beyondgreypinstripes.org.

Chapter 6 Four Habits of Thought

1   Hersch, T. (2002) 'Cod's warning from Newfoundland', *BBC Online*, 10 December.

2   An increasingly organized academic research group, the Resilience Alliance, is studying the way natural ecological systems manage resilience and trying to draw theoretical models to help human beings live sustainably within the natural systems. It's tough going at times, but very interesting with lots of important insights. Buzz Hollings is the recognized father of this way of thinking. See www.resalliance.org for references to his writings.

3   Report by the Commission on the Measurement of Economic Performance and Social Progress, www.stiglitz-sen-fitoussi.fr.

4   Policy Network Progressive Governance Conference, April 2008.

5   US Department of Defense news briefing, 12 February 2002.

Chapter 7 New Perspectives and Broad Knowledge

1   A dogma (settled opinion) or an ideology (way of thinking) are sometimes used synony-
    mously with world view, but strictly speaking are not the same thing. A political ideology,
    like socialism, or a dogmatic approach to how financial markets operate, say, may be the
    consequence of a world view, but equally may be maintained despite a change of world
    view.
2   Scruton, R. (2007) 'The sacred and the human', *Prospect*, August.
3   Kate Rawles, quoted in *The Engineer of the 21st Century Inquiry Report*, July 2000, Forum
    for the Future, London.
4   Puddington, A. (2010) 'Freedom in the world 2010: Erosion of freedom intensifies',
    12 January, Freedom House, London, www.freedomhouse.org. This essay anticipates the
    results of the full report to be published in spring 2010.
5   Lovins, A. (2004) 'More profit with less carbon', *Scientific American*, September,
    www.rmi.org.
6   *The Guardian*, 1 September 2008.
7   Daly, H. E. (2008) *A Steady State Economy*, paper for the UK Sustainable Development
    Commission project on Redefining Prosperity, 24 April, www.sd-commission.org.uk/
    pages/redefining-prosperity.html.

Chapter 8 Principles of Practice and Tools of the Trade

1   Khurana, R. and Nitain, N. (2008) 'It's time to make management a true profession',
    Harvard Business Review, October.
2   Desmond Tutu, quoted in Hallencreutz, C., Palmberg, F. and Palmberg, M. (eds) (1995)
    Religion and Politics in South Africa (seminar proceedings), The Nordic Institute, p72.
3   Franklin, B. (1732–1758, this edition 2007) *Poor Richard's Almamack*, Elibron Classics
    series, Adament Media Corporation, Boston.
4   Offerman, L. R. (2004) 'When followers become toxic', *Harvard Business Review*, 1 Janu-
    ary.
5   Goleman (1995) p119, citing Hoffman, M. L., 'Empathy, social cognition and moral
    action', in Kurtines, W. and Gerwitz, J. (eds) (1984) *Moral Behaviour and Development:
    Advances in Theory, Research, and Applications*, John Wiley & Sons, New York, NY.
    www.positivedeviance.org.
6   *Harvard Business Review* Special Centennial Issue, July–August 2008, p2 (directory
    section).
7   Quoted in a useful website (www.ecoliteracy.org).
8   Greenstock, J. (2008) 'Nations have to act locally in a globalised world', *Financial Times*,
    16 May.
9   *The Guardian*, 12/13 October 2006.
10 Thorpe, A. (2009) 'The uncertainty principle', in *Planet Earth*, NERC, Spring.
11 See for example, Prahalad, C. K. and Ramaswamy Venkat (2004) *The Future of Competi-
    tion*, Harvard Business School Press.
12 See for example, WWF Chemicals and Health Campaign, www.wwf.org.uk.

13   Lueneburger, C. and Murray-Bruce, R. (2009) *Sustainability Leadership: Making Change Happen. Part 1: The Executive*, Egon Zehnder International, March.

14   See for example Edvinsson and Malone (1997). A good starting point for organizational learning is online via Smith, M. K. (2001) 'The learning organization', *the encyclopedia of informal education*, www.infed.org/biblio/learning-organization.htm. See also www.solonline.org for the institution established by Peter Senge's Society for Organisational Learning.

15   *Learning and Skills for Sustainable Development: Guidance for Higher Education Institutions*, Forum for the Future, February 2004, www.forumforthefuture.org. The word 'competencies' was used in the tool, which was designed and first tested by Heloise Buckland and Andy Johnston in a project for the Chilean government in Antofagasta University.

16   See, for example, Georgescu-Roegen (1971) on the environment; Hirsch (1976) on social limits to conventional economic growth; Dasgupta and Seregeldin (1999) on social capital; and Sen (2000) on development economics. Also Daly and Cobb (1990) and Seregeldin and Steer, 'Epilogue: Expanding the capital stocks' in Seregeldin and Steer (eds) (1994).

17   See for example the Social reports of Wessex Water at www.wessexwater.co.uk, or Anglo American at www.angloamerican.oc.uk.

18   For examples see Forum for the Future's Higher Education Partnership for Sustainability (HEPS) Final Report, 2004, and Tourism, 2009. See also Chemical Leadership Council vision for the sustainable production and use of chemicals derived from their table, all at www.forumforthefuture.org/library.

19   More detail about The Natural Step and how it works at www.thenaturalstep.org. See also Robèrt et al (2004).

20   Chambers, T., Porritt, J. and Price-Thomas, P. (2007) *Sustainable Wealth Creation within Environmental Limits*, October 2007, Forum for the Future, www.forumforthefuture.org/library.

21   Forum for the Future has several examples of scenario planning in its library: see Climate Futures and Retail Futures for the retail sector, www.forumforthefuture.org/library.

22   PESTLE: Political, Economic, Social, Technology, Legislative, Environmental.

23   Parliamentary Office of Science and Technology (2008) *ICT and CO2 Emissions*, Postnote 319, December.

24   See UK government *Waste Strategy for England 2007*, Defra, London, and the year-on progress report.

25   www.forumforthefuture.org and search for Streamlined LCA.

26   Use Google to get at examples of LCA, industrial ecology and EMS. Look too at Janine Benyus (1997) for how innovation in the natural world can inspire human processes. For an (American) eye-opener on the life cycle of a car, cheeseburger, aluminum, a computer chip and more see Ryan, C. R. and Durning, A. T. (1997) *Stuff: The Secret Lives of Everyday Things*, New Report No 4, Northwest Environment, Seattle. It is short and expensive but very good at illustrating the boundaries for life cycle analyses of very different types of stuff.

27   Amongst other things ACCA run annual awards for sustainability reporting, www.acca.org.uk, and CIPFA collaborated with Forum for the Future on a reporting framework for public services published in 2006, www.cipfa.org.uk. Search the sites with the word sustainability.

28   See for example, www.st-andrews.ac.uk/~csearweb and the work of Jan Bebbington and Rob Gray.

29   www.sustainabilityatwork.org.uk/decision/ to see the report, then further click on 'appraisal and evaluation techniques' to get at the Sustainability Decision-Making Methodology.

30   www.wwf.org; www.globalactionplan.org.uk; www.actonco2.direct.gov.uk.

31   Walter Anthony, K. (2009) 'Arctic climate threat – Methane from thawing permafrost', *Sciencific American*, December.

32   Forum for the Future and Clean Air Cool Planet (2008) *Getting to Zero: Defining Corporate Carbon Neutrality*, at www.forumforthefuture.org/library.

33   *Nichomachean Ethics*, Book VI, Chapter 5 [1141b], translated by David Ross (1925) Oxford University Press, Oxford.

Chapter 9 The Global Sustainability To Do List

1   A biome is a large geographical area characterized by certain types of plants and animals. A biome is defined by the complex interactions of plants and animals with the climate, geology (rock formations), soil types, water resources and latitude (position north or south on the globe) of an area.

2   Sen, A. (2003) 'The importance of basic education', address to 15th Triennial Conference of Commonwealth Education Ministers, Edinburgh, 28 October.

3   Greenstock, J. (2008) 'Nations have to act locally in a globalised world', *Financial Times*, 16 May.

4   Giles, J. (2009) 'Eating less meat could cut climate costs', *New Scientist*, 10 February.

5   www.fao.org/docrep/010/ag049e/AG049E03.htm, last accessed 20 May 2009.

6   Ehrlich, P. R. and Holdren, J. P. (1971) 'Impact of population growth', *Science*, vol 171, pp1212–1217.

7   Commoner, B. (1971) *Closing the Environmental Circle: Confronting the Environmental Crisis*, Jonathan Cape, London, and Commoner, B. (1972) 'The Environmental Cost of Economic Growth', in *Population, Resources and the Environment*, US Government Printing Office, pp339–363.

8   Pacala, S. and Socolow, R. (2004) 'Stabilisation wedges: Solving the climate problem for the next 50 years with current technologies', *Science*, vol 305, pp968–972. The website of the Carbon Mitigation Initiative at Princeton: www.princeton/edu/~cmi.

Prologue: The Future Starts Here

1   Turner, G. M. (2008) 'A comparison of *The Limits to Growth* with 30 years of reality', *Global Environmental Change*, no18, pp397–411.

2   Editorial (2010) 'Climate of fear', *Nature*, 464, p141, 11 March.

Bibliography

A good read

A lightly annotated bibliography of texts referenced in this book, and a few extra that have influenced or informed me. I've come up with a top 15 (couldn't get it down to ten, sorry!) that should give you a good foundation. There are also five other 'starter' texts for each of the four knowledge themes, a highly selected few of the 'golden oldies' that set me off, and, so you can see the colour of their eyes, a couple of examples from the naysayers.

Top fifteen
Brown (2008)
Goleman (2007)
Grint (2000)
Jackson (2009)
Layard (2005)
MacDonaugh and Braungart (2002)
Mackay (2009)
Meadows (2009)
Neiman (2009)
Nye (2008)
Porritt (2006)
Reich (2007)
Sire (1997)
Wilson (1992)

Ethics and values
Des Jardins (2000)
Grayling (2003)
Midgley (2003)
Sandel (2009)
Spretnak (1997)

Science
Angier (2007)
Arthur (2009)
Harding (2006)
Smil (2006)
Wilsdon and Willis (2004)

A few 'golden oldies'
Capra (1982)
Carson (1962)
Ehrlich (1968)
Goldsmith and Allen (1972)
Khor (1957)
Leopold (1949)
Lovelock (1979)
Robertson (1973)
Schumacher (1973 and 1977)
Skolimowski (1981)

Even fewer naysayers
Lawson (2009)
Lomborg (2000)

People and community
Argyle (2001)
Handy (1993) and/or Hudson (1995)
Irwin (2001)
Mcfarlane (2005)
Warburton (1998)

Economics
Ariely (2008)
Daly and Cobb (1990)
Ekins et al (1992, 2000 edition)
Heilbroner (1953)
Lunn (2008)

Abrahamson, E. and Freeman, D. (2006) *A Perfect Mess: The Hidden Benefits of Disorder*, Little Brown, New York, NY

Adair, J. (1979) *Action Centered Leadership*, McGraw Hill, London

Adams, J. (1995) *Risk*, UCL Press, London

Angier, N. (2007) *The Canon: The Beautiful Basics of Science*, Faber and Faber, London
> The whole lot – from scientific process through physics, chemistry, evolutionary and molecular, geology to astronomy – told with gripping zest by a Pulitzer Prize winning journalist.

Ariely, D. (2008) *Predictably Irrational: The Hidden Forces that Shape our Decisions*, Harper Collins, London
> A very entertaining description of some of the experiments proving we often act in complex and unpredictable ways – undermining the model of rational predictable *homo oeconomus*.

Aristotle (1991) *The Art of Rhetoric*, Penguin, Harmondsworth

Argyle, M. (2001 edition) *The Psychology of Happiness*, Routledge, Hove
> A new edition of a hugely popular book first published in 1987. Lots of insights into both the outcomes and the methodologies of the psychological research into well-being.

Armstrong, K. (1993) *A History of God: The 4,000-year Quest of Judaism, Christianity and Islam*, Ballantine Books, New York City, NY

Armstrong, K. (2000) *The Battle for God: A History of Fundamentalism*, Ballantine Books, New York City, NY

Arthur, W. B. (2009) *The Nature of Technology: What it is and how it Evolves*, Allan Lane, London
> More accurately this is about our relationship with technology, how we use it, why we fear it, yet often have blind faith in it. But excellent too on what it is.

Azapagic, A., Perdan, S. and Clift, R. (eds) (2004) *Sustainable Development in Practice: Case Studies for Engineers and Scientists*, Wiley, London

Bannock, G., Baxter, R. E. and Davis, E. (2003) *The Penguin Dictionary of Economics*, Penguin Reference, London
> A good enough reference for economics, though it doesn't cover environmental or behavioural economics at all well. For consistency I've use its definitions throughout my book; I found the 2007 edition harder to understand.

Barton, H. (ed) (2000) *Sustainable Communities*, Earthscan, London

Bass, B. M. and Avolio, B. J. (eds) (1994) *Improving Organisational Effectiveness Through Transformational Leadership*, Sage, California

Bateson, G. (2000 edition) *Steps to an Ecology of Mind*, University of Chicago Press, Chicago, IL

Benyus, J. (1997) *Biomimicry*, Harper Collins, New York, NY

Biggs, J. and Tate, C. (2007 edition) *Teaching for Quality Learning at University*, Open University Press, Maidenhead

Brittan, S. (1996) *Capitalism with a Human Face*, London, Fontana Press

Brown, L. (2008) *Plan B (3.0): Mobilizing to Save Civilization*, W. W. Norton, New York, NY

A leading thinker on how to make sustainability work, this book is full of things for the global to do list. Unlike me, Lester Brown does go into cost and politics.

Bruce, S. (2000) *Sociology: A Very Short Introduction*, Oxford University Press, Oxford

An clear overview of sociology including: social construction, causes and consequences, the modern world and imposters.

Buchan, J. (2003) *Capital of the Mind: How Edinburgh Changed the World*, John Murray, London

Capra, F. (1982) *The Turning Point*, Wildwood House, London

The story of how we became disconnected from the natural world.

Capra, F. (1996) *The Web of Life: A New Scientific Understanding of Living Systems*, HarperCollins, London

More from the theoretical physicist, explaining how we are part of an indivisible whole that is life on Earth – a rich, readable intellectual tale; no formulae.

Capra, F. (2002) *The Hidden Connections*, Doubleday, New York City, NY

Capra takes the logical next step: translating the way life organizes into our social and institutional arrangements.

Carson, R. (1962) *Silent Spring*, Houghton Mifflin, Boston, MA

Huge at the time, including the disgraceful behaviour of the chemical industry and their political supporters (for which JFK apologized – somewhat late). Modern versions of the impact of chemical pollution abound, but tell the same story of corporate and political irresponsibility.

CEML (2002) *Managers and Leaders: Raising our Game*, Council for Excellence in Management and Leadership, London

Chambers, T., Porritt, J. and Price-Thomas, P. (2007) *Sustainable Wealth Creation Within Environmental Limits*, October, Forum for the Future, www.forumforthefuture.org/library

Chambers Dictionary (2003, 9th edition) Chambers Harrap, London

Chandler, A. D. (1977) *The Visible Hand: The Managerial Revolution in American Business*, Harvard University Press, Cambridge, MA

Clover, C. (2008) *The End of the Line: How Overfishing is Changing the World and What we Eat*, University of California Press, Berkeley, CA

A horror story.

Collins, J. (2001) *Good to Great*, Harper Business, London

Wishful thinking about what makes corporations successful.

Covey, S. (1992) *Principal Centred Leadership*, Simon & Schuster, London

A long-established management 'guru' used by *The Economist* Magazine to illustrate the habits of 'highly irritating management gurus', October 2009, p84

Cowe, R. and Porritt, J. (2002) *Government's Business*, Forum for the Future, London

Daly, H. E. (2008) *Ecological Economics and Sustainable Development, Selected Essays of Herman Daly*, Edward Elgar, Cheltenham

Daly, H. E. and Cobb, J. (1990) *For the Common Good: Redirecting the Economy Toward Community, the Environment and a Sustainable Future*, Greenprint, London
> An economist and a theologian give one of the very best journeys around what an economy that delivers sustainable development might look like. US oriented, but excellent for getting to grips with new economics without getting bogged down in equations.

Dasgupta, P. (2001) *Human Well-being and the Natural Environment*, Oxford University Press, Oxford
> For proper economists (lots of equations!), from a pioneering ecological economist.

Dasgupta, P. and Seregeldin, I. (eds) (1999) *Social Capital: A Multifaceted Perspective*, World Bank, Washington DC
> A collection of essays from many of the most important thinkers on social capital – what it is and how to measure its contribution to economic progress.

Dawkins, R. (1989) *The Selfish Gene*, Oxford University Press, Oxford

Dawkins, R. (2006) *The God Delusion,* Houghton Muffin, New York

Des Jardins, J. R. (2000) *Environmental Ethics: An Introduction to Environmental Philosophy*, Wadsworth, Belmont, CA
> An excellent guide to ways of thinking ethically about the environment.

De Soto, H. (2000) *The Mystery of Capital: Why Capitalism Triumphs in the West and Fails Everywhere Else*, Basic Books, New York, NY
> A robust and fascinating look at capitalism in practice in poor countries – and why it doesn't seem to work.

Diamond, J. (2005) *Collapse: How Societies Choose to Fail or Succeed*, Viking, New York, NY
> Salutory lessons from case studies of how past civilizations have collapsed – including Easter Island, Maya civilization. A baggy book that makes worrying parallels with what is happening in the US state of Montana today.

Doppelt, B. (2003) *Leading Change Towards Sustainability*, Greenleaf, Sheffield
> Based on a change management tool derived from Dana Meadows's systems thinking, a good guide to organizational change with sustainability in mind.

Dresner, S. (2002, 2nd edition 2008) *The Principles of Sustainability*, Earthscan, London
> Not principles as such, but a good stroll through the key intellectual milestones of sustainable development. Has a rather inconclusive and glum ending.

Drucker, P. F. (2001) *The Essential Drucker*, Collins Business, New York, NY
> Remains one of the few management gurus worth reading because he thinks and writes on the larger canvas of human existence.

Edvinsson, L. and Malone, M. S. (1997) *Intellectual Capital*, Harper Collins, New York, NY

Edwards, M. (2004) *Civil Society*, Polity Press, Cambridge
> A slightly academic but interesting look at what makes a society civil, and how to get it and keep it.

Ehrlich, P. R. (1968) *The Population Bomb*, Buccaneer Books, Cutchogue, New York, NY
> The book that caused a sensation, when the world population was half it is now.

Ehrlich, P. R. and Ehrlich, A. H. (2009) *The Dominant Animal: Human Evolution and the Environment*, Island Press, Washington DC
  An update 40 years on, with all the problems magnified.

Ekins, P. (ed) (1986) *The Living Economy*, Routledge & Kegan Paul, London
  A series of edited essays, based on contributions to The Other Economic Summit, which brought together pioneering thinkers about the 'new economics'. Worth a visit by newly initiated.

Ekins, P. (2000) *Economic Growth and Environmental Sustainability: The Prospects for Green Growth*, Routledge, London and New York, NY
  There are some formulae in this book but several chapters are excellent in discussing the key elements of environmental economics.

Ekins, P., Hillman, M. and Hutchinson, R. (1992, see 2000 edition) *Wealth Beyond Measure: An Atlas of New Economics*, Gaia Books, London
  Fabulous way to understand the new economics if you have no background at all.

Ekins, P. and Jacobs, M. (1995) 'Environmental sustainability and the growth of GDP: Conditions of compatibility', in Bhaskar, V. and Glyn, A. (eds) (1995) *The North, the South and the Environment*, Earthscan, London

Elkington, J. and Hartigan, P. (2008) *The Power of Unreasonable People*, Harvard Business Press, Cambridge, MA
  An analysis of and examples from social entrepreneurs who are breaking the mould of business models and motivations.

Elliot, L. and Atkinson, D. (2008) *The Gods that Failed: How Blind Faith in Markets has Cost us our Future*, The Bodley Head, London
  A rattling explanation of how the financial crash happened. Elliot is the economics correspondent of *The Guardian*.

Engelman, R. (2008) *More: Population, Nature, and What Women Want*, Island Press, Washington DC

Etzioni, A. and Carney. D. (eds) (1997) *Repentance: A Comparative Perspective*, Rowman and Littlefield, Oxford

Ferguson, N. (2008) *The Ascent of Money*, Allan Lane, London (Also a Channel 4 TV series)

Flannery, T. (2005) *The Weathermakers: The History and Future Impact of Climate Change*, Allan Lane, London

Florida, R. (2002) *The Rise of the Creative Class*, Basic Books, New York, NY

Frey, B. S. and Stutzer, A. (2002) *Happiness and Economics: How the Economy and Institutions Affect Human Well-being*, Princeton University Press, Lawrenceville, NJ

Galbraith, J. K. (1958) *The Affluent Society*, Houghton Miffin, New York, NY

Galbraith, J. K. (1977) *The Age of Uncertainty*, BBC-André Deutsch, London

Georgescu-Roegen, N. (1971) *The Entropy Law and the Economic Process*, Harvard University Press, Cambridge, MA
  From one of the founding father of ecological economics – very hard going!

Gibson, C. C., Andersson, K., Ostrom, E. and Shivakumar, S. (2005) *The Samaritan's Dilemma: The Political Economy of Development Aid*, Oxford University Press, Oxford

Gilbert, D. (2006) *Stumbling on Happiness*, HarperPress, London

Gintis, H., Bowles, S., Boyd, R. and Fehr, E. (eds) (2005) *Moral Sentiments and Material Interests: The Foundations of Cooperation in Economic Life*, The MIT Press, Cambridge, MA

> A very scholarly exposition of the truth that we are, at heart, moral beings who like to cooperate with each other.

Goldsmith, E. and Allen, R. (1972) 'Blueprint for survival', *The Ecologist*, vol 2, no 1, January; republished (September 1972), Penguin, London

> Massive impact at the time with a great definition of sustainability:
>
> *The principal conditions for a stable society – one that to all intents and purposes can be sustained indefinitely:*
> *1 minimum disruption of ecological processes*
> *2 maximum conservation of materials and energy – or economy of stock rather than flow*
> *3 a population in which recruitment equals loss*
> *4 a social system in which the individual can enjoy, rather than feel restricted by, the first three conditions.* (p30, Penguin edition)

Goleman, D. (1995) *Emotional Intelligence*, Bantam Books, New York, NY

> The book that started the modernization of management and leadership education. It gave permission to feel.

Goleman, D. (2007) *Social Intelligence: The New Science of Social Relationships*, Arrow Books, London

> One of the best overviews of why we evolved as social animals and what that means to the way we get on with each and do things in a modern world. Covers the basics of neuro-physiology.

Gore, A. (2006) *An Inconvenient Truth*, Bloomsbury, London

> The book of the PowerPoint presentation. A good way into the science, but weak on what is to be done.

Gore, A. (2007) *Assault on Reason*, Bloomsbury, London

> Big seller in US for its critique of the Bush administration and Congress for using fear and ideology to mask truth and reason.

Graedel, T. E. and Allenby, B. R. (1994) *Industrial Ecology*, Prentice Hall, Englewood Cliffs, NJ

Grayling, A. C. (2003) *What Is Good? The Search for the Best Way to Live*, Weidenfeld & Nicolson, London

> Particularly good and easy read on the classical ideas of the 'good life' through to how we lost the plot via various enlightenments and the need to return to ethics as a solution to our various crises. Gets sidetracked by his life mission to disprove the existence of God. Comprehensive bibliography into philosophy and ethics.

Grint, K. (2000) *The Arts of Leadership*, Oxford University Press, Oxford

> Four 'arts' of leadership – Philosophical Arts (identity); Fine Arts (strategic vision); Martial Arts (organizational tactics); Performing Arts (persuasive communication) – are used for an unsentimental analysis of the performance of leaders ranging from Hitler to Martin Luther King. If you read only one book on leadership *per se*, let it be this one.

Grint, K. (2005) *Leadership: Limits and Possibilities*, Palgrove McMillan, Basingstoke
  On the same theme as his 2000 book, a 'who, what, where, how' look at leadership with the same goal – how to guard against the consequences of bad leaders.

Hale, S. (2008) *The New Politics of Climate Change: Why We Are Failing and How We Will Succeed*, Green Alliance, London

Hampden-Turner, C. (1994) *Charting the Corporate Mind*, Blackwell, Oxford

Hampden-Turner, C. and Trompenaars, F. (1993) *The Seven Cultures of Capitalism*, Doubleday, New York, NY

Handy, C. (1987, 4th edition 1993) *Understanding Organizations*, Oxford University Press, Oxford
  Wise in a timeless way about running an organization.

Handy, C. (1997) *The Hungry Spirit*, Hutchinson, London
  The quest for purpose in the modern world – and a call to use our initiative to find out what it is.

Harding, S. (2006) *Animate Earth: Science, Intuition and Gaia*, Green Books, Totnes
  Whole earth science – a holistic view of the systems of life on Earth and a great introduction to James Lovelock's concept of Gaia (a modern revision of James Hutton's 18th century theory, backed by modern observations) and Deep Ecology.

Hart, S. (2005) *Capitalism at the Crossroads*, Wharton School of Publishing, University of Pennsylvania, Philadelphia, PA
  A practical business education look at how companies can 'go beyond greening' and find opportunities at the bottom of the pyramid to do good and make profit.

Hawken, P. (2008) *Blessed Unrest: How the Largest Movement in the World Came into Being and Nobody Noticed*, Viking Press, New York, NY
  An optimistic look at some of the many people and organisations doing the right thing in the USA.

Hawken, P., Lovins, A. and Hunter Lovins, L. (1999) *Natural Capitalism: Creating the Next Industrial Revolution*, Earthscan, London

Heifetz, R. (1994) *Leadership without Easy Answers*, Harvard University Press, Cambridge, MA

Heifetz, R. and Linsky, M. (2002) *Leadership on the Line: Staying Alive Through the Dangers of Leading*, Harvard Business School Press, Cambridge, MA

Heilbroner, R. (1953, latest edition 2000) *The Worldly Philosophers*, Penguin, Harmondsworth, London
  The perfect antidote to awe about economics and economists; a very readable book about the thoughts and foibles.of some of the classical theorists. The fact this book has been in print since 1953 speaks for itself.

Hemel, G. (2007) *The Future of Management*, Harvard Business School Press, Cambridge, MA

Herman, A. (2003) *The Scottish Enlightenment: The Scots' Invention of the Modern World*, Fourth Estate, London

Hines, C. (2000) *Localisation: A Global Manifesto*, Earthscan, London

Hirsch, F. (1976) *Social Limits to Growth*, Harvard University Press, Cambridge, MA

Huber, J. and Robertson, J. (2000) *Creating New Money*, New Economics Foundation, London

Hudson, M. (1995) *Managing without Profit*, Penguin, Harmondsworth, London
> A really good and straightforward book about setting up and managing a not-for-profit organization. Lots of tips for profit makers too.

Hutton, J. (1795) *Theory of the Earth*, Kessinger Publishing, www.kessinger.net

Irwin, A. (2006) *Sociology and the Environment: A Critical Introduction to Sociology, Nature and Knowledge*, Polity, Cambridge
> A cogent explanation of why environmental problems are the business of sociologists as much as natural scientists, and what insights they have to offer.

IPCC (Intergovernmental Panel on Climate Change) (2007) *Climate Change 2007: The Fourth Assessment Report*, www.ipcc.ch

Jackson, T. (1996) *Material Concerns*, Routledge, London
> Explains the universal laws governing the way energy and raw materials are processed through the economy in a very easy to understand way, and shows how the economy and industrial process would be different if this knowledge was applied in pursuit of sustainability.

Jackson, T. (2009) *Prosperity without Growth: Economics for a Finite Planet*, Earthscan, London
> Can we flourish without the growth-based economy we have now? Well, yes, but we will need a new definition of prosperity and a new ecological-macro-economics to help us organize to get there. Drawing on the now substantial body of 'new' economic thinking, this is a brilliant exposure of where it has got to now – and what needs to happen next.

Jacobs, M. (ed) (1996) *The Politics of the Real World*, Earthscan, London

James, K. and Burgoyne, J. G. (2001) *Leadership Development: Best practice guide for organisations*, Council for Excellence in Management and Leadership, London

Jasonoff, S. (2005) *Designs on Nature*, Princeton University Press, Princeton, NJ

Kellerman, B. (2008) *Followership: How Followers are Creating Change and Changing Leaders*, Harvard Business Press, Cambridge, MA
> As much about leadership as followership, from the author of *Bad Leadership: What it is, How it Happens, Why it Matters*.

Kelly, G., Mulgan, G. and Muers, S. (2002) *Creating Public Value*, www.strategy.gov.uk

Khanna, .(2008) *The Second World: Empires and Influence in the New Global Order*, Allen Lane, London

Khurana, R. (2007) *From Higher Aims to Hired Hands: The Social Transformation of American Business Schools and the Unfulfilled Promise of Management as a Profession*, Princeton University Press, Princeton, NJ

Kohr, L. (1957, 1978 edition) *Breakdown of Nations*, Dutton, London
> Kohr's self-depreciating style kept him less influential than Schumacher, whom Kohr influenced significantly: 'A teacher from whom I have learned more than from anyone else', he said. Kohr's thesis: 'There seems only one cause behind all forms of social misery: bigness.'

Kolb, D. A. (1984) *Experiential Learning: Experience as the Source of Learning and Development*, Prentice Hall, Englewood Cliffs, NJ

Kotter, J. (1990) *A Force for Change: How Leadership is Different from Management*, Free Press, New York, NY

Kotter, J. (1996) *Leading Change*, Harvard Business School Press, Cambridge, MA

Krosinsky, C. and Robins, N. (2009) *Sustainable Investing: The Art of Long-term Performance*, Earthscan, London

    Investments with a sustainability purpose are already outperforming the mainstream. What are they, how do they do it, and what is the future for them. Well written and easy to understand.

Krugman, P. (2008) *The Return of Depression Economics*, Penguin, London

Kübler-Ross, E. (1969) *On Death and Dying*, Scribner, New York, NY

Lane, R. E. (2000) *The Loss of Happiness in Market Democracies*, Yale University, New Haven, CT

    A scholarly but readable explanation of how and why subjective well-being is reducing in more affluent economies, and what might be done to change this, including questions about the role of democracy and freedom of choice.

Lang, T. and Heasman, M. (2004) *Food Wars: The Battle for Mouths, Minds and Markets*, Earthscan, London

Lawson, N. (2009) *An Appeal to Reason: A Cool Look at Global Warming*, Duckworth, London

Layard, R. (2005) *Happiness: Lessons from a New Science*, Penguin, London

    An economist's take on the scientific evidence that happiness (subjective well-being in a moral, well-lived life) makes a better (more realistic) goal for economics, with a nine-point recommendation to policy makers on how to make it happen.

Layard, R. and Dunn, J. (2009) *A Good Childhood: Searching for Values in a Competitive Age*, Penguin, London

Leggett, J. (2005) *Half Gone: Oil, Gas, Hot Air and the Global Energy Crisis*, Portobello Books, London

Leighton, A. (2007) *On Leadership: Practical Wisdom from the People Who Know*, Random House, London

Leopold, A. (1949) *A Sand County Almanac*, Oxford University Press, New York, NY

Famous for his 'land ethic'.

Levitt, R., Christie, I., Jacobs, M. and Therivel, R. (2003) *A Better Choice of Choice*, The Fabian Society, London

Lomborg, B. (2000) *The Skeptical Environmentalist*, Cambridge University Press, Cambridge, New York, NY, Oakleigh, Madrid and Cape Town

    A very long book from a statistician denying that environmental degradation is a problem. He got into trouble for the ethics of the way he manipulated statistics, and proves the importance of using quality sources.

Lovelock, J. (1979) *Gaia: A New Look at Life on Earth*, Oxford University Press, Oxford

    A Nobel Prize worthy insight into how the world really works.

Lovelock, J. (2006) *The Revenge of Gaia*, Allan Lane, London

    An angry man reflects on the consequences of not acting on the evidence he and others presented a long time ago.

Lovins, A., Datta, K., Bustes, O.E. and Koomey, J. (2005) *Winning the Oil Endgame: Innovation for Profits, Jobs and Security*, Rocky Mountain Institute, Boulder, CO

Lunn, P. (2008) *Basic Instincts: Human Nature and the New Economy*, Marshall Cavendish, London

> Contrasting the model of Marketopia with that of Muddleton, Lunn exposes a basic flaw in the way orthodox economics understands human behaviour.

Macfarlane, A. (2005) *Letters to Lily: On How the World Works*, Allen and Unwin, London

> Letters from a grandfather, an anthropologist to his granddaughter explaining why the world and people are the way they are.

Macintyre, A. (1981) *After Virtue: A Study in Moral Theory*, Duckworth, London

Mackay, D. J. C. (2009) *Sustainable Energy: Without the Hot Air*, UIT Cambridge, Cambridge, and on-line

> Quite the best source for reliable figures on climate change and energy options.

Margulis, L. (1998) *The Symbiotic Planet: A New Look at Evolution*, Phoenix, London

McMahon, D. (2006) *The Pursuit of Happiness*, Allan Lane, London

> Of the canon of 'happiness' books this one gives an overview of the history of the search for human happiness that is not about just feeling good, but being good too. It has a happy ending.

McDonough, W. and Braungart, M. (2002) *Cradle to Cradle: Remaking the Way we Make Things*, North Point Press, New York City, NY

> Excellent on how to close technological and biogeochemical material loops.

MEA (Millennium Ecosystem Assessment) (2005) *Ecosystems and Human Well-being: Synthesis*, Island Press, Washington DC

Meadows D. (2009) *Thinking in Systems*, Earthscan, London

> From the lead author of *The Limits to Growth*, a painless entry into the world of systems thinking – finalized by friends after her sudden death.

Meadows, D. H., Meadows, D. L., Randers, J. and Behrens III W. W. (1972) *The Limits to Growth: A Report for the Club of Rome's Project on the Predicament of Mankind*, Earth Island Press, London

Midgley, M. (2003), *The Myths We Live By*, Routledge, London

> We need myths and symbols to help us find meaning in life. But have we got the right ones? See also her other writings.

Mill, J. S. (1848, 2004 edition) *Principles of Political Economy*, Prometheus Books, Amherst, NY

Millennium Development Goals, www.un.org/millenniumgoals

Miller, G. (2009) *Spent: Sex, Evolution and the Secrets of Consumerism*, William Heinemann, London

> About the turbo-consumption motor at the heart of our economy. Is this as good as it gets? Still time to evolve differently. Read in conjuction with Levitt et al on a better choice of choice.

Mintzberg, H. (1994) *The Rise and Fall of Strategic Planning*, Pearson Education, Harlow, Essex

Mintzberg, H., Ahlstrand, B. and Lampel, J. (2005) *Strategy Bites Back: It is a lot More and Less, Than you ever Imagined*, FT Prentice Hall, London
> A real miscellany of contributions including an admiring Gary Hamel interview with the criminally indicted (and now late) Kenneth Lay, former CEO of Enron. Definitely for fun, and confirmation of one of the contributor's assertions that 'there is more vacuity about strategy than about any other topic in business today'.

Monbiot, G. (2000) *The Captive State*, MacMillan, London
> A no-holds-barred on how government's dependence on business and wealthy individuals undermines democracy.

Monbiot, G. (2007) *Heat: How to Stop the Planet Burning*, Allan Lane, London
> A gripping account of Monbiot's attempt to work out how to get the heat, power and light we currently use without fossil fuels.

Mulgan, G. (2006) *Good and Bad Power*, Allan Lane, London
> An excellent review of how states originated and how power is both accumulated and circumscribed in the modern world. An argument for government as servant to the whole world and the future. An excellent summary of the arguments at the end offers a model that others could follow with benefit.

Mulgan, G. (2009) *The Art of Public Strategy: Mobilising Power and Knowledge for the Public Good*, Oxford University Press, Oxford
> A little old-fashioned in the chapter on leadership, but excellent on strategies for implementing and evaluating public policy.

Myers, I. B. and McCaulley, B. H. (1985), *Manual: A Guide to the Development and Use of the Myers-Briggs Type Indicator*, Consulting Psychologists Press, Palo Alto, CA

Naess, A. (Rothenburg, D. tr) (1990) *Ecology, Community and Lifestyle: Outline of an Ecosophy*, Cambridge University Press, Cambridge
> Not for the fainthearted, but lots of learning from an intellectual pioneer.

Neiman, S. (2009) *Moral Clarity*, Bodley Head, London
> A brilliant analysis of the 'metaphysic' of the right (ambiguous) and left (non-existent) in the US. A delicious settling of political scores but a most readable book that doesn't let the reader off the hook of clarifying their own morality.

NIC (2008) *Global Trends 2025: A Transformed World*, National Intelligence Council (US), November, US Government Printing Office, Washington DC or www.dni.gov/nic.

Nye, J. (2008) *The Power to Lead*, Oxford University Press, New York, NY
> From the man who introduced soft and hard power to the political toolbox – what every leader should know.

Ostrom, E. (1990) *Governing the Commons: The Evolution of Institutions for Collective Action*, Cambridge University Press, Cambridge
> Alternatives to state or market-based solutions for looking after the environment – proving that locally crafted solutions work better in theory and backed by lots of practical examples to learn from.

O'Toole, J. (1995) *Leading Change: The Argument for Values-based Leadership*, Jossey-Bass, San Francisco, CA

Owen, D. (2009) *The Hubris Syndrome: Bush, Blair and the Intoxication of Power*, Politicos, London

Palmer, M. (1992) *Dancing to Armageddon*, Aquarian/Thorsons, London
  An exploration, via science and religion, of how to fuse the spiritual and physical stories of human development and our future.

Parkin, S. (2000) 'Sustainable development: The concept and the practical challenge', *Civil Engineering*, vol 138, November, paper 12398, pp3–8

Pearce, F. (2007) *When the Rivers Run Dry*, Bantam, London

Porritt, J. (2000) *Playing Safe: Science and the Environment*, Thames & Hudson, London
  A brief and enjoyable excursion through (mostly) the politics of science and how it has variously ignored or misinterpreted its role in safe-guarding the environment and supporting sustainable development.

Porritt, J. (2006) *Capitalism: As if the World Matters*, Earthscan (paperback for US edition 2007, also Earthscan), London
  A deeper insight into the different sorts of capital that matter in the world, and the challenges of change.

Postel, S. and Richter, B. (2003) *Rivers for Life*, Island Press, Washington DC
  Excellent on the importance of protecting watersheds and the dangers of failing to arrest the rate of degradation.

Putnam, R. (2000), *Bowling Alone: The Collapse and Revival of American Community*, Simon & Schuster, New York, NY
  The great title conjures an image of lonely people going bowling on their own instead of in convivial teams and leagues and serves well to examine the drop in participation in community and democratic life in America, why it has happened and how it may be reversed.

Randers, J. and Meadows, D. (2005) *Limits to Growth: The 30-year Update*, Earthscan, London

Ravetz, J. (2006) *The No-nonsense Guide to Science*, New Internationalist, London
  'Post-normal science' (enquiry that is issue driven, where facts are uncertain and values in dispute, stakes high and decisions urgent) means recognizing the need of multiple perspectives from science and the affected public.

Real World Coalition and Jacobs, M. (1996) *The Politics of the Real World*, Earthscan, London
  What the UK NGOs recommended the incoming administration should do – sadly still salient.

Real World Coalition, Christie, I. and Warburton, D. (eds) (2001) *From Here to Sustainability: Politics in the Real World*, Earthscan, London
  Another good overview of sustainability from the point of view of UK NGOs.

Rees, M. (2003) *Our Final Century*, William Heinemann, Portsmouth, NH
  A far-reaching (literally) exploration of the question: Will the human race survive the 21st century? The Astronomer Royal joins the green movement in explosive fashion. Not a solutions-oriented book, but it ends contemplating the odds that our biosphere is 'the unique abode of intelligent and self aware life within our Galaxy'.

Reich, R. B. (2007) *Supercapitalism: The Transformation of Business, Democracy and Everyday Life*, Knopf, New York, NY
  Of the many critiques of capitalism, this is one I like a lot – it tackles head-on the intertwined world of business and government.

Riddle, J. M. (1992) *Contraception and Abortion from the Ancient World to the Rennaissance*, Harvard University Press, Cambridge, MA

Robèrt, K.-H., Basile, G., Broman, G., Byggeth, S., Cook, D., Haraldsson, H., Johansson, L., MacDonald, J., Ny, H., Oldmark, J. and Waldron, D. (2004) *Strategic Leadership towards Sustainability*, Blekinge Institute of Technology, Karlskrona, Sweden

> A bit techie, but one of the first course books devoted to sustainability. Light on the leadership side.

Robertson, J. (1978) *The Sane Alternative: A Choice of Futures*, James Robertson, Cholsey

> One of the earliest syntheses of environmental and social outcomes as goals for progress, the SHE (sane, humane, ecological) economy is explained along with strategies for change, and scenarios should we choose differently.

Rosenzweig, P. (2007) *The Halo Effect*, Free Press, New York, NY

Rowe, W. D. (1977) *The Anatomy of Risk*, Wiley, New York, NY

Sandel, M. (2009) *Justice: What's the Right Thing to Do?*, Allan Lane, London

> A brilliant book based on Sandal's Reith lectures. So well written it is a page turner.

Sarkissian, W., Vaida, S., Hofer, N., Shore, Y. and Wilkinson, C. (2009) *Kitchen Table Sustainability*, Earthscan, London

> Lots about how to do community engagement and local initiatives to tackle unsustainability.

Schumacher, E. F. (1973) *Small is Beautiful*, Abacus (1975 edition), London

> Straplined: *A Study of Economics as if People Mattered*, this book provided important intellectual underpinning for the green movement's view of the economy.

Schumacher, E. F. (1977) *A Guide for the Perplexed*, Jonathon Cape, London (see Vintage 1995 edition)

> A philosophical map for navigating the massive change implicit in being on the wrong path of progress, though understanding four fields of knowledge – my inner world, the inner world of others, myself as an objective phenomenon, the world around me – and ensuring all are properly 'cultivated'.

Schumpeter, J. (1942) *Capitalism, Socialism and Democracy*, Harper and Brothers, New York, NY

Scruton, R. (2002) *The West and the Rest: Globalisation and the Terrorist Threat*, ISI Books, Wilmington, DE

Sen, A. (2000) *Development as Freedom*, Anchor Books, New York, NY

> In a world where deprivation is to be found even in the richest countries, Sen argues that social commitment to individual freedom is the route to justice and equality.

Sen, A. (2006) *Identity and Violence*, London, Allen Lane

> A great explanation of why our search for identity, as an individual or a culture, does not need to be prosecuted through conflict and war. How to obtain peace by respecting the humanity and diversity of others rather than resorting to tribalism. Should be read by every head of state and newspaper editor in the world.

Sen, A. (2009) *The Idea of Justice*, Allan Lane, London
A synthesis of Sen's thinking to date. A philosophical tour de force from an economics Nobel Prize winner. Start with this one – though it is longer and you'll need to concentrate.

Senge, P. (1990) *The Fifth Discipline: The Art and Practice of the Learning Organization*, Doubleday, New York, NY
A seminal text on systems thinking to create a learning organization.

Senge, P. (1990) *The Dance of Change: The Challenges of Sustaining Momentum in Learning Organizations*, Nicholas Brearley, London
Full of ideas, tools, stories about managing organizational change in a systemic way. Lots of good insights but hard to pull out a practical process to use straightaway.

Seregeldin, I. and Steer, A. (eds) (1994) *Making Development Sustainable: From Concepts to Action*, World Bank, Washington DC
An early exploration of the role of different types of capital in an economy.

Sims, A. and Smith, J. (eds) (2008) *Do Good Lives Have to Cost the Earth?*, Constable & Robinson, London
Uneven contributions, but some zingers, including Adair Turner on Dethroning Growth.

Sire, J. W. (1997) *The Universe Next Door: A Basic Worldview Catalog*, InterVarsity Press, Downers Grove, IL
Although he comes from an unapologetically Christian perspective, his catalogue of world views focuses on philosophical rather than political 'isms' – from Christian Theism via Nihilism to Postmodernism. I particularly enjoyed his critique of the New Age.

Skolimowski, H. (1981) *Eco-philosophy: Designing New Tactics for Living*, Marion Boyars, New York, NY
An early influence on philosophers and the green movement.

Smil, V. (2006) *Technological Innovations and Their Consequences*, Oxford University Press, Oxford
Contains some technical drawings, equations and acronyms but refreshingly interdisciplinary in describing key technological changes, for example, in the speed and mode of transporting stuff and information. Directly tackles sustainability concerns and reflects on accomplishments and concerns of where we are now, as well as outlooks for the future.

Smith, A. (1759, 2006 edition) *The Theory of Moral Sentiments*, Dover Philosophical Classics, New York, NY

Smith, A. (1776, 1986 edition) *The Wealth of Nations Books I-III*, Penguin Classics, London

Spretnak, C. (1997) *Resurgence of the Real*, Addison Wesley, New York, NY
Described as 'nothing less than a spiritual guidebook for life in the next millennium' this book sweeps wide over history, literature and spirituality to make a 'post modern' analysis of how we need to 'get real' for the future. The bibliography leads the reader to a range of intellectual and spiritual traditions and even sideways into green politics!

Stern, N. (2006) *The Economics of Climate Change*, HMSO, London
Had finance departments around the world shaking in their boots, but at last able to see climate change described in their own language.

Stern, N. (2009) *A Blueprint for a Safer Planet*, The Bodley Head, London
A heroic but unsuccessful attempt to influence the climate change negotiations with costs and policies for mitigation and adaptation.

Stibbe, A. (ed) (2009) *The Handbook of Sustainability Literacy*, Green Books, Totnes
Collection of essays on many aspects of sustainability. Mostly from writers and academics, raising hope universities are beginning to pick up their responsibilities.

Stiglitz, J. (2006) *Making Globalization Work*, Allan Lane, London
Another Economics Nobel Prize winner, making a positive case for reform of organizations like the UN, IMF and the World Bank to overcome international financial instability – ahead of the crash!

Stirling, A. (1999) *On Science and Precaution in the Management of Technical Risk*, Final Report to the EC Forward Studies Unit, European Commission, Brussels

Stogdill, R. M. (1974) *Handbook of Leadership: A Survey of the Literature*, Free Press, New York, NY

Tett, G. (2009) *Fools Gold: How Unrestrained Greed Corrupted a Dream, Shattered Global Markets and Unleashed a Catastrophe*, Little Brown, London
An assistant editor of the *Financial Times* takes a social anthropologist's eye (because she is one) to the debacles in the financial markets. A no-jargon, gripping tale of how shockingly bad management, *laissez-faire* leadership and zero understanding of human relationship dynamics brought the global economy to its knees.

Thaler, R. H. and Sunstein, C. R (2008) *Nudge: Improving Decisions about Health, Wealth and Happiness*, Yale University Press, New Haven, CT, and London
This book describes how knowing how people think means 'choice environments' can be designed to make it easier for people to choose what is best for themselves, their family and society. Lots of good examples of how neither we nor the market necessarily know best instinctively, and a nudge in the right direction is in fact welcome as choices reach bamboozling levels of complexity.

Tudge, C. (2000) *The Variety of Life: A Survey and a Celebration of all the creatures that have ever Lived*, Oxford University Press, Oxford

Turner, A. (2001) *Just Capital: The Liberal Economy*, Macmillan, London

Uglow, J. (2002) *The Lunar Men: The Friends who made the Future*, Faber & Faber, London

UNDP (2005) *International Cooperation at a Cross Roads: Aid, Trade, and Security in an Unequal World*, Oxford University Press, New York, NY and Oxford

Vernadsky, V. I. (1945, 1998, in Russian 1926) *The Biosphere*, Springer-Verlag, New York, NY

Victor, P. A. (2008) *Managing without Growth: Slower by Design not Disaster*, Edward Elgar, Cheltenham
A Canada-centric book with a lot of universally useful knowledge and discussions. Falls into equations and policies at the end, but that does not diminish its utility to the non-specialist reader.

Warburton, D. (ed) (1998) *Community and Sustainable Development*, Earthscan, London

Weizsäcker, von E., Lovins, A. B. and Lovins, L. L. (1997) *Factor Four: Doubling Wealth – Halving Resource Use: A Report to the Club of Rome*, Earthscan, London

Weizsäcker, von E., Hargroves, K., Smith, M., Desha, C. and Stasinopoulus, P. (2009) *Factor Five: Transforming the Global Economy Through 80% Improvements in Resource Productivity*, Earthscan, London

Western, S. (2008) *Leadership: A Critical Text*, Sage, Los Angeles, CA
> An attempt to develop a critical theory approach to leadership that doesn't really come off.

Williamson, O. (1999) *The Mechanisms of Governance*, Oxford University Press, Oxford
> Far from easy, but an important book that melds organizational theory with transaction-cost economics to understand why a range of internal factors means everything is more complicated than institutions care to think.

Wilsdon, J. and Willis, R. (2004) *See-through Science: Why Public Engagement Needs to Move Upstream*, Demos, London

Wilsdon, J., Wynne, B. and Stilgoe, J. (2005) *The Public Value of Science: Or How to Ensure that Science Really Matters*, Demos, London
> Looks at how science can benefit by including the public 'upstream' in the definition and design of research projects. A very readable pamphlet.

Wilson, E. O. (1992) *The Diversity of Life*, Penguin Books, London
> A best-seller and perfect introduction to how evolution gets its resilience. Final section on human inpact includes an environmental ethic.

Wilson, E. O. (1998) *Consilience*, Little Brown, London
> Full of reasons why the real bottom line is not economic, but ecological. The biological case for sustainability, if you like, but done in a way that synthesizes knowledge in search of wisdom rather than just catalogues it.

Wilson, E. O. (2002) *The Future of Life*, Little Brown, London

Wirtenberg, J., Russell, W. G. and Lipsky, D. (eds) (2009) *The Sustainable Enterprise Fieldbook*, AMACOM Books, New York, NY
> Written very much from an American business case perspective. Lots of jargon but with tips and examples of current good practice to stir ideas.

Woodin, M. and Lucas, C. (2004) *Green Alternatives to Globalisation*, Pluto Press, London

Worldwatch Institute (annually) *Vital Signs 200X–200X: The Trends that are Shaping our Future*, Earthscan, London
> An annual publication that is very good for keeping track of changes in different trends. See also the annual *State of the World* from Worldwatch. Although US focused, lots of good information and ideas. Impeccably researched.

World Commission on Environment and Development (1987) *Our Common Future*, Oxford University Press, Oxford
> Very influential with its definition of sustainable development: 'development that meets the needs of the present without compromising the ability of future generations to meet their own needs' is still widely used.

Index

Body Shop 126, 131, 264, 266
borrowers 72, 77, 266, 273
Botswana 270
boundaries 112–13, 137, 183, 192, 221, 227
Bowling Alone (Putnam) 149
BP (British Petroleum) 131
brains 7, 52, 153, 164
Braungart, Michael 219, 247
Brazil 69, 84, 102, 159
Brecht, Berthold 156
British Airways (BA) 108
British Library 91
British Waterways 221
Brown, Lester 237
BT (British Telecom) 244, 249
Buddhism 157, 159
Burke, Tom 42
Burma 95, 190
Bush, George W. 108
business 14, 23, 31, 65, 72, 74–5, 77–8, 83, 85, 108, 119–20, 124–37, 176–7, 209–10, 227–8, 254
business benefits of sustainable development 129
Business Council for Sustainable Development (BCSD) 128
Business Principles for Countering Bribery 128
business schools 49, 89, 91, 123–5, 137, 140, 144
  betrayal by 123–38
business sector 131, 133

Cadbury 126
Caddick, David 98, 264
Cambodia 20
Cambridge Network 41
Cameron, James 265
campaigns/campaigners 32, 45, 128–9, 157, 176, 184–6
Canada 210
  Index of Wellbeing 82
capacity 9, 16, 45, 52–3, 64, 92, 100, 145–6, 182, 203, 206, 209–10, 230, 234, 252, 268
  environment's 206, 228
capital 14, 65–8, 75–7, 79, 81–2, 130, 170, 201–2, 204–8, 222, 265
  circulating 66–7
  financial 66, 68, 203–4, 206

manufactured 203–4, 206
  stocks 76–7, 202–6
capitalism 66–7, 130, 133, 135–6, 273
Capitalism As if the World Matters (Porritt) 130
Capra, Fritjof 58
carbon 25–6, 30–1, 33–4, 37–8, 40, 48–9, 61, 69, 77, 142, 192, 200, 220, 223–4, 227, 236–7
  accounting for 223
  family of understanding 26
  global warming potential 224
  management hierarchy 228
  pricing 34
  what is it? 224
carbon dioxide 20, 22, 26–7, 33, 223–5
Carbon Mitigation Institute 253, 256
Carbon Reduction Committee 34
Carbon Trust 223, 229
Carrot Mob 265
Carson, Rachel 192, 258
Caulkin, Simon 123
CBI (Confederation of British Industry) 119
CCC (Committee on Climate Change) 31, 223, 226–7
CEML (Council for Excellence in Management and Leadership) 89–90, 110, 123
central bank 77–8
CEOs (chief executive officers) 44, 108, 124, 128, 131–2, 140, 186, 193, 267
Chain of Being 50
Chandler, Alfred 124
change 1, 28–30, 39, 73, 92, 94, 107, 114–16, 119, 125, 127, 130–1, 136–7, 142, 192, 212–16
  behavioural 192, 194
  disruptive 215
  managing, contrasting views on 214
chaos 45, 88, 104–6, 107
Chapman, Jake 110, 12
charisma 100, 102–3, 183
Charles, HRH Prince of Wales 221, 271
Charter 77 268
Chartered Institute of Personnel Development 281
chemicals 22–4, 45, 57, 147, 192, 225
children 3, 7, 23, 43–4, 55–6, 68, 82, 120, 148–9, 176, 213–15, 239–42, 263
Chime Communications 126

316 *The Positive Deviant: Sustainability Leadership in a Perverse World*

visioning 211
Vodafone 43

W.L. Gore & Associates 106, 267
Walkers Crisps 219
Wal-Mart 118
Washington Consensus 74, 159
waste 34–5, 45–6, 113, 203, 225–6, 237,
    247, 253
  generation 22–5
  hierarchy 24
  overdose 18
  squeezing out of system 25
water 8, 18–20, 24, 26, 30, 33–4, 48, 61,
    110, 112, 138, 148, 203–4, 236–8,
    244–5, 247–8
  shortages 20
WBCSD (World Business Council for
    Sustainable Development) 131–2
wealth 7, 54, 59, 64, 66–7, 83, 160, 203
Wealth of Nations, The (Smith) 5
Weber, Max 100
Wedge Card 69, 264
wedges 235, 249, 254–6
weight 23–4, 166, 218
Weizsäcker, Ernst von 218
Welanschauung 155
well-being 18–19, 69, 72, 76, 82–3, 170,
    178, 203, 206, 236, 241–2, 253
West Bank 263
Wharton, Joseph 124, 126
Wharton School 123

Whistler Resort 210
Wikipedia 42
Williams, Rowan 59
Williamson, Oliver 148
Wilson, Edward 153
women 43, 55–6, 80, 84, 91, 104, 114–21,
    139, 176, 236, 239, 240–1, 245, 264,
    268, 270, 272–3
  emancipating 239, 241
  resistance to leadership by 117
Women for Women International 119
World Bank 42, 68, 119, 159
World Business Council for Sustainable
    Development (WBCSD) 131–2
World Coal Institute 22
World Economic Forum 115
World Health Organization (WHO) 24
World Resources Institute 227
World Trade Center terrorist attack 108, 159
WorldCom 128
Worthington, Bryony 38, 272
WWF (World Wide Fund for Nature) 18,
    24, 59, 222

Yemen 116
you and positive deviance 175–7
YouTube 126
Yunus, Muhammad 273

Zimbabwe 160
ZOPA (Zone of Possible Agreement) 78,
    273